001 Mikhail Lychkovskiy GEO— SDGS FLOWERS FOR THE HUMANITY

Poster for the SDGS Taiwan International Image Design Invitational Exhibition (Tunghai University and National Taiwan Normal University). Sustainable development goals (SDG) lead to the flourishing of humanity, which is literally interpreted through the prism of flowers.

MULTI DIMENSIONAL

3D—a technology that has completely changed our idea of spaces and shapes. Spatiality was used in art and architecture long before the digital era, but it wasn't until the first computer graphics in the 1960s that the real revolution began. What once began as simple wireframes has now evolved into impressive, realistic 3D worlds that have become indispensable in areas such as film, art, and product design. The works in this chapter offer an exciting insight into the creative diversity made possible by 3D techniques.

002 Dennis Hoelscher DEU—[J]UGGERNAUT

As part of a series these letter sculptures blew up to reveal certain parts inflated by force and others pinned to keep the shape. This letter "J" is also projected as a texture on the surface which adds a second layer of abstraction through deformation. [J]UGGERNAUT—a massive inexorable force.

003 Stella Kornfeld
DEU—WELCOME TO THE MACHINE

Stella Kornfeld's project WELCOME TO THE MACHINE investigates the potential of 3D programs in graphic design to generate innovative forms. By leveraging advanced 3D software, Kornfeld explores how these tools can create new visual languages and challenge traditional design conventions. Her work demonstrates the transformative power of 3D technology by expanding the boundaries of graphic design, offering fresh, dynamic perspectives that push the field into new, uncharted territories.

004 Sam Steiner CHE— NEUBAD MONATSPROGRAMM 23/24

Every season, the Neubad Luzern commissions a new designer to create 10 illustrations for the monthly program. The inspiration is based on the tiles of the former swimming pool and the varied and multi-layered program of the cultural center. The lively, almost chaotic atmosphere of the Neubad is reflected in the project.

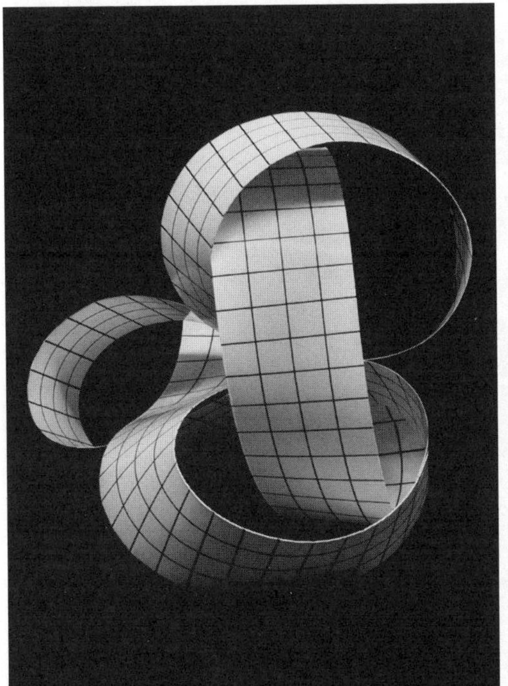

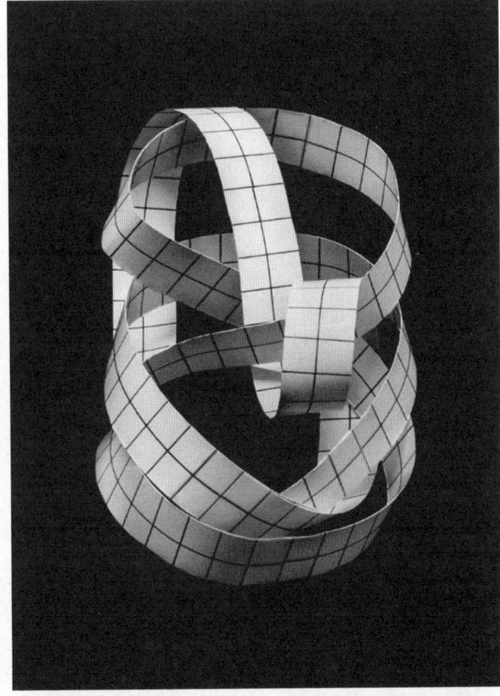

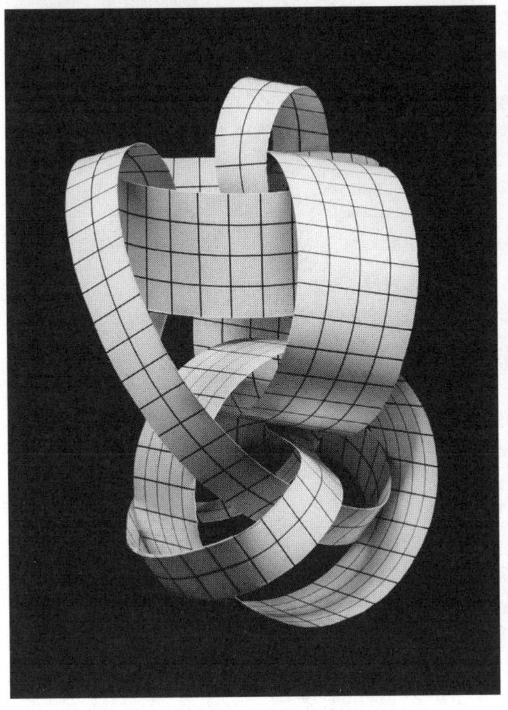

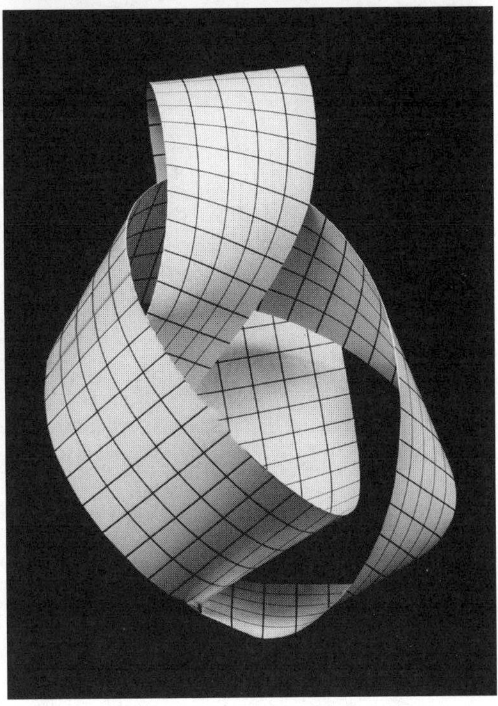

005 Nihal Tuerkyilmaz DEU—COEXIST

This 3D animation draws inspiration from a brutalist concrete building in Dortmund: Hannibal 2. It also explores Homi K. Bhabha's "Third Space" theory, where hybrid identities emerge effected by spaces.

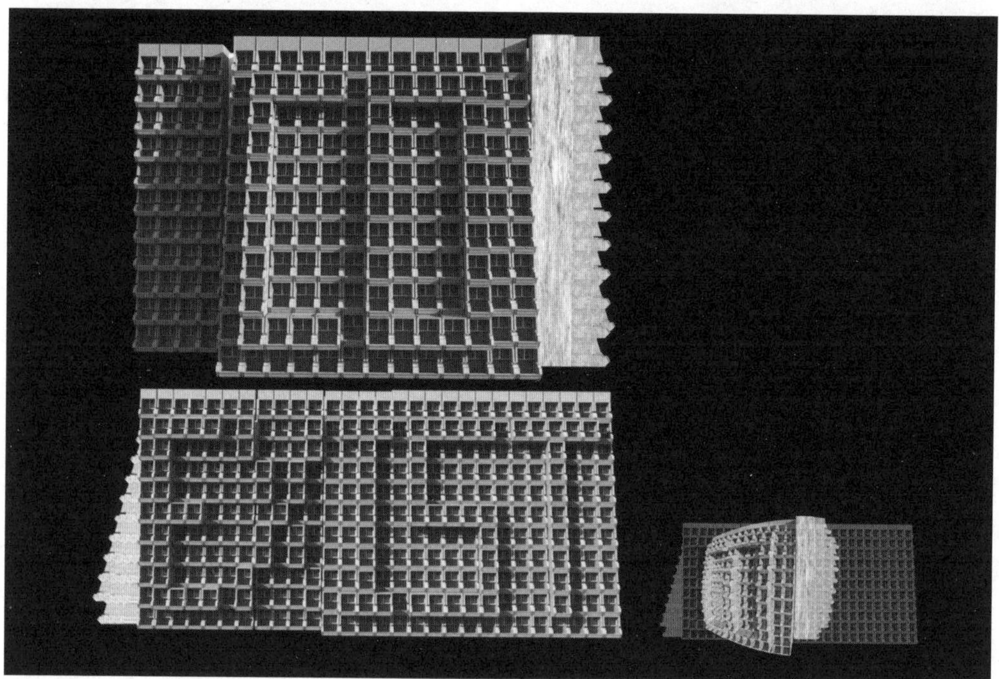

006 Niclas Kötting DEU—
CHROME AND GLASS
Chrome letters, enclosed in a glass box,
exploring light and reflection.

007 Nathalie Knappik DEU-
TOMORROW NEVER COME

A phrase associated with the rise of glob
warming and the fear it evokes. It depic
the destruction and deformation of lette
using the random principles of the Shrir
wrap tool in Blender 3D, to create an ima
of a fragile status qu

008 Nathalie Knappik DEU—YOUR DATA IS THEIR PROFIT

A phrase distorted using the random principles of Blender 3D's Shrinkwrap tool. The fragmented letters symbolize the fragmentation and commercialization of data, while also visualizing personal data exploitation.

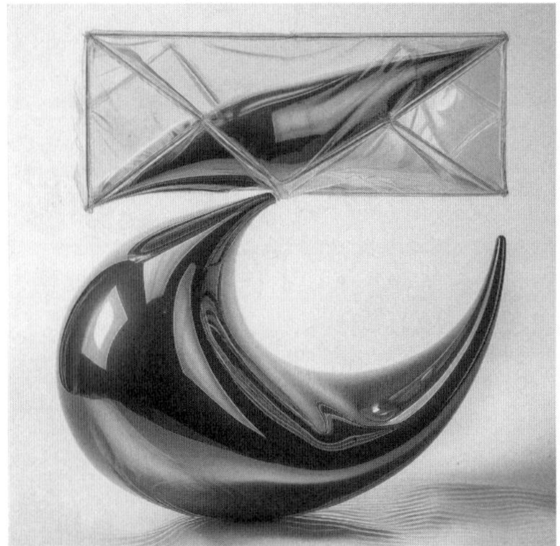
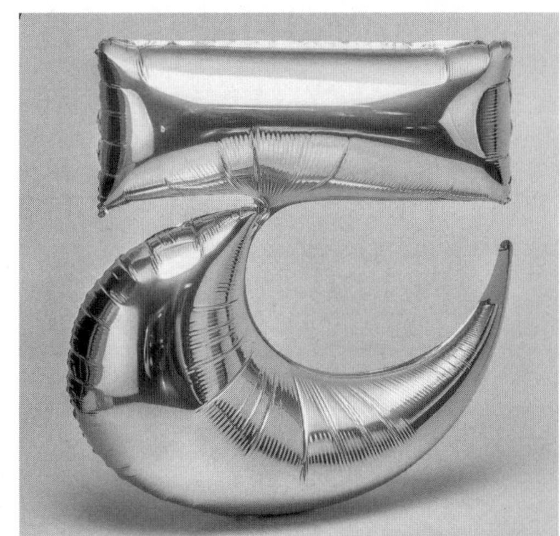

009 Alexandra Steffan DEU— SOFT METAL

The artwork reveals an intriguing blend of flowing fabric and hard metal. The challenge was to make the metal appear so soft that it seems as if it would yield to touch. The indefinable fabric looks like it's blowing in the wind, yet remains perfectly still. The delicate background suggests the object is very light, showing no sign of giving way.

010 Anja Bolender DEU—POLLUTION

Experimental poster typography.

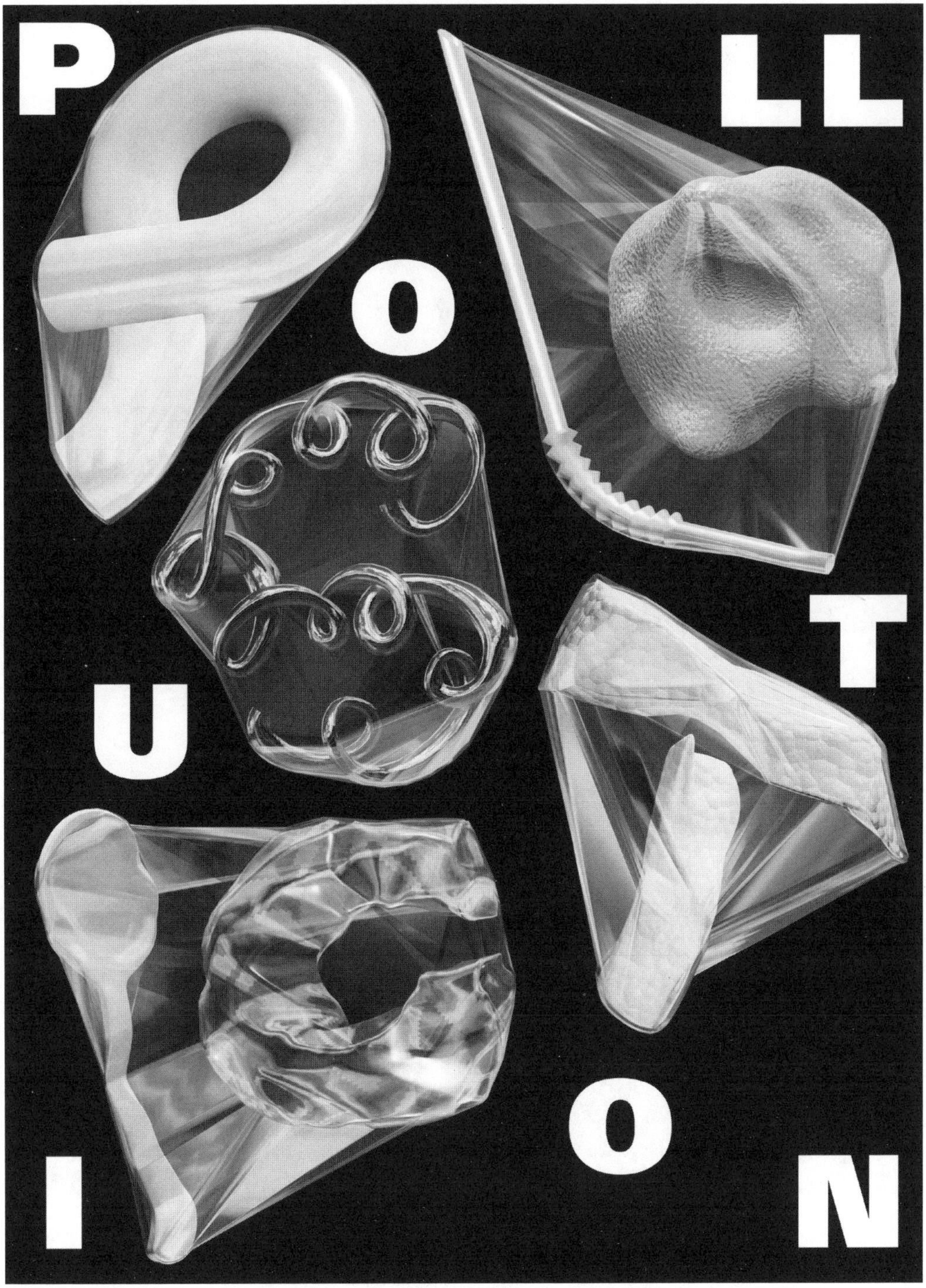

011 .Anton Burmistrov ESP—AI EXPLORATIONS

While many creators, designers, and artists are hesitant to use AI in their work due to copyright concerns, Anton is exploring how to incorporate this technology into his projects. He experiments with shapes and textures to create entirely new, unique type designs.

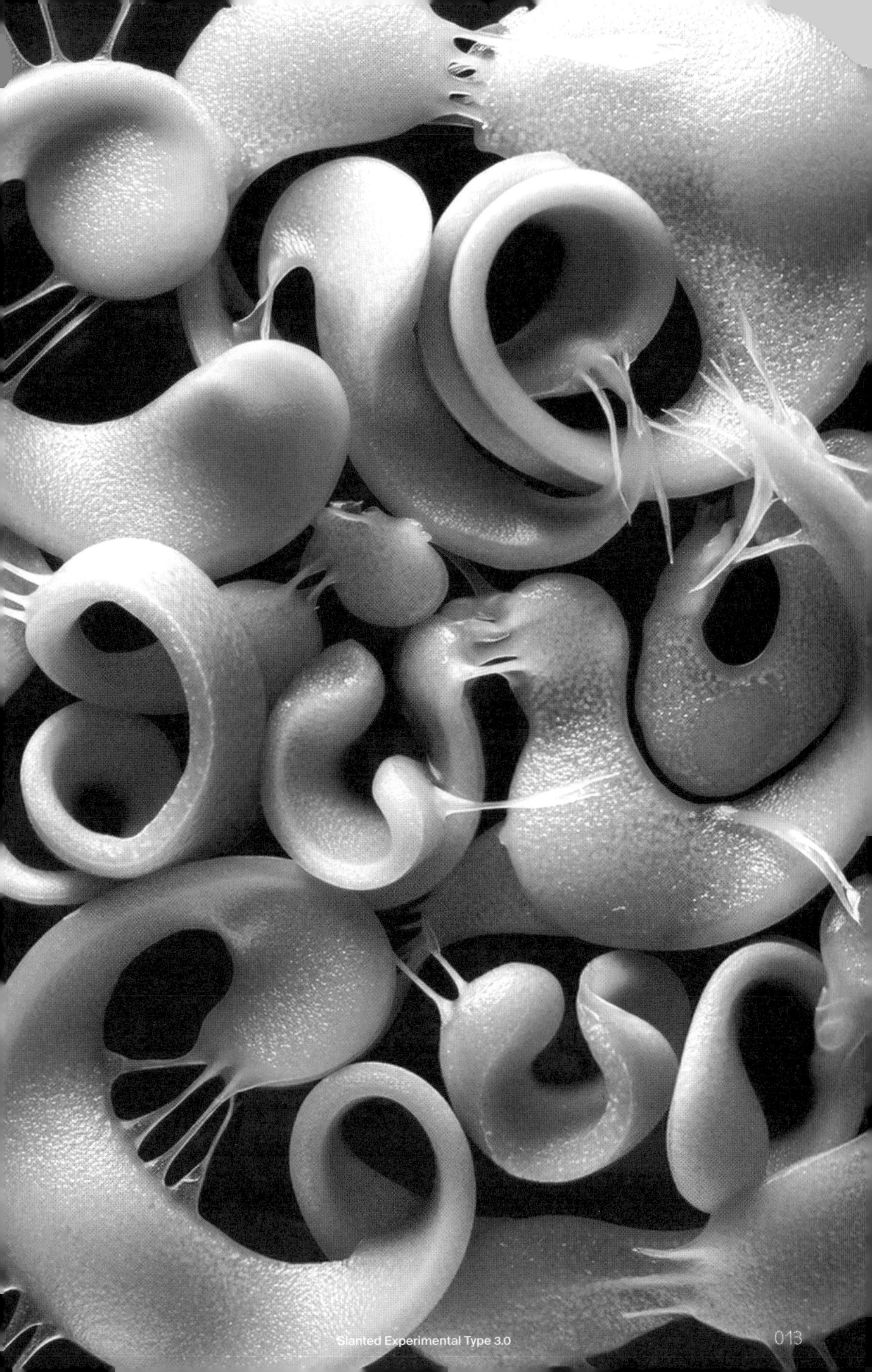

012 Abdulhadi Aldarwich DEU— PERCEPTION OF TYPE

Aldarwich experimented with geometric shapes to develop a new typographic font. They combined simple elements such as circles, triangles, and lines to create a modern and aesthetic typeface. This approach pushes the traditional boundaries of typography and redefines the perception of type in communication design.

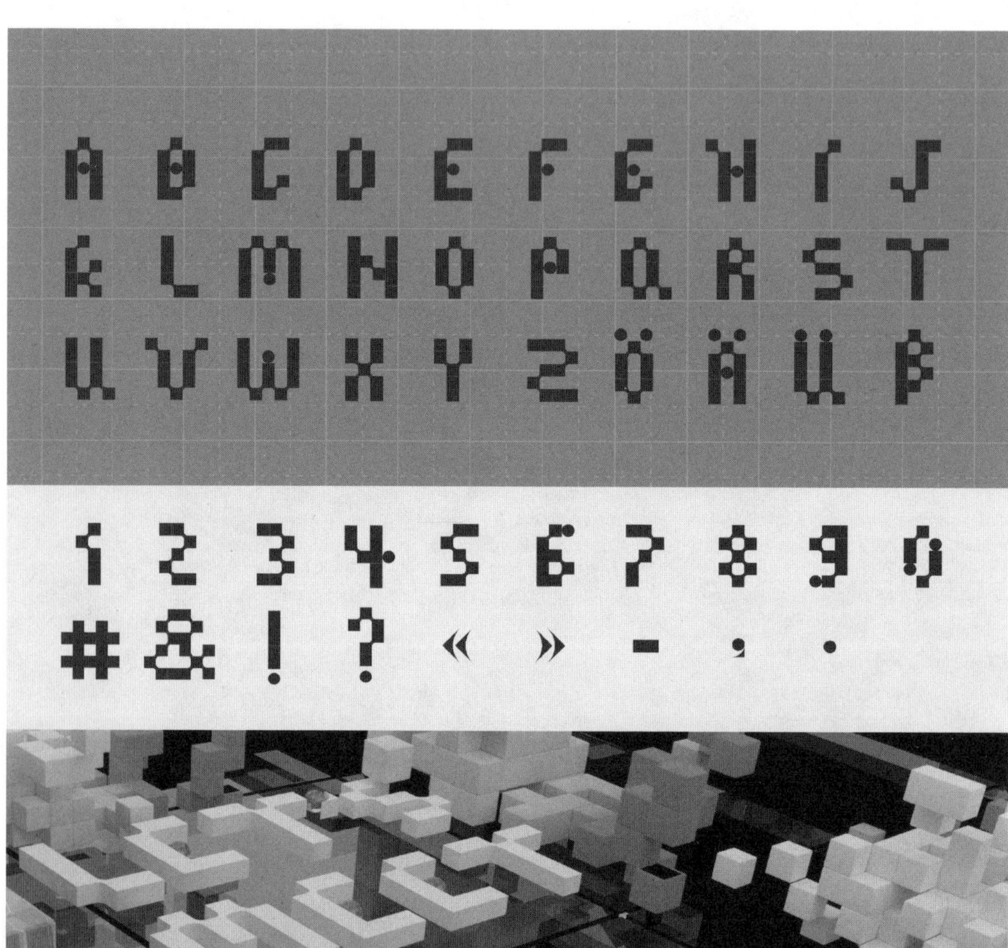

013 Anna Fay DEU—
LATENT TYPE

AI tools for image generation and manipulation are developing very fast. Yet, their utility for designing typography remains limited. LATENT TYPE explores different ways of working with Text-to-Image models—as one of the most recent additions to said tools. It analyzes available settings, inputs, and finetuning options, both with the aim of creating experimental letter shapes as well as fonts. It moreover explores the role of human and artificial intelligence in a shared design process.

014 Ricardo Gantschnigg AUT—

VIENNA TYPEFACE

Vienna Typeface is a three-dimensional portrait of Vienna in 26 letters. The project captures the essence of this majestic city by illustrating the Latin alphabet. Each of the illustrated letters is a 3D miniature that picks up an aspect of the Viennese lifestyle or a monument and portrays them in a diorama.

015 NEOMATTER DEU—ABC3D

The people of NEOMATTER believe type can fly! An additional axis in typography adds further possibilities by nature. Outlines turn into raw or soft surfaces, the volume takes spatial presence. There is a great bandwidth of aesthetic and functional paths to go, and they want to go high in the sky. NEOMATTER encourages to create new perspectives on type as a sculptural object.

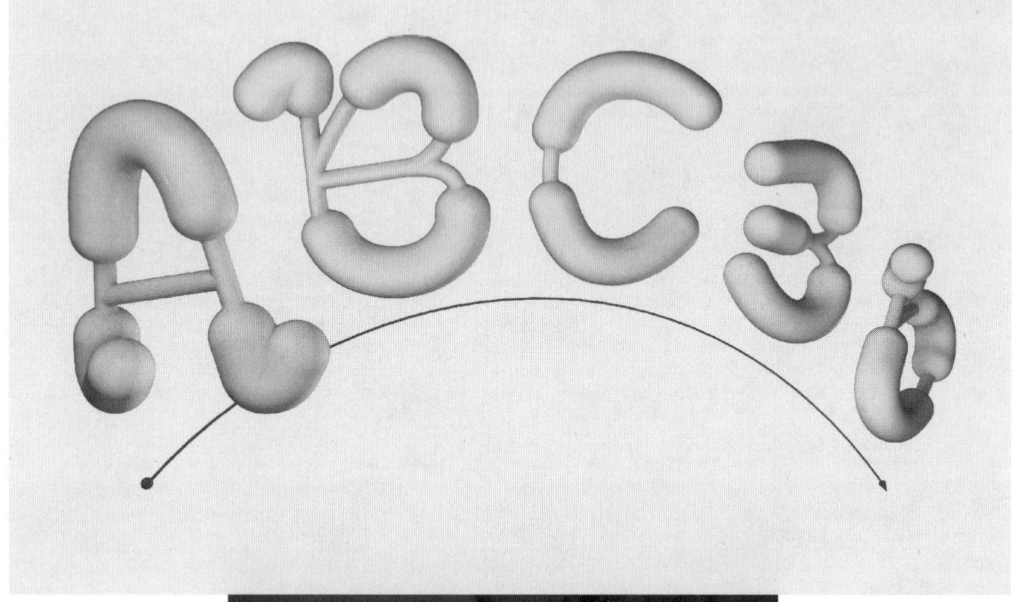

016 NEOMATTER
DEU—NM ORIGIN
NM ORIGIN in physical reality, captured by Timo Matthies at NEOMATTER's Launch Event in 2023. The material is extruded polystyrene, usually used for isolation purposes.

017 Franziska Stetter USA—
COTTON CANDY

This poster was created for the Fight for Kindness open call, a project designed to spread the values of kindness through a typographic message. In her contribution, Stetter aimed to raise awareness about the overwhelming amount of money spent each year on war, highlighting how these funds could benefit humanity in numerous other ways. In 2023 alone, 2,443 billion US dollars were spent globally on military activities.

018 Anton Burmistrov ESP—
AI EXPLORATIONS

While many creators, designers, and artists are hesitant to use AI in their work due to copyright concerns, Burmistrov is exploring how to incorporate this technology into his projects. He experiments with shapes and textures to create entirely new, unique type designs.

019 Chanel Enya Wloka DEU—
BOOGIE FONT

As a reference for the project, steel was chosen as the basic material for the typography. BOOGIE shows the robust character and a technical aesthetic that can be observed in the modern industrial world. It appears simple and yet is very complex and detailed. BOOGIE was created in Blender and can therefore be displayed in various positions.

020 Anton Burmistrov ESP— AI EXPLORATIONS

While many creators, designers, and artists are hesitant to use AI in their work due to copyright concerns, Burmistrov is exploring how to incorporate this technology into his projects. He experiments with shapes and textures to create entirely new, unique type designs.

021 Monica Sharoubime DEU— PUFFY FONT

3D typeface exploration.

022 Mikhail Lychkovskiy GEO— THE GHOST BREW

Conceptual typographic poster for a theatrical show Der Geisterbräu (the ghost brew) made at poster workshop with Peter Bankov. Although posters with a room-space-feeling are common, Lychkovskiy tried to partially bend the right side of the poster, so that the viewer would not be completely sure if they were really looking into the room. The cat is used as a counterweight to the curvature and leads the viewer to the space of the room. A good cat.

023 Mikhail Lychkovskiy GEO—
THE SPOILSPORT

Conceptual poster for a theatrical show Die Spielverderber or Das Erbe der Narren ("the spoilsport" or "the legacy of fools") held at Theater Köln Süd.

024 Liad Shadmi DEU—
EYES OFF MIT MONOH

Poster design for Monoh playing at Neubad Luzern.

025 Beyza Duyuran DEU— CYBER THORN

CYBER THORN is a futuristic type design made from solder. The letters are pointed and angular and have an impressive shiny metallic 3D effect thanks to the use of solder.

Daniel Bausch DEU— SHAPESHIFT

Analogously created letterforms were digitally captured and interpreted by an image-generating AI. Influences such as transparent foil, Y2K product design, X-ray images, and anatomical visualizations shaped the process. The sketches were interpreted and refined using a real-time image-to-image model and repeatedly blended to create new perspectives and expressions. Through the process, static forms transformed into more abstract and organic shapes.

027 Julian Tillmann
DEU—NOPE YES

Experimental poster typography.

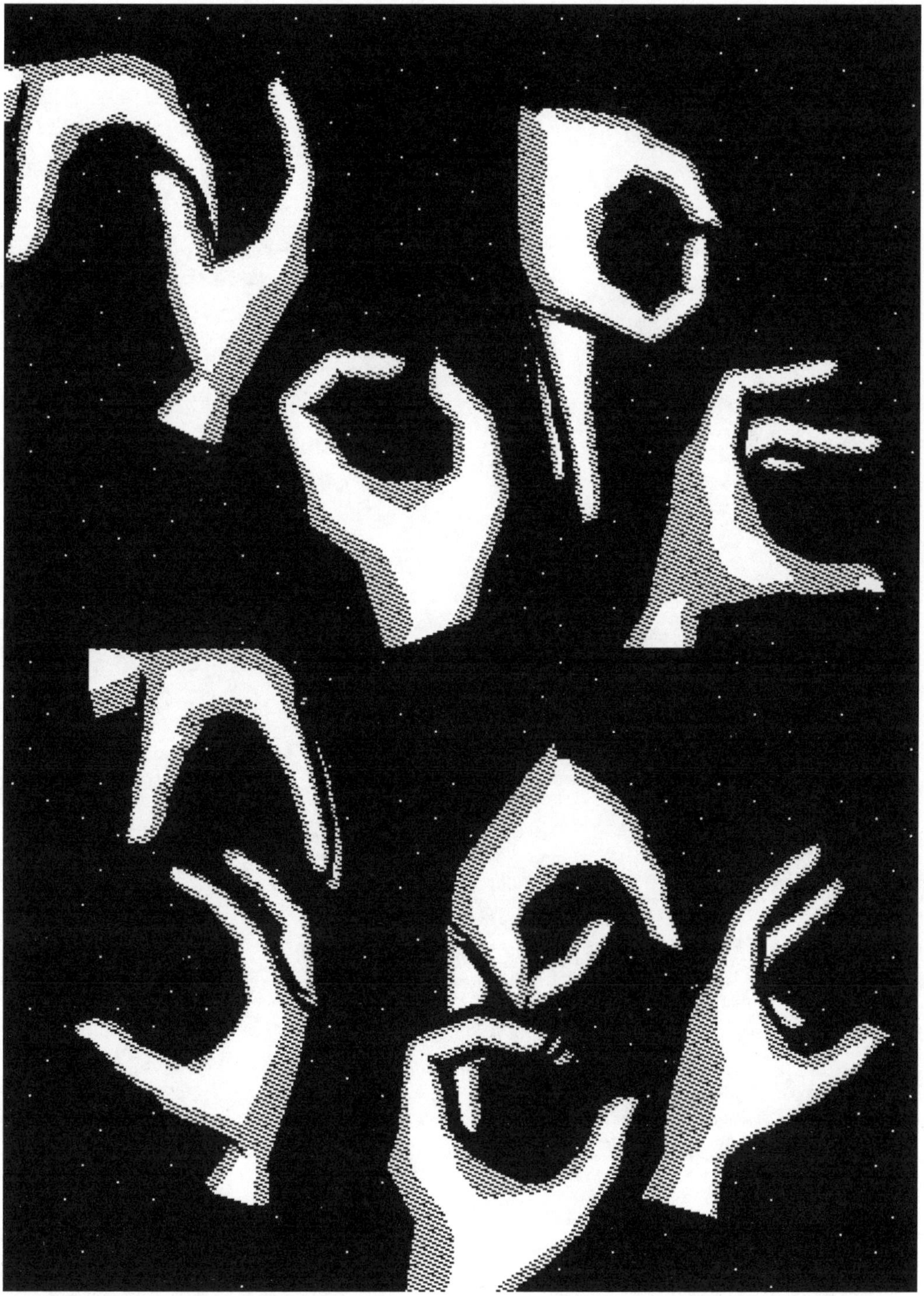

028 Isobel Connelly / CRYBABY STUDIOS© USA— NICOLE × ISOBEL

A collaboration with Nicole Saldana to showcase some of the new shoes from her SS24 collection.

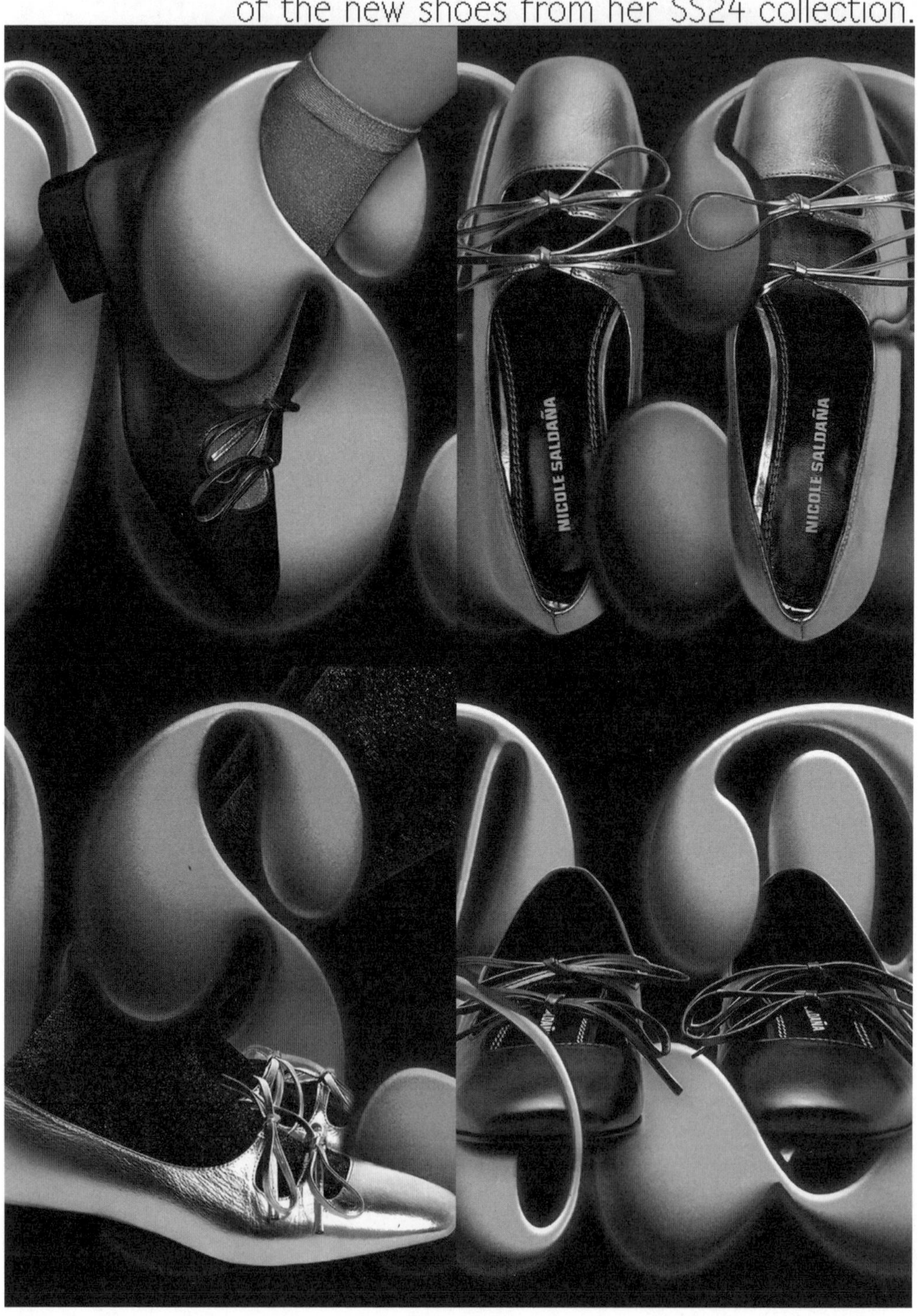

029 JLF Müller DEU—LANAGE

LANAGE, a made-up word made up of latex and drainage, comes from the creation process of this experimental typeface. In PLEXIGLAS® plates, screws with long nuts were turned according to a certain grid, and a balloon as known from circus clowns was braced and inflated in the shape of the letters. The font is a tribute to the contrast of man-made and nature, soft and hard, cold and warm, artificial bone and flesh

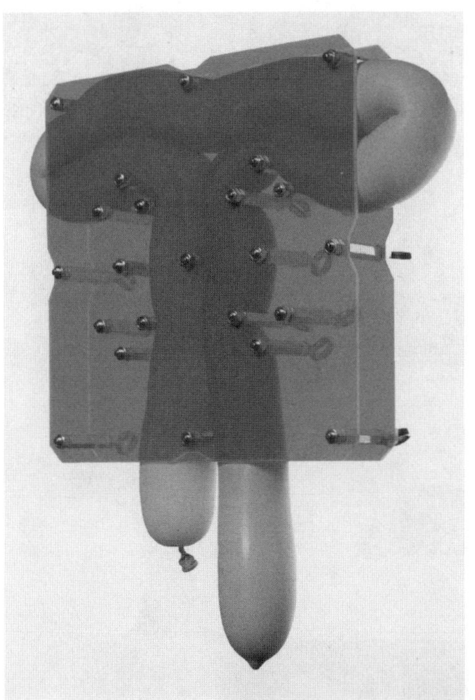

030 Melissa Smajic DEU—FAQ LMAO

Experimental 3D typography.

031 Mikhail Lychkovskiy GEO—TRANSMISSION
Experimental poster for the show Transmission held at Maison de la Culture de Tahiti. Readability is significantly complicated here, but the poster has retained an information structure that still allows it to be read. In the word "transmission" letters are divided into component parts to convey possible distortions in the transmission of information.

032 Ian Mayer DEU—LUFTDICHT

The font LUFTDICHT is sealed airtight
to ensure its preservation.

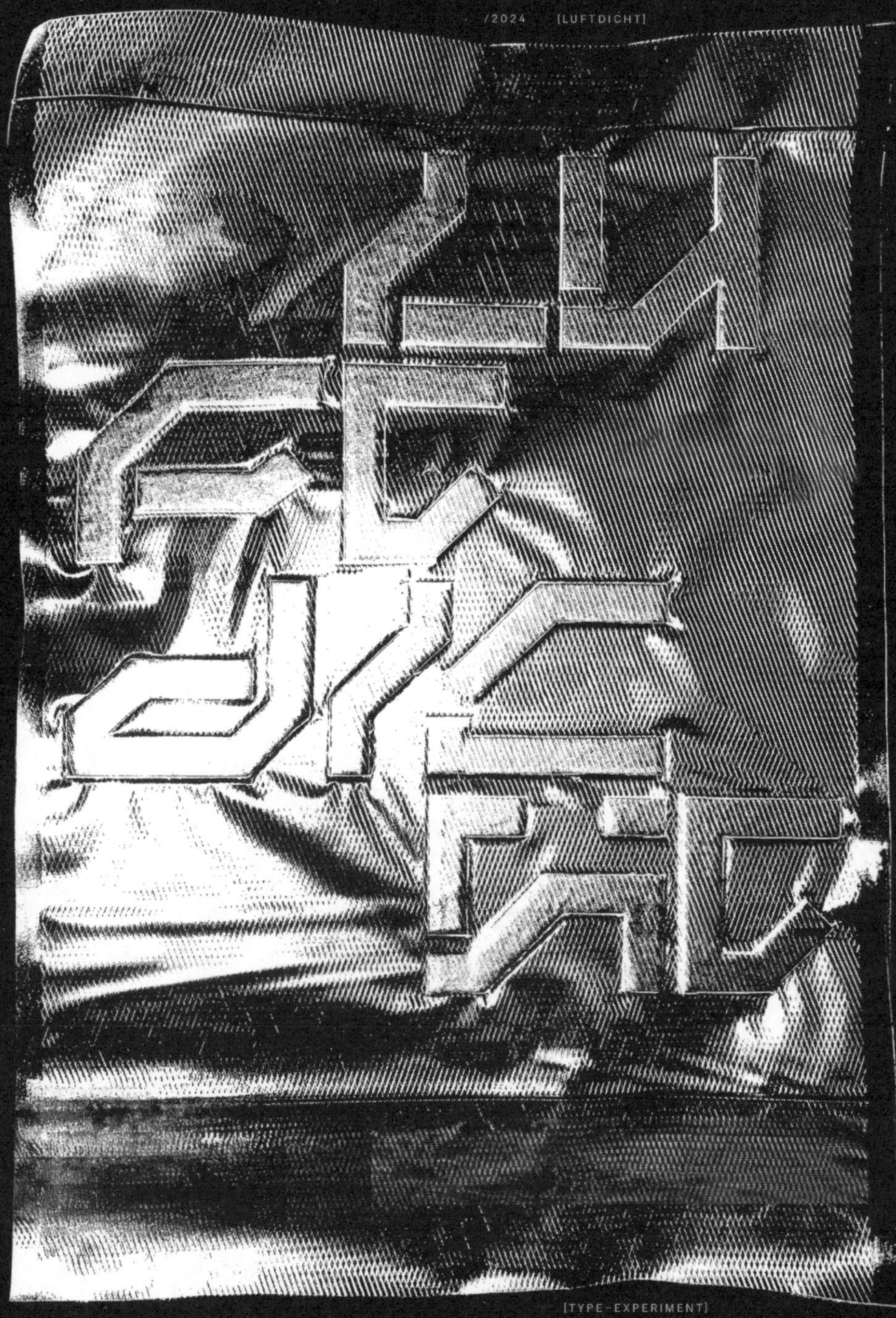

033 Nele Kreuger, Julian Ratay DEU— GROWING OBSCURITY

Font design Spikes combined with 3D.

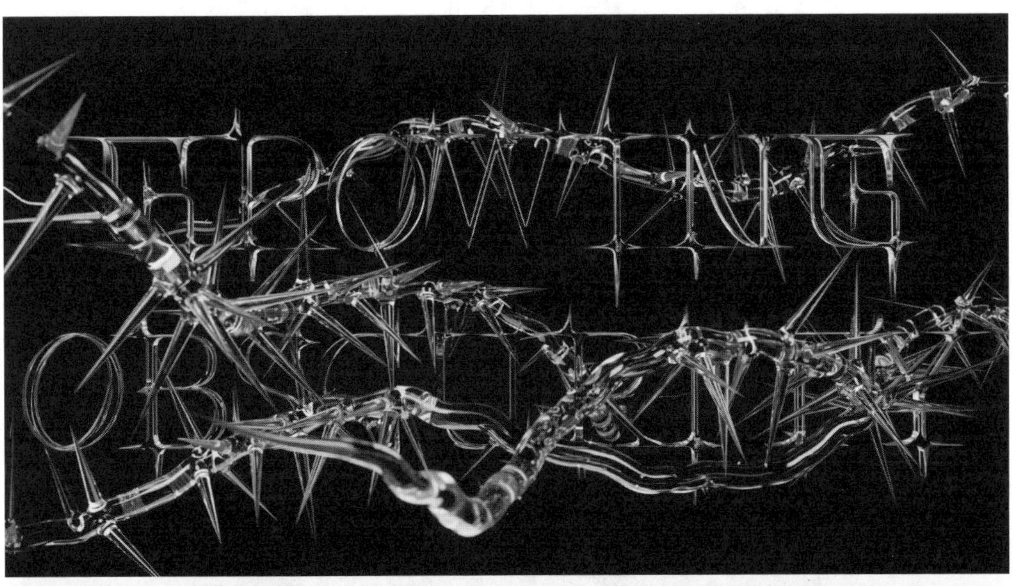

034 Nassim Mokarami DEU—KHANE

Experimental typographic exploration.

035 Lilith Dolch DEU— WHO CARES WHAT TEXT IS SUPPOSED TO BE

Dolch used text as the base for a sculptural image in Blender. The shapes and textures were achieved by adding another object multiple times onto 3D text with Geometry Nodes and altering the object's parameters like scale, rotation, count, and density.

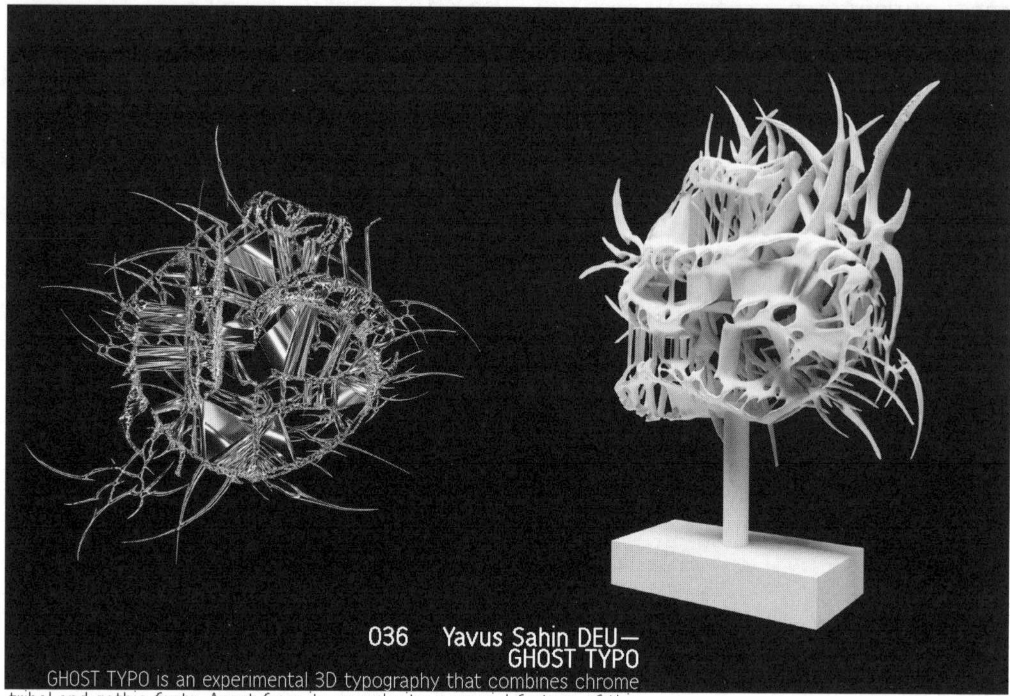

036 Yavus Sahin DEU—
GHOST TYPO

GHOST TYPO is an experimental 3D typography that combines chrome tribal and gothic fonts. Apart from its complexity, a special feature of this typography is that the characters themselves are not visible, only the chrome that adheres to them. The font was created in Blender so that it can be viewed from all sides. It was also reworked so that it could be printed with a 3D printer.

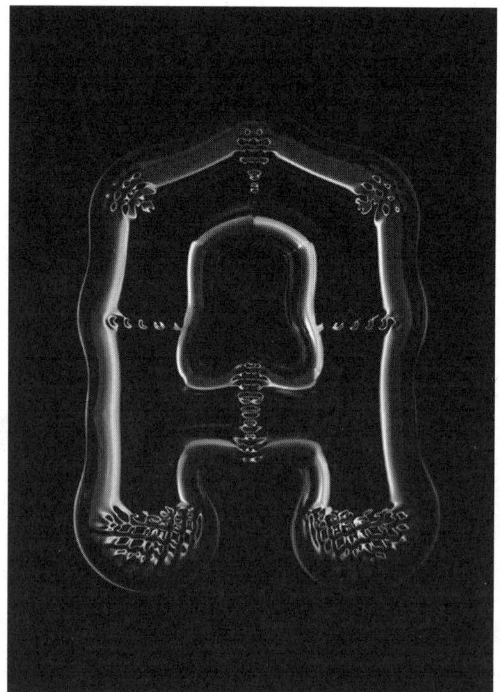

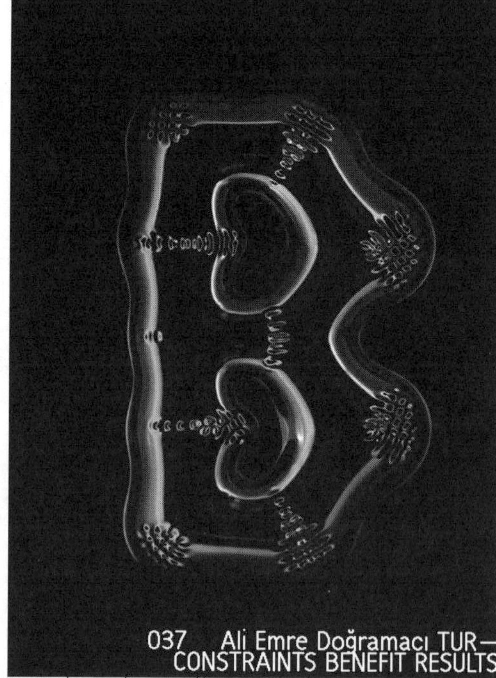

037 Ali Emre Doğramacı TUR—
CONSTRAINTS BENEFIT RESULTS

Experimental typography made using the reaction between ferrofluid and neodymium magnets for Stefan Sagmeister's class "Can Design Touch Someone's Heart" at School of Visual Arts MFA Design Department.

038 ANTIDOTE.PSD / CHRISTIAN GOSS UK/DE—Y-9

This is a collection of the creator's favorite experimental/abstract typographic pieces. They were all created at separate points and places approximately in the last year. Wherever the creator goes, they carry a sketchbook, often sketching during journeys and drawing inspiration from their immediate surroundings.

039 Dennis Hoelscher DEU—GROWING COMMUNICATION

With the introduction of Geometry Nodes in Blender 3D software, a transition happened in Hoelscher's workflow. The final result of a creative process is now the product of a procedural system, which can be subsequently adjusted at any point in the pipeline and in return delivers a completely new output each time. Nodes are connected into networks that define a recipe, which can be adjusted to refine the outcome and repeated to produce similar yet unique results.

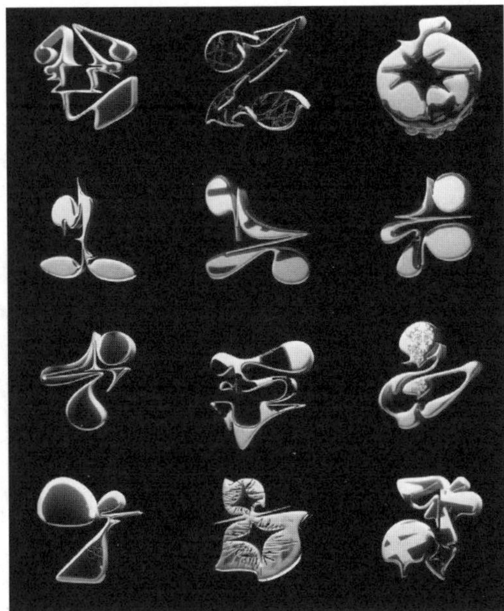

040 Adson Rodrigues BRA—36D0T10

36 experimental letter designs for the 36 days of type initiative.

041 **Anu Manohar IND—NICE**
Expressive 3D typography.

042 **Anu Manohar IND—NICE**
Experimental 3D alphabet for the 36 days of type initiative, made with Adobe Dimension.

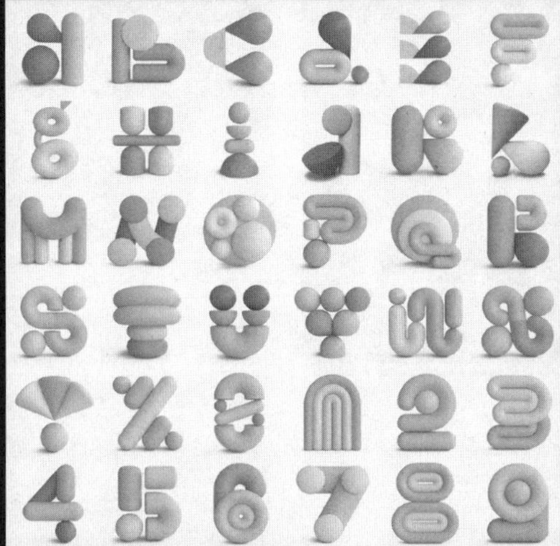

043 **Daniel Escudeiro BRA—13 POSTER**
Bubbly 3D type exploration for a poster for the 2022 election.

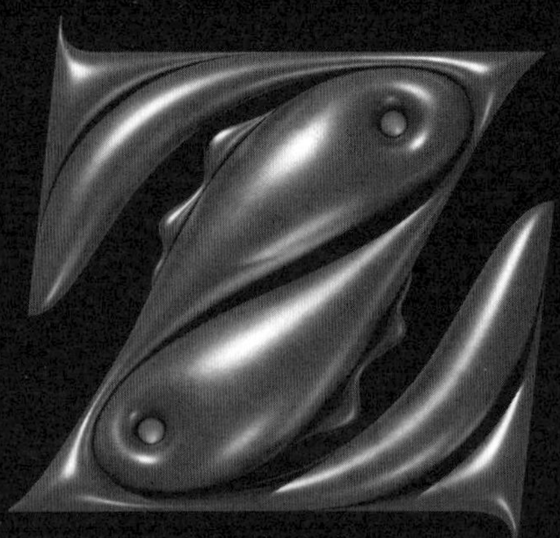

044 **Daniel Escudeiro BRA—13 POSTER**
"Z" for 36 days of type with interconnected yin-yang like faux-symmetry and little fins.

045 Txaber Mentxaka ESP—NEON X

3D type experimentation.

PROGRAMMER POETRY

Coding is a vital skill in today's world, enhancing problem-solving, logic, and creativity. It offers opportunities in fields like software development, design, and science. Recently, coding has merged with creative disciplines, powering gener ative art, inter active installations, and al gorithmic design to create dynamic visual experiences.

046 Philip Popek DEU—

I ATE COOKIES WHILE CHAT GPT CODED THIS

Creation of various type generators, coded by ChatGPT. A new approach to font design: what is possible with AI and basic knowledge of Java?

047 Jasmin Sonderegger CHE—GSCALC.PY

Visual research based on the Gray-Scott model, which simulates a chemical process. Two substances react with each other. One substance is consumed, the other is formed. By adjusting the parameters accordingly, new, distorted characters are created. The implementation was done in Python. The parameters for controlling the reaction are very sensitive, so the process is mainly based on trial and error, which on the other hand always leads to surprising results.

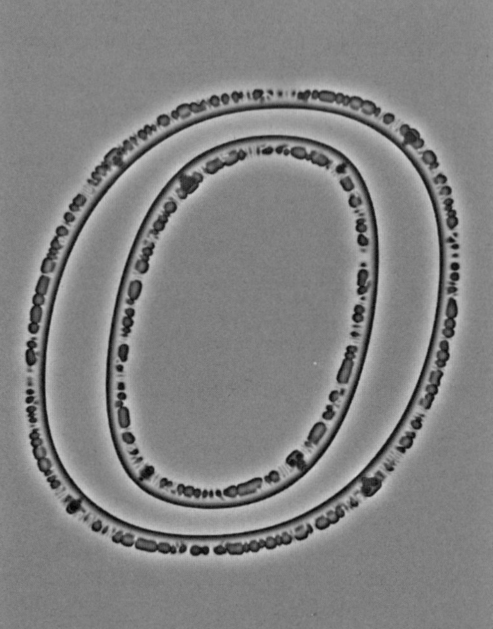

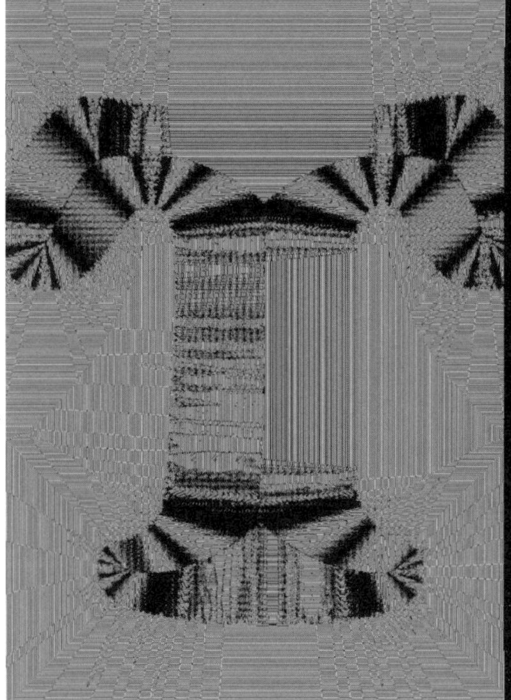

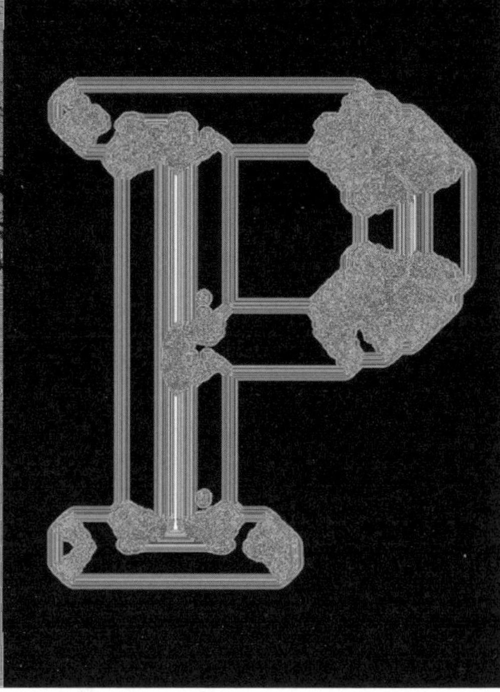

048 Emelie Gannert, Chantal Meilick DEU—
WORKSHOP-WEEK-POSTER

Poster for the Workshop-Week of the type department of the Bauhaus University Weimar (Germany). Grids, patterns, outlines, and the interplay between typography and background—exploring the boundaries between the readability of text and pattern.

049 Michelle Duong DEU— PERSPEKTIVEN IN BEWEGUNG

For the graduation show at the University of Applied Sciences Düsseldorf, animations were projection mapped in the hallway. Students showcased insights and gave perspectives into various aspects of student life through motion. The poster design was for the Projection Mapping course led by Kilian van de Water.

Perspektiven in Bewegung

Animationen über den studentischen Alltag

26.–27.01.2024

im Atrium

Animationen von
Seher Akbaba
Noah Chen
Michelle Duong
Marie Fischer
Sven Goldschmidt
Eva Hilden
Daniel Klauser
Laura Licata Tiso
Theresa Nguyen
Sinem Özcan
Chiara Pizzichillo
Lisanne Roloff
Charlotte Schneeloch
Carina Thomae
Paula Timmermann
Sarah Vollbach
Elena Wüllner
Sena Yüksel

Kurs von
Kilian van de Water

Beleuchtet werden das Uni-Leben, Studium und Arbeitsprozesse auf dem Campus. Studierende präsentieren durch Animationen vielfältige Einblicke in verschiedene Facetten des Studentenlebens.

HSD PBSA

Gestaltung von Michelle Duong

050 Michelle Duong DEU—CLOCK
The clock serves as a tool for conscious perception and decision-making about how we want to use our time. Everything is part of the day, and we decide every second, minute, and hour how we want to spend time. With each second, a task keeps on adding up. This animation works generative and is part of Duong's Bachelor Project at University of Applied Sciences Düsseldorf.

**051 Michelle Duong DEU—
WORK-LIFE IMBALANCE**
The coexistence of personal life and work requires a flexible adjustment of both areas. Can work and personal life exist together without one overshadowing and dominating the other?

**052 Michelle Duong DEU—
TIME'S PASSAGE**
The words "Past," "Present," and "Future" are broken into individual letters that move up and down the screen. The word "Present" uniquely drifts between the top and bottom of the screen, which display the words "Past" and "Future." This reflects how our thoughts and perceptions of time wander between different stages. The movement of these words symbolizes the intertwining of time and identity, illustrating how we navigate between past, present, and future.

053 Antonin Waterkeyn FRA— DIGITAL RHYTHMS

Antonin Waterkeyn, a Belgian motion designer living in France, has been exploring the Cavalry software with various typographic experiments for over a year. It's a graphic experiment. It's one of Antonin's many experiments. He wanted to play with time lag and rhythm, so that the result becomes almost musical. The animations always work in loops. Antonin has always been fascinated by optical art, which comes across in this experiment.

054 Tim von Bischopinck DEU— GENERATE SANS

GENERATE SANS is a typeface based on a single generated line. The line loosely follows a template using creative code to generate two messy-looking typefaces. In 3D, a new dimension is added to create large, sculptural letter forms.

055 Michael Zöllner DEU— UNICODE SPACE

There are invisible characters in the UTF-8 Unicode character encoding standard: Hair space, thin space, punctuation space, and many more. This experiment measured the width of each invisible character with p5.js to dynamically manipulate the kerning of single characters. By analyzing the brightness of individual pixels of an image and inserting them at the corresponding lines and characters, image patterns are emerging in the text through white space and densification.

Dianthus caryophyllus, commonly known as carnation or clove pink, is a species of Dianthus native to the Mediterranean region.
Its exact natural range is uncertain due to extensive cultivation over the last 2,000 years. Carnations are prized for their vibrant
colors, delicate fringed petals, and enchanting fragrance. The scent of carnations is often described as spicy, clove-like, or
reminiscent of a combination of cinnamon and nutmeg, hence the common name "clove pink". This delightful aroma has
made car n atio ns a popular choice for use in perfumes, Potpourri, and scented products. They have cultural significance
and are a s so cia ted with love, distinction, and motherly affection. With numerous cultivars and hybrids, carnations of fer
a wide variety of colors and forms, making them popular for gardens, floral arrangements, and scented products. Overall,
carnations are enduring symbols of beauty and grace, treasured by flower enthusiasts and used to convey heartfelt emotions.
Taxonomy: C arnations were mentioned in Greek literature 2,000 years ago. T he term dianthus was coined by Greek botanist
Theophrastus, and is derived from the Ancient Greek words for divine ("d i o s ") and flower ("anthos"). The name "carnation"
is believed to come from the Latin corona-ae, a "wreath, g arlan d , c ha p let , cr own" ,[7] as it was one of the flowers
used in Greek and Roman ceremonial crowns, or possibly f r o m t he L a ti n c a r o (genitive carnis), "flesh",
which refers to the natural colour of the flower, or in C h r is t i a n i c o n o gra ph y incarnatio, "incarnation",
God made flesh in the form of Jesus. Carl Lin n ae us de s c rib e d t he carn a t i o n in volume one of his
Species Plantarum in 1753, giving it the nam e D i a n th us c ary o phy ll us . A l t h oug h originally applied
to the species Dianthus caryophyllus, the n a me c ar n ati on i s a l s o oft e n a pp lied to some of the
other species of Dianthus, and more pa r t ic ul ar ly to gar d e n hyb r id s bet w e e n D. caryophyllus
and other species in the genus. Descrip ti o n : Dia n t h us c a r yop h y llus is a her bac eous perennial
plant growing up to 80 cm (31+1⁄2 in) tall. Th e l e a ves a re gla u cous gr e yish gr een to blue -green, slender,
up to 15 cm (6 in) long. The flowers are prod u c e d s in g l y o r up to five t oge th e r in a cyme; they
are around 3–5 cm (1+1⁄4–2 in) diameter, a nd s w eet l y sc en t ed ; t he o rigin a l n at u ral flower color
is bright pinkish-purple, but cultivars of o t h e r c ol o r s , incl u d i ng re d, p i nk, yel l o w, white,
and green have been developed. While s o m et i me s d yed b lue f o r cut b ou que t s, there are
no known carnation cultivars that produc e a t r u e blu e f l o w e r. T h e frag rant, h e r maphrodite
flowers have a radial symmetry. The fou r t o s i x s urroun d i n g th e calyx, egg-sha pe d , sti n g-pointed
scales leaves are only ¼ as long as the caly x t u b e . D istri but i o n an d h ab i t at : T he wil d ca rnation
is found in the Mediterranean countries of Spain , I t a l y, C roa tia , A lba n ia, Greece a nd Turkey. Carnations
require well-drained, neutral to slightly alkaline so i l , a n d full sun. N u m e r ou s cultiva rs ha v e b een
selected for garden planting. Typical examples inclu d e ' G i n a P o rt o ', ' Hel en ' , 'L aced Romeo',
and 'Red Rocket'. They are used for medical purpose s , s u ch as f o r up se t st o m ach and f ev er. Their
fragrance was historically used for vinegar, beer, wine, s a uc e s a n d sa lad s. Cros s b ree di ng D. c a ryophyllus
with D. capitatus results in a hybrid that is resistant to bacterial wilt f rom P ara b urkholderi a c a ry op hyl l i. However,
the flower is less attractive and so more breeding and backcrossing i s nee de d t o im prov e the f l ower. Carnation
cultivars with no fragrance are often used by men as boutonnières o r "but t o nh o l es ". H olida y s and ev ents:
Carnations are often worn on special occasions, especially Mother' s Day an d w e d d i n gs. I n 190 7, Anna Jarvis
chose a carnation as the emblem of Mother's Day because it was h er mothe r ' s f a v o u ri t e f lo w er.[20]
This tradition is now o bs erved in the United States and Cana d a o n the seco n d S u nd ay in Ma y. A nn Jarvis
chose the white car n a tion because she wanted to represen t t h e p urity of a m othe r 's love. This meaning
has evolved over tim e , a nd now a red carnation may be w o rn i f one's m other is alive, and a white one if she has
died. In Slovenia, red c arnat io ns are sometimes also give n to wo men on Women's Day, the 8th of March, however,
nowadays orchids or ro s e s a re often given as well. In K or e a, carnation s express admiration, love and gratitude.
Red and pink carnations a r e wo rn on Parents Day (Kore a does not sepa rate Mother's Day or Father's Day, but has
Parents Day on 8 May). So me t i mes, parents wear a corsag e o f carnation(s) on their left chest on Parents Day. Carnations
are also worn on Teachers Da y (1 5 May). Red carnation s are worn on May Day as a symbol of socialism and the labour
movement in some countries, su c h a s Austria, Italy, and successor countri es of the former Yugoslavia. The red carnation
is also the symbol of the Carnatio n Rev olution in Portug al. Green carnat ions are for St. Patrick's Day and were famously
worn by the Irish writer Oscar Wild e . T he green carna tion thence bec ame a symbol of homosexuality in the early
20th century, especially through the b o o k The Green C arnation and N o ël Coward's song, "We All Wear a Green Carnation"
in his operetta, Bitter Sweet. In commu n i s t Czechosl ovakia and in P o land in times of the People's Republic of Poland,
carnations were traditionally given to w o m e n on the w idely celebrat e d Women's Day, together with commodities that
were difficult to obtain due to the countries' c o mmunist system, such a s t ights, towels, soap and coffee. After the 1990
uprisings against Soviets in Azerbaijan in which 14 7 Azerb aijani civil i ans were killed, 800 people were injured and five people
went missing, the carnation has become a symbol o f the B lack Janu a ry tragedy associated with the carnations thrown into
the puddles of blood shed in the streets of Azerbaijan subse quent t o the massacre. At the University of Oxford, carnations
are traditionally worn to a l l e x aminations; w hite f or the first exam, pink for exams in between, and red for the
last exam. One story e xplaining t hi s tradition r e lat es t hat initially a white carnation was kept in a red inkpot between
exams, so by th e last exam it was fully r e d; the stor y is t hought to originate in the late 1990s. Carnations are the
traditional first wedding anniversary flower. C arnation s ar e also known as the "Flower of God". The Greek name for
Carnation is a fusion of "dios" and "anthos". D io s is us e d the described Zeus while Anthos means flower; thus the name
"flower of God" is attached to it . Symbols of te rr i t or i a l entities and organizations: The carnation is the national
flower of Spain, Monaco, and Slov enia, and the pr o v inc i al flower of the autonomous community of the Balearic Islands.
The state flower of Ohio is a scarlet carnation, which w a s introduced to the state by Levi L. Lamborn. The choice
was made to honor William McKinley, Ohio governor and U.S . president, who was assassinated in 1901, and regularly wore
a scarlet carnation on his lapel. Colours : Carnations do not naturally produce the pigment delphinidin, and thus a blue
carnation cannot occur by natural selecti on or be created by traditional plant breeding. It shares this characteristic with
other widely sold flowers like roses, lilies, tu lips, chrysanthemu ms and gerberas. Arou n d 1996, a company, Florigene, used
genetic engineering to extract certain genes fr om petunia and snapdragon flowe r s t o p r o duce a blue-mauve carnation,
which was commercialized as Moondust. In 1 99 8, a violet carna tion called Moo n shadow was commercialized. As of

056 Andreas Gysin CHE— ASCII PLAYGROUND

The ASCII PLAYGROUND is an attempt of a browser-based live-code environment with text-only output. It is born from the joy and pleasure ASCII, ANSI, and text-based art in general can give. It is a homage to all the artists, poets, and designers who used and use text as their medium. From the design perspective it is also an exercise in reduction: there is almost no interface, just a preview window and a code editor; margins and line numbers are removed as well.

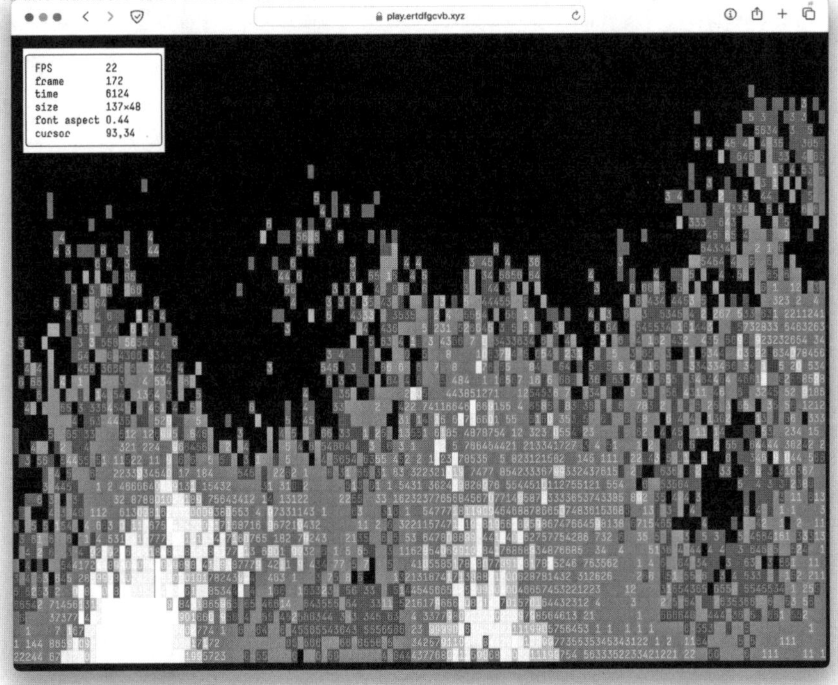

057 Luca Schlosser DEU—ARTICLE ABOUT VIDEOGAME GLITCHES

The designers task was to create an article on a topic relating to mistakes while incorporating "mistakes" in the typography. Schlosser chose to make it about video game glitches. To match the topic, the designer used ASCII art for illustrations and text boxes.

SELF CRITICISM

058 PHILIP POPEK
DEU—SELF CRITICISM
Typographic experimentation.

059
Philip Popek
DEU—MORE TSUNAMIS EVERY YEAR

Typographic experimentation.

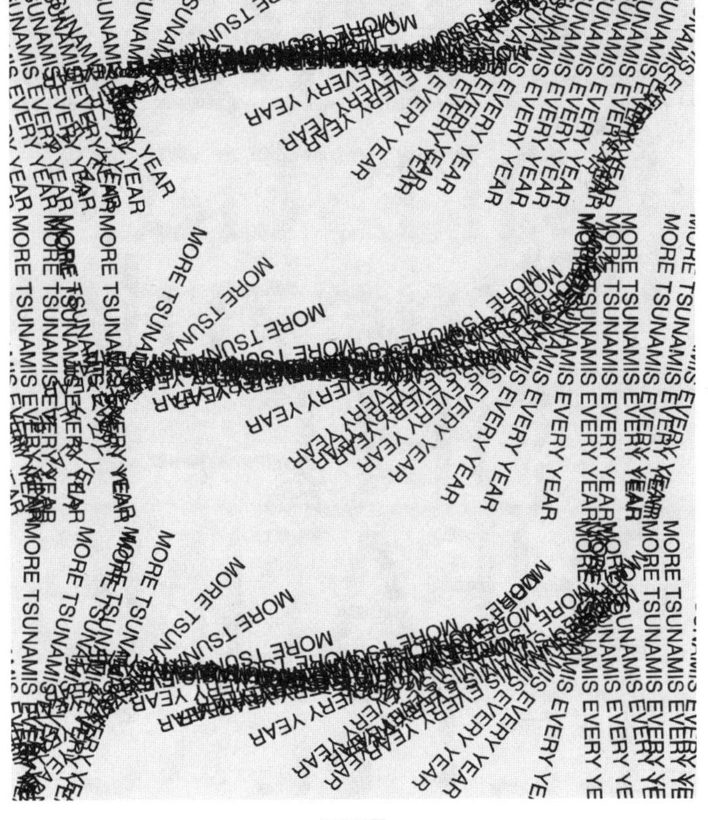

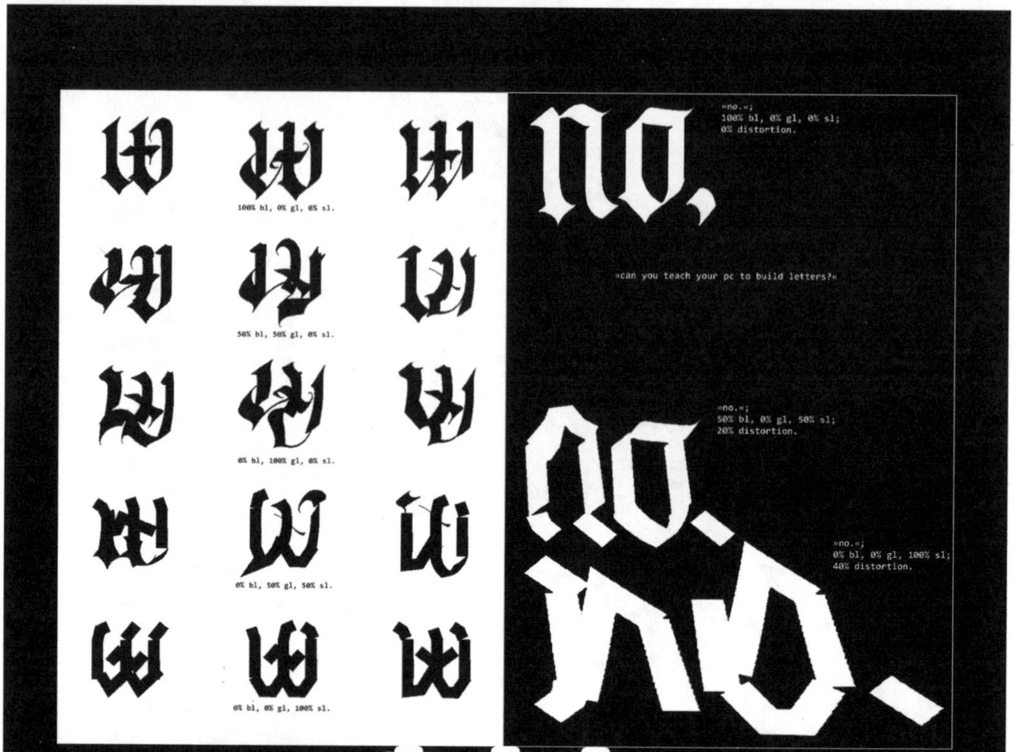

100% bl, 0% gl, 0% sl.

50% bl, 50% gl, 0% sl.

0% bl, 100% gl, 0% sl.

0% bl, 50% gl, 50% sl.

0% bl, 0% gl, 100% sl.

no,

»no.«;
100% bl, 0% gl, 0% sl;
0% distortion.

»can you teach your pc to build letters?«

»no.«;
50% bl, 0% gl, 50% sl;
20% distortion.

»no.«;
0% bl, 0% gl, 100% sl;
40% distortion.

060 Christian Tkaczuk DEU— CHEATING LETTERS

Experimental typographic exploration.

061 Yaroslava Kovalchuk
UKR—FLOWERS

This poster is the outcome of a design exercise where Kovalchuk has been investigating type as a visual element. It's part of a broader series that delves into the theme of nature. The combination of experimental typography and typeart create a whole image where all elements are constructed with type. For the poster FLOWERS, she used transformed graphic elements to create the letters. In this case, the individual elements combine to form the typography.

062 Mike van der Sanden, Bas van Brandwijk NL—
SAVE OUR SOUND

A sound-based motion system coded in p5js.

FOR YOUR FONT COLLECTION

This chapter showcases experimental type design and unique type books. Experimental typography emerged in the early 20th century with movements like Dada and Bauhaus, where artists broke traditional rules by blending forms, materials, and techniques. Today, designers mix modern technology with craftsmanship to create innovative, expressive typefaces that blur the lines between language, art, and design.

063 Hana Bernardová CZE— OSPALI

This project's primary objective is to conduct experiments promptly using readily available materials to achieve immediate results. One aspect of the project involved creating a new experimental type called OSPALI, derived from colored bath oil.

064 Alex Ortiga ITA—21 TYPE FACE

The typeface N21 in thee Regular (bottom) and Retro (top) weights was designed on a squared grid: one square subdivided into nine smaller squares. The whole grid is then again subdivided in the middle by a horizontal and a vertical line.

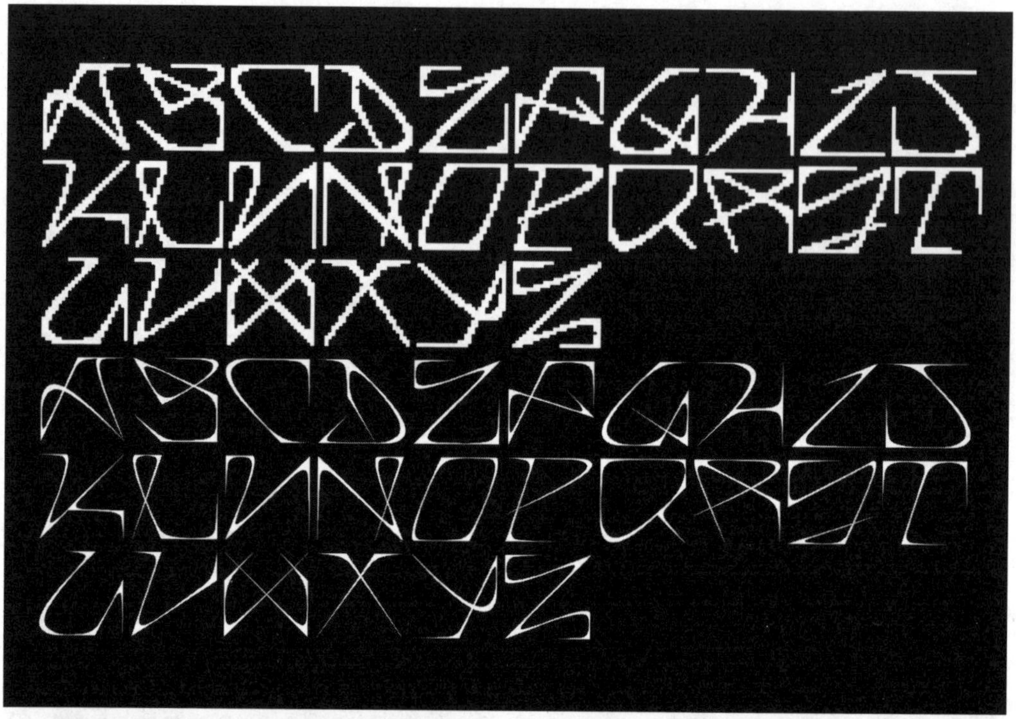

065 Daniel Chillerón Mora ESP—STAL TYPE

STAL TYPE emerges as an innovative and bold typeface that defies conventional norms. It is a Display typeface, meaning it is only used for headlines and highlights, not for running text.

066 Awista Montagne FRA—GG

Experimental lettering engraved on glass.

067 Miriam Goldschmidt DEU— ROOSTER-SPIKE TYPEFACE

Extremely spiky experimental typeface.

068 Miyoun Park DEU—SCALE

Inspired by the precision of a ruler, the SCALE typeface embodies the principle, “If you cannot measure it, you cannot improve it.” This font also serves as a measuring tool, with each character capable of representing a unit of measurement—be it 1 cm or 1 inch. By enabling precise measurements through its characters, SCALE supports both creative and practical applications. Beyond its beauty, the interactions it encourages during use uncover deeper meanings, enhancing understanding and performance.

IF YOU CAN NOT MEASURE IT YOU CAN NOT IMPROVE IT

069 Carmen Draxler DEU—
GRAPHIS SCRIPTA

GRAPHIS SCRIPTA is a variable display typeface that abstractly traces the symbiotic nature of lichen. It has its roots in gravestone inscriptions from different epochs and grows along two axes into ornamental allegories of ecological grief. Printed with bioluminescent ink made from lichen pigment, the typeface comes to life on paper and offers a playful approach to the complex process of mourning over dying landscapes and changing ecosystems.

070 Bureau Progressiv DEU—
MUT ZUR WUT—12TH INTERNATIONAL POSTER COMPETITION

Call to boldly express your own opinion.
Poster for the competition Mut zur Wut—12th International Poster Competition.

071 Özkan Kandir DEU—
EXHAUSTION

Experimental type exploration.

072 Giorgos Zavakos
GRC—VANITY FONT

Helvetica is considered to be the perfect font. However, is perfection possible? Is there a one and only one answer to a question? What if we consider all possibilities? This font is the result of using all the different weights of Helvetica at once. A vain effort to find the gray between the absolute white and black.

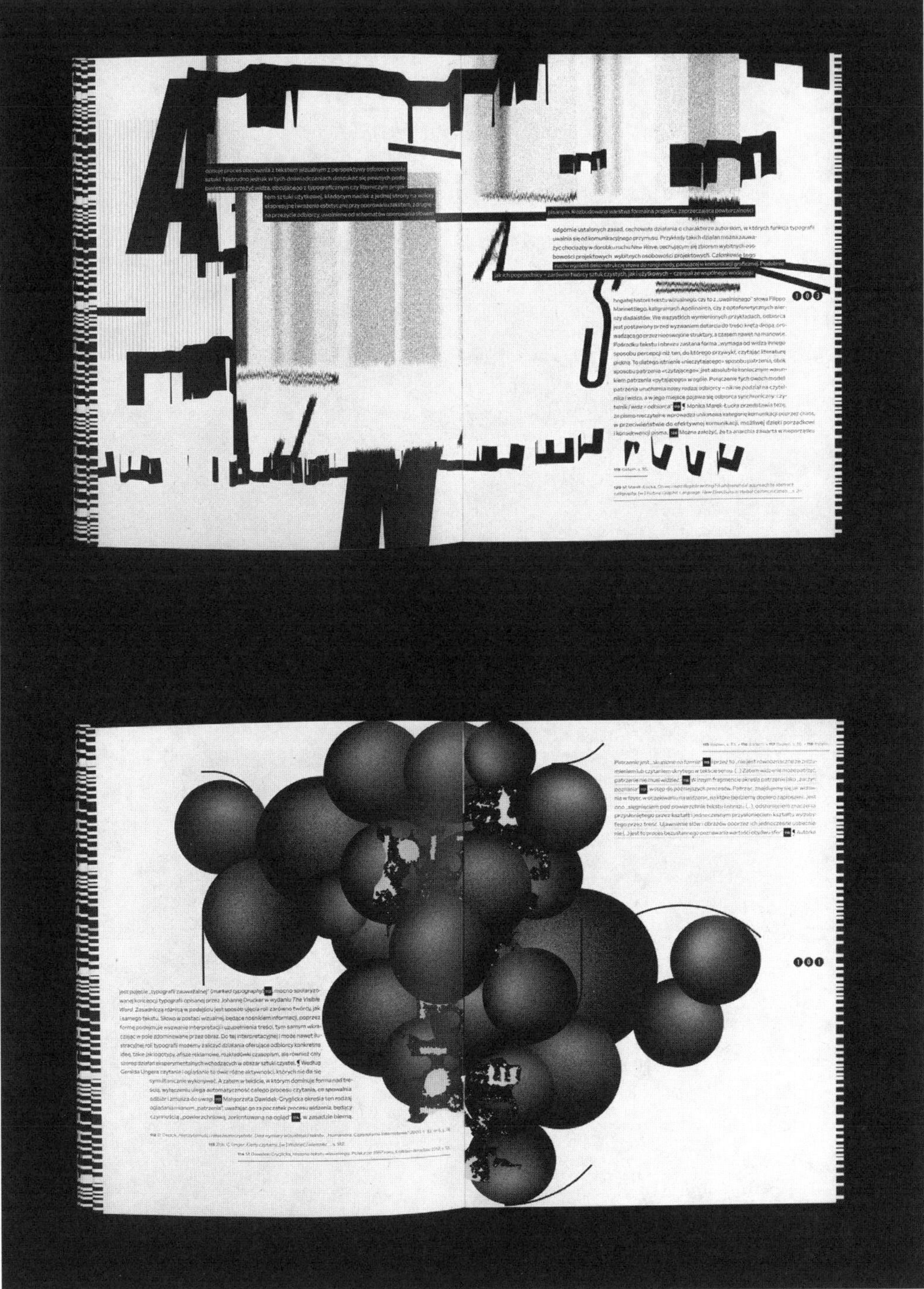

073 Joanna Tyborowska POL— ILLEGIBILITY—THE DICHOTOMY OF FUNCTION AND FORM IN GRAPHIC DESIGN ON THE BASIS OF TYPOGRAPHY AND LETTERING DESIGN

This work examines the issue of text legibility in the domain of graphic design—a field of art that has had a significant influence on the development of contemporary social communication. Due to the functional character of the letter, the aspect of legibility is a basic requirement for the realization of the superior function of text, which is to convey content. For centuries, however, the letter has been entangled in a relationship between the message it carries and its visual representation.

074 Andreas Trenker /
Normplusultra ITA — OUT OF THIN AIR

Andreas Trenker typeset poems in the South Tyrolean dialect, exploring fleeting moments and ephemeral feelings. To visualize the emotions, he created letters from air bubbles in water. By filling an aquarium with fizzy mineral water and treating the surface, bubbles formed words that continually shifted, capturing the poems' essence. This process was documented in a video, accessible via AR on postcards featuring the poems, merging physical and digital realms in a dynamic visual representation.

075 Christopher Sleboda, Kathleen Sleboda USA—DROIT

DROIT is a distinctive display typeface characterized by its straight, fragmented lines that form round and diagonal shapes. The typeface creates a unique texture and rhythm through the interplay of wide and narrow letters, resulting in an unconventional look rooted in the application of a narrow set of parameters.

DROIT
SHIP—BREAKERS 98
BACKPAY
23 MEMORANDUMS
PROTONS
BOOKMAKERS
CRINGE—MAKING STROLL
MINERALISTS

076 Taller Torrents ESP—DIFRACCIONS

DIFRACCIONS is an experimental music festival for which Taller Torrents designed the visual identity. In 2023, the festival revolved around reinterpretation. Inspired by concrete poetry of the mid-20th century, dynamic forms that interact with the theme of this edition were created.

077 Vlad Boyko BEL—PROCESSED-REGULAR

PROCESSED REGULAR—a collaborative AI-generated typeface, result of the first Processed Lab workshop led by Vlad Boyko. Born out of digital tools, PROCESSED-REGULAR becomes a tool itself; an environment for exploring experimental type forms.

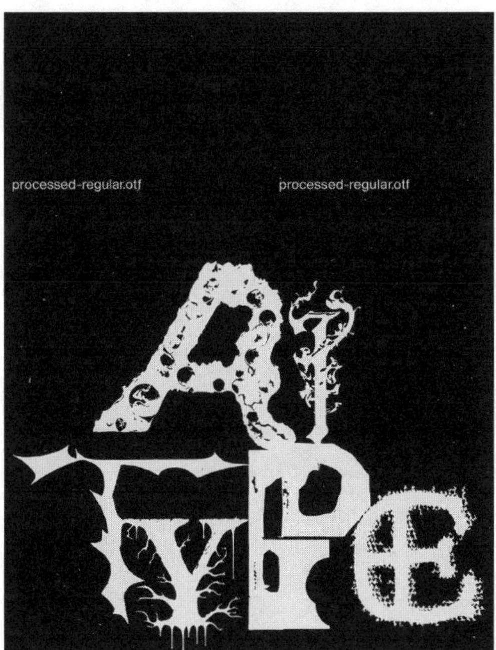

078 Hana Bernardová CZE—EXPERIMENTAL TYPE DEVELOPMENT AND THE CREATION OF THE OSPALI FONT

This project's primary objective is to conduct experiments promptly using readily available materials to achieve immediate results. One aspect of the project involved creating a new experimental type called OSPALI, derived from colored bath oil.

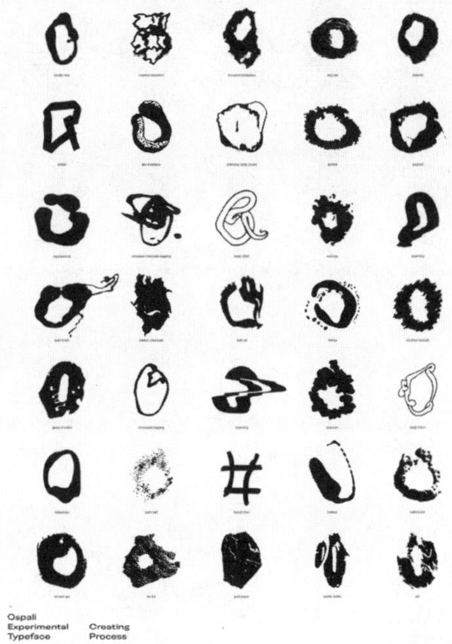

079 Franziska Prüsener DEU—
AGAINST FORGETTING

The Sütterlin script has largely been forgotten today. Its decline began during the Nazi era, when it was banned from schools by the state. Since then, the spread of this script has been dwindling, especially among the generations who still learned it in school. This work sees itself as a symbolic representation of the history of the Sütterlin script and examines its use in an analog and digital context. To counteract the threat of disappearance, the script was digitized with the help of glyphs. This opens up a new level of utilization that makes it possible to preserve and reinterpret Sütterlin in contemporary media and formats.

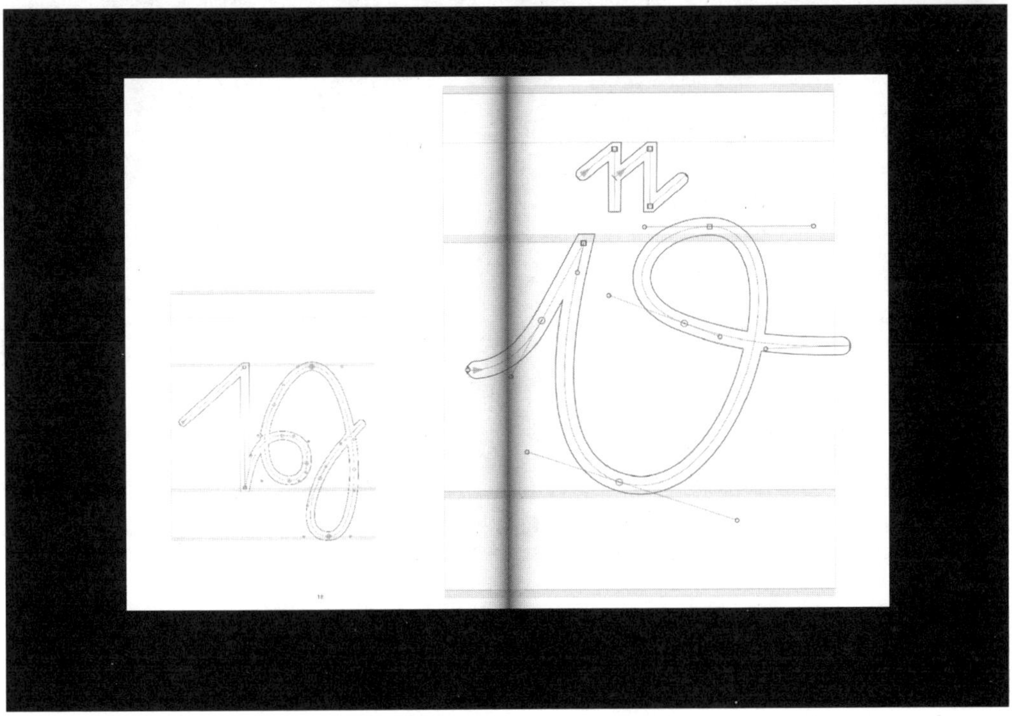

080 Anne-Dauphine Borione FRA— BALEZE TYPEFACE

BALEZE is a contemporary typeface inspired by a Fraktur alphabet, dated around 1825–1850 from Pennsylvania. The source material was used as the basis for a pixel typeface, which was then generatively modified via heavy use of custom filters on the Glyphs software. The result was then refined by hand, preserving the spirit and aesthetic of the original pixel typeface as much as possible. Several stylistic interpretations of the pixel typeface are to be added in the future.

081 Jérémy Landes DEU— NAN SUCCESS

Drawing inspiration from late Art-Nouveau typefaces, the likes of De Vinne and Louis Jou (alongside a healthy dash of alien goo), Jérémy Landes brought the *Success Titling* sub-family to life, packing the Display typefaces with an absolutely insane amount of ligatures (280 to be precise), for both the Latin and Cyrillic scripts. To that end, welcoming its own wonderful absurdity, *Success* embraces its role as an out-of-the-box tilting machine, doubling down on the title with the inclusion of innovative multi-width ligatures and alternates.

082 Carlotta Krämer DEU— LIGA ORNAMENTS

This work is part of a Bachelor Thesis titled *The Sin of Decoration*, in which the gender constructions inherent in modernism and the role played by the rejection of the decorative in relation to this, is revealed. By analyzing design-theoretical texts from a feminist design-historical standpoint, the positioning of the term decorative was revisited in a critical way. „[...]Typography and decoration—is nonsense." is a quote by Max Bill from 1953, directly inspiring the *Liga Typeface*.

083 Wanwai Shum NLD— SLIME REGULAR - BOLD

The SLIME REGULAR - BOLD type design explores the dynamic interplay of form and shadow. The concept revolves around the idea of "slime"" where dragging or manipulating the type module generates overlapping shapes and subtle shadow effects, creating a visually intriguing and but not fluid typographic experience.

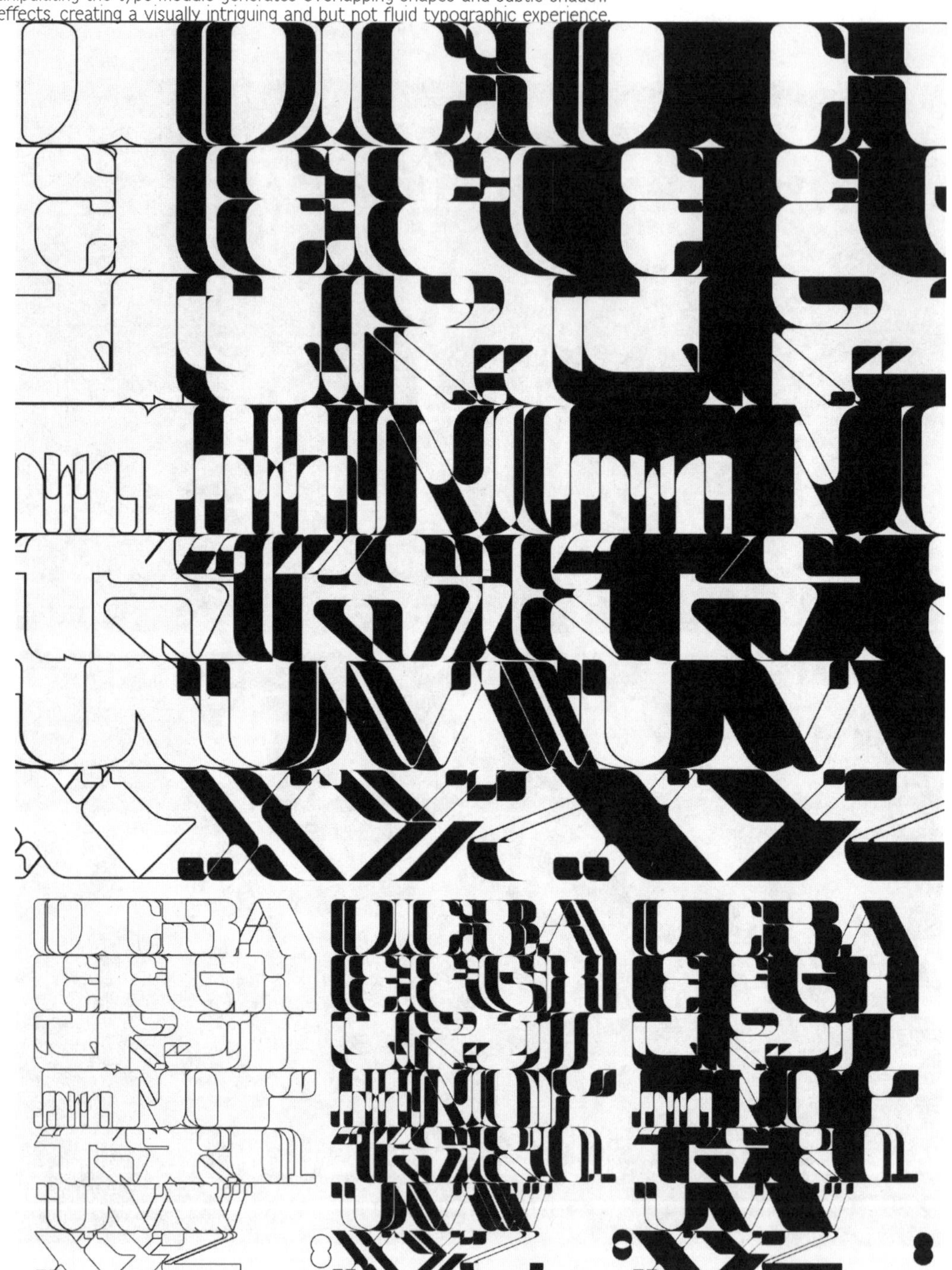

084 Font Spectrum NLD / CHE—PURPLE HAZE

Typographic exploration of numerals by Font Spectrum: The type of playground of Dutch graphic designer / animator Daniël Maarleveld and Swiss type designer Edgar Walthert.

085 Jan Šindler DEU—ROTOR

ROTOR (read from both directions)—just like the typeface. From decoded to encoded message along with the rotation axis! It's a monospaced monolinear typeface that merges surprise and joy together into a unique experience. Why condense letters, when you can rotate them?

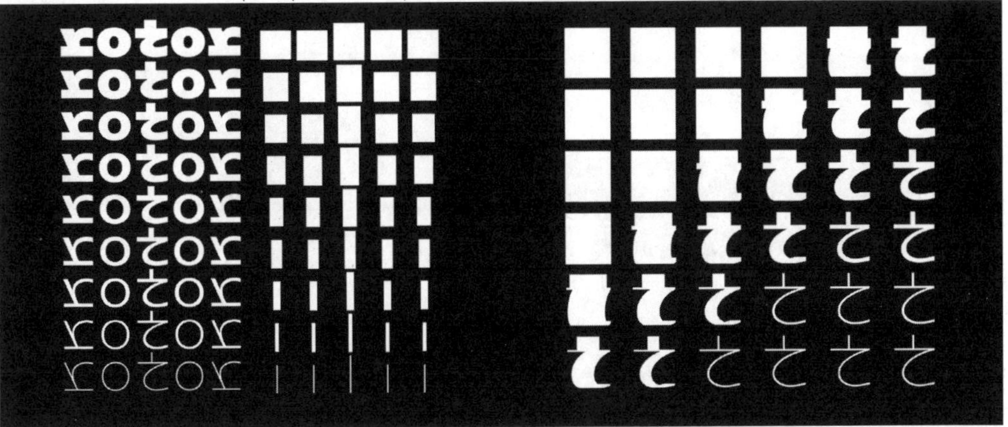

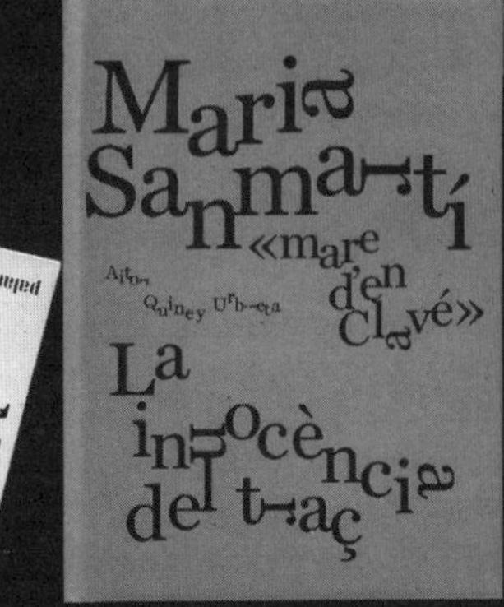

086 David Torrents ESP—
MARIA SANMARTÍ

This work is a catalog about Maria Sanmartí, a mid-20th century painter. She was the mother of the painter Antoni Clavé and highly recognized in Europe and Spain, but absurdly forgotten. In this project, the designers have created a dialog between her work and typography.

087 Thomas Maier DEU—FELSEN

The FELSEN font or rather its character set consists of six basic forms that are programmed to compose each character. Random parameters were programmed into the font to create the font's unusual characteristics. There are different random details in each font style. In addition, a theoretically unlimited number of font styles can be created. The font was not subsequently reworked in order to preserve its unique character which has an unmistakable appearance especially in the extreme weights.

088 Luis Rutz

DEU— BRUTALE

Paris brutal typeface— a shifted, destructed system.

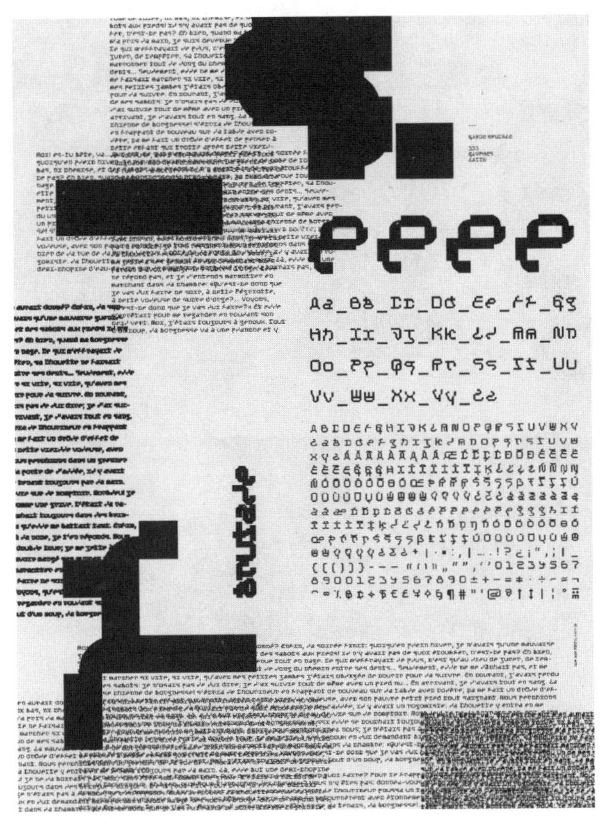

MORE IS MORE

Experimental collages and illustrations invite you to explore type as a living component of design. They show how type not only communicates, but also conveys aesthetic and emotional mes sages. Through the use of abstract forms, the visu al identity of type is re interpreted and trans formed, giving the works a unique and inno vative touch.

089 Lilli Gölz DEU— FUTURE OF DESTRUCTION

Follow the path. Can you still follow?

090 Julie Doriath FRA— COLIBRI

COLIBRI is a typeface family inspired by 90s rave flyers, created by Julie Doriath. Available in three weights, with two of them being encoded, which is inspired from animal mimicry and rave culture codes for confidential communication hypotheses. BPM stems from the deconstruction of the character through techno vibrations (130 to 200 BPM), while Fluid explores the fluidity and the wrapping of electronic music. Its name references the hummingbird's heartbeat, ranging from 250 BPM at rest to 1000 BPM in flight.

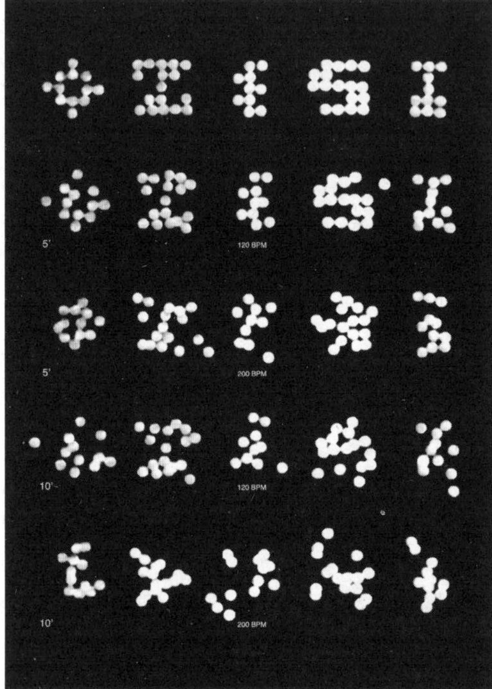

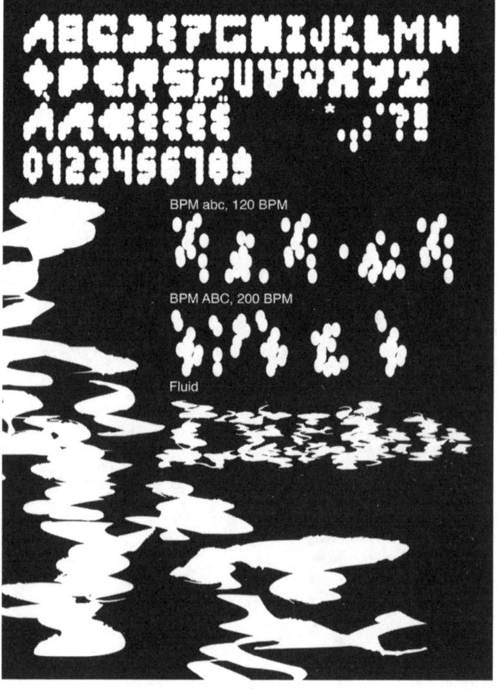

091 Juliane Lipp DEU—
TEASING TYPOGRAPHY

An exploration of the anatomy and structure of typography, delving into the hidden frameworks and tactile qualities that emerge when dissecting and manipulating its form.

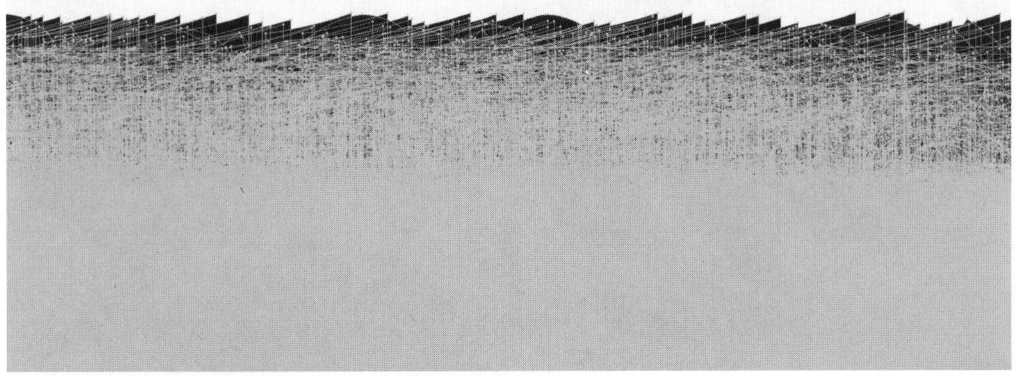

092 Slawomir Jakub POL—
SAVAGEDESIGN

This project is a fun branding project for SavageDesign, a digital studio run by a friend of the designer. It involves experimenting with a blend of physical and digital media, combining mixed analog techniques with 3D rendering in postproduction.

093 Cihan Tamti DEU—
DOXS RUHR-REBELS & REALITIES

Every year, DOXS RUHR hosts a festival with a new theme, for which a special lettering design is created. For the title Rebels & Realities, the word "Rebels" was designed experimentally with simple curves and connections between the letters. It was important to keep the lower part, "Realities," simple to maintain balance in the design and create a good typographic contrast.

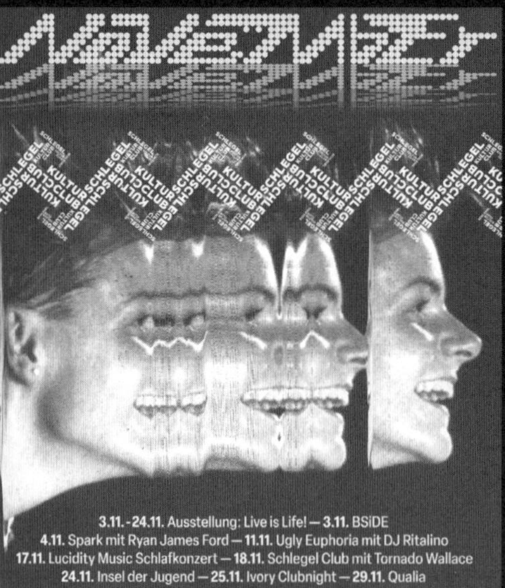

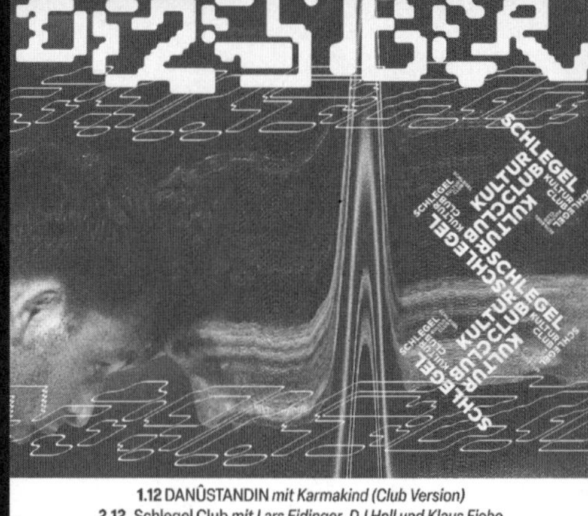

094 Emma Märschenz, Anna Maurer DEU— SCHNITTBLUMEN

The SCHNITTBLUMEN project addresses the environmental impact and working conditions in the global cut flower industry. It shows how the massive use of pesticides and the exploitation of labor call the sustainability and ethics of the industry into question.

095 Marie Sadlo DEU—
PLASTIC WASTE BEHIND CLOSED DOORS

By now everyone should be reflecting their own waste habits and working towards improvement. But the fact that the majority of plastic waste is hidden behind the doors of industry and commerce often remains unnoticed. The plastic waste typography was crafted from discarded plastic from the automotive industry, symbolizing the tons of plastic that leave these sectors as unusable remnants.

096 Marcus Diamond GBR—FEEL THE BURN

FEEL THE BURN Is an experimental typeface made from discarded waste produced by a mechanical machine tool. A day-to-day working laser cutter uses selective burning away of material to create precision-cut artwork. The surplus produced is saved in the leftover tray. The offcuts, embers, and detritus are collated, digitally scanned, and constructed into letter forms. The use of byproducts and speculative production techniques makes the works an ambiguous piece of visual communication.

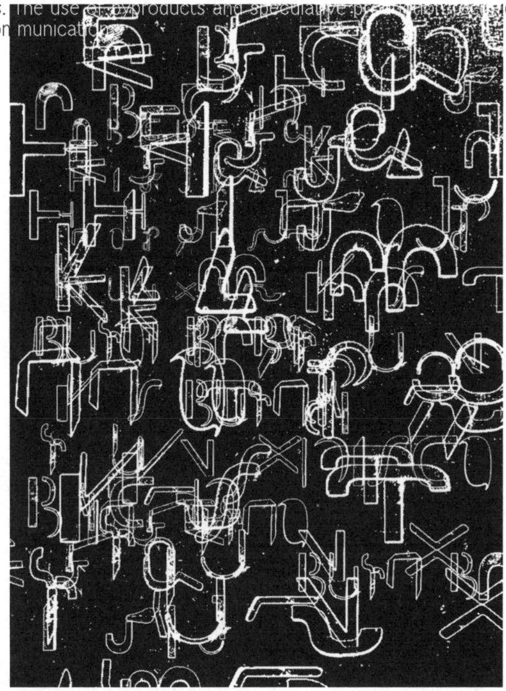

097 Jona Kranzusch DEU—FOAMTYPE

The idea for these works came to Kranzusch while cleaning their stovetop. They had used too much foam and began drawing shapes in it with the sponge. The resulting textures and surfaces were so interesting that Kranzusch scanned them with their phone using the Notes app. This process inspired the aesthetic of the works. With the stovetop, a sponge, and plenty of foam, they created a new typeface called FOAM-TYPE, which were used to design these type posters.

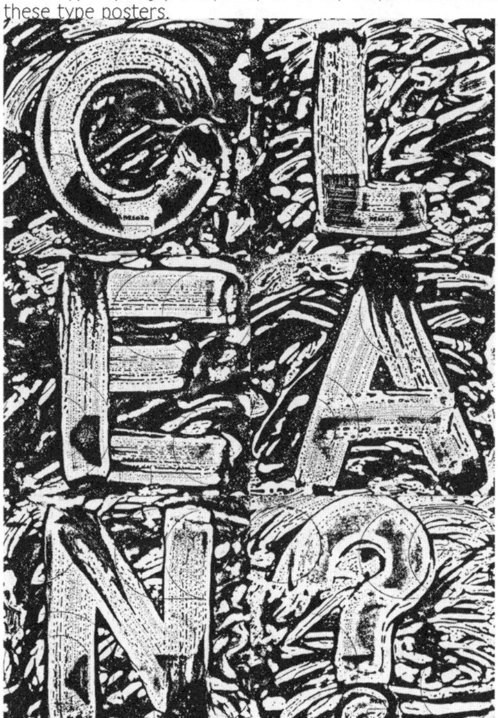

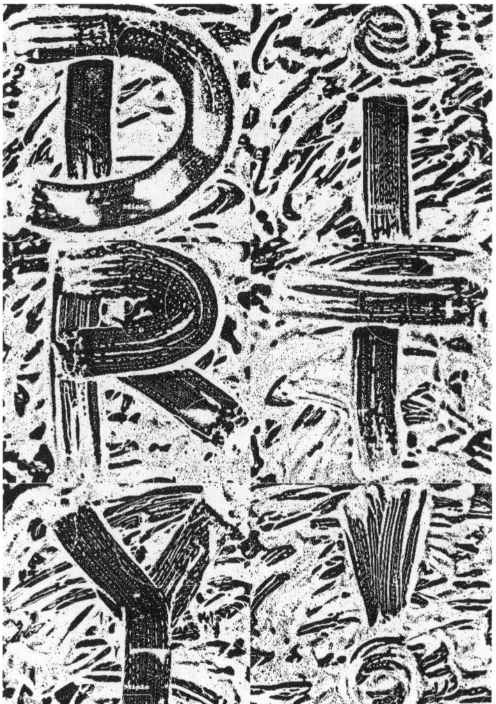

098 Matej Vojtus CZE— A DREAM ABOUT AN EXHIBITION

Experimental exhibition poster.

099 Andrei Turenici ROU—
FICTION TUESDAYS
Poster for the 2024 spring edition of Fiction Tuesdays—a film screening series organized by the Czech Centre Bucharest.

100 Simon Alexander-Adams USA—FLOW DRIP MELT MOLD

This piece combines generative text with a classic reaction diffusion simulation based on the Gray-Scott model. The system simulates two chemicals reacting and diffusing with each other. By driving this simulation's parameters with text, one can generate typography of a fluid and melted quality.

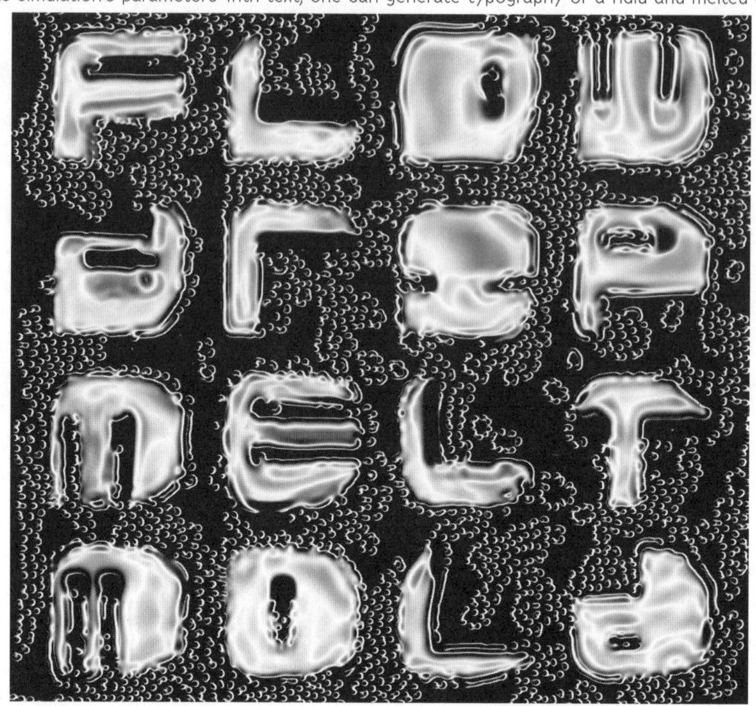

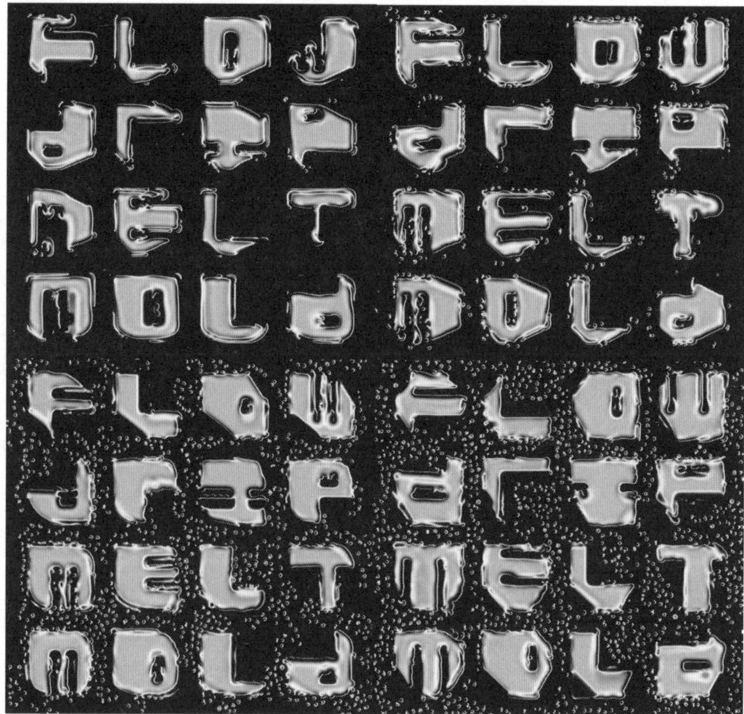

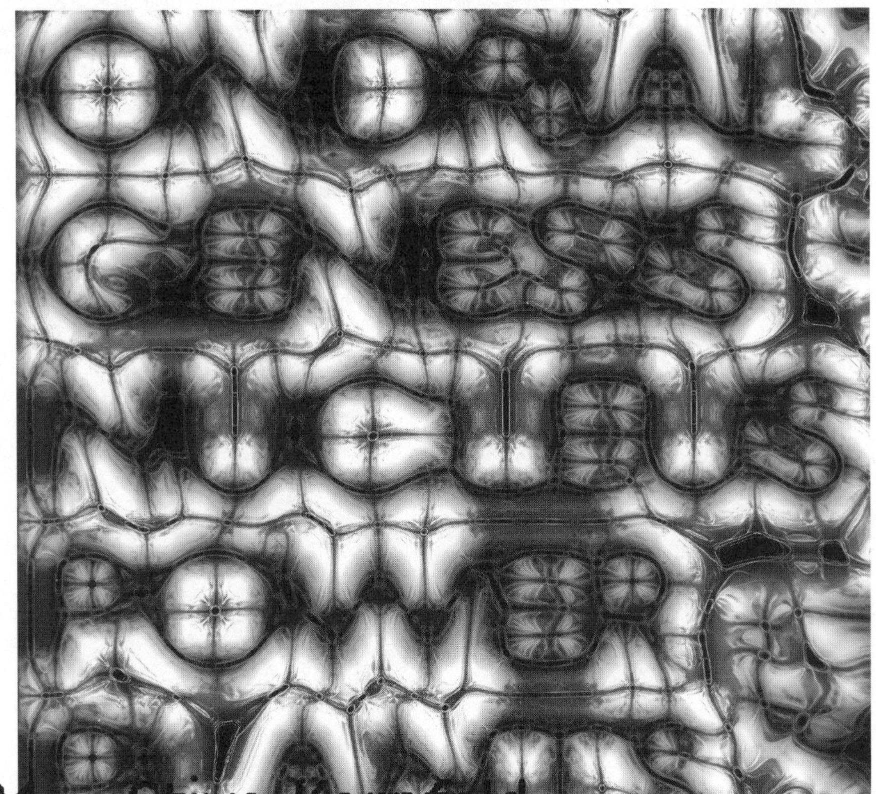

101 Stiva Kornfeld DEU — NUCLEUS

Stiva Kornfeld's project NUCLEUS delves into experimental typography inspired by his fascination with organic cell structures. By pushing the boundaries of digital design tools, Kornfeld generates new, unexpected forms that challenge traditional design norms. NUCLEUS shows how accidents and imprecision can lead to innovative designs, offering a fresh perspective on type creation. This project highlights the fusion of technology and creativity, embodying experimental graphic design.

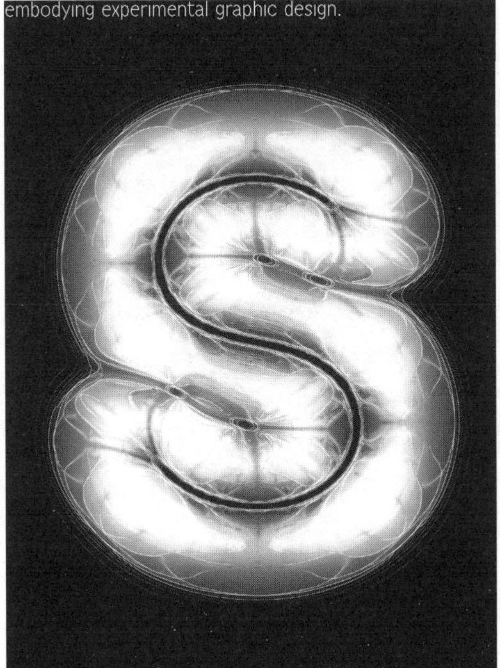

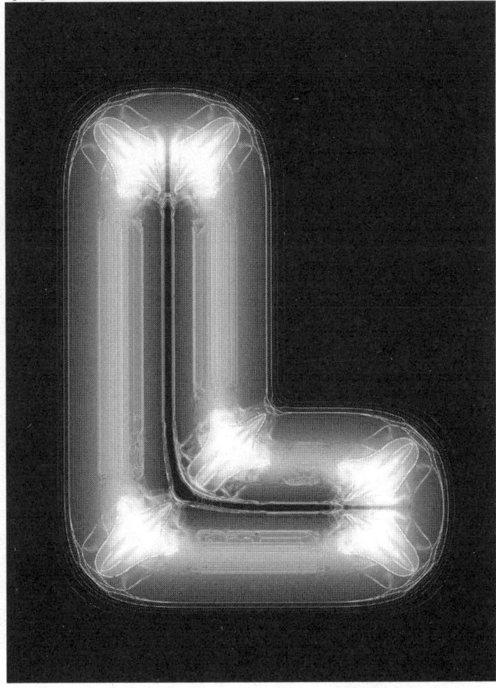

102 Martin Egrt CZE—EPHEMERAL MOTION

A fluid essence of movement in a symphony of perpetual transformation. This experimental piece explores the delicate interplay between motion and perception, inviting the viewer to witness the ethereal choreography of kinetic artistry.

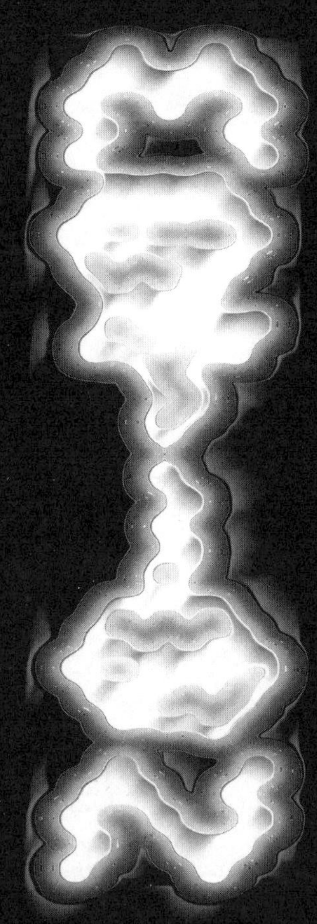

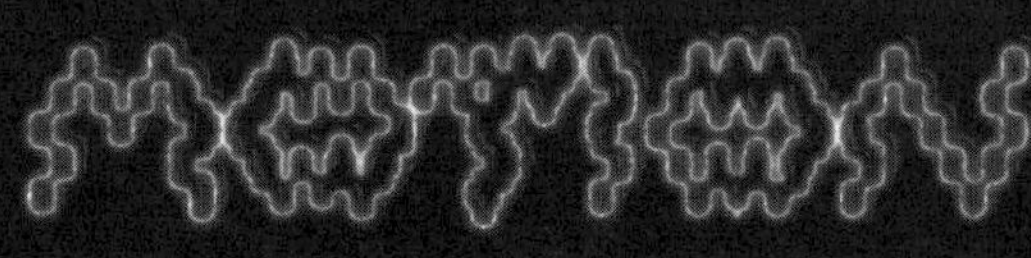

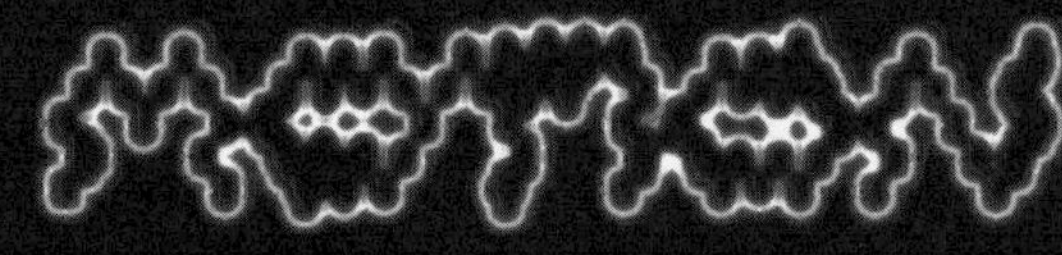

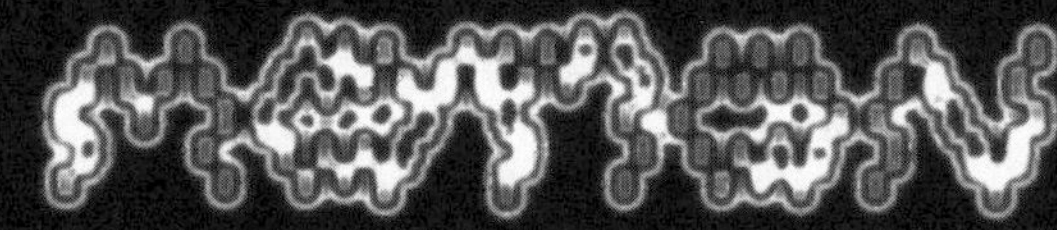

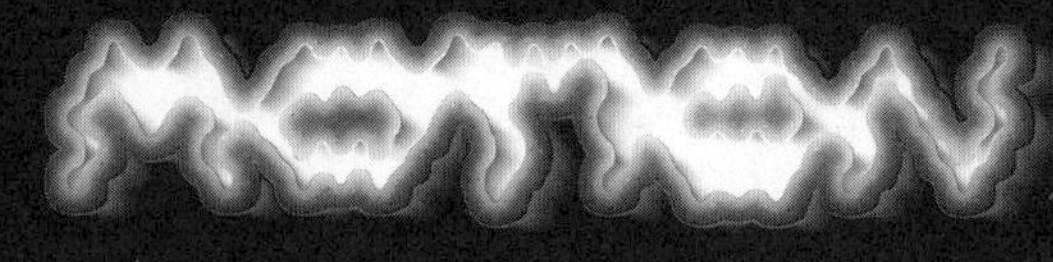

103
Nelli Kamaeva
GEO—TYPE STUDIES

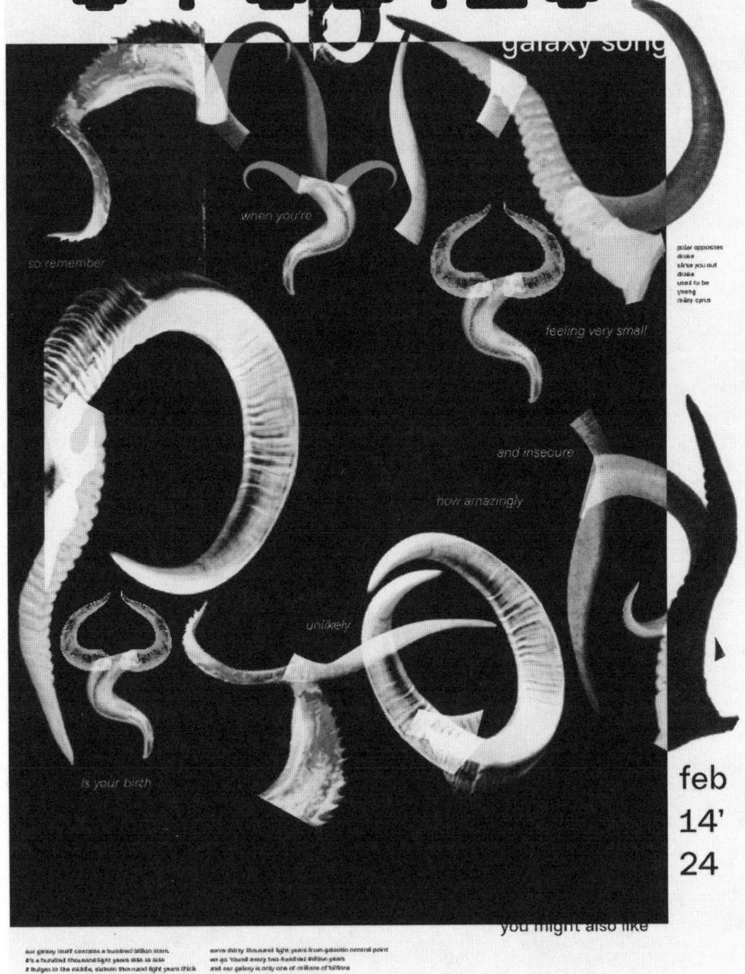

Tbilisi Posters
studio experiments, 2024.

104 Muriel Labadi DEU—FEMME

Experimental typography made out of flowers, specifically the Gloriosa. A poster series around the topic of gender equality and elementary feminism.

105 Vladyslav Boyko UKR— PROCESSED LIFESTYLE NO.4

Getting inspired, we process contexts and meanings around us and produce an outcome, influenced by our personal vision, taste, and reflection. In a world so overloaded with everything, most likely any noise we perceive is already covered in layers of processed contexts. That's probably what Processed Lifestyle means—though the designer isn't entirely certain, either way.

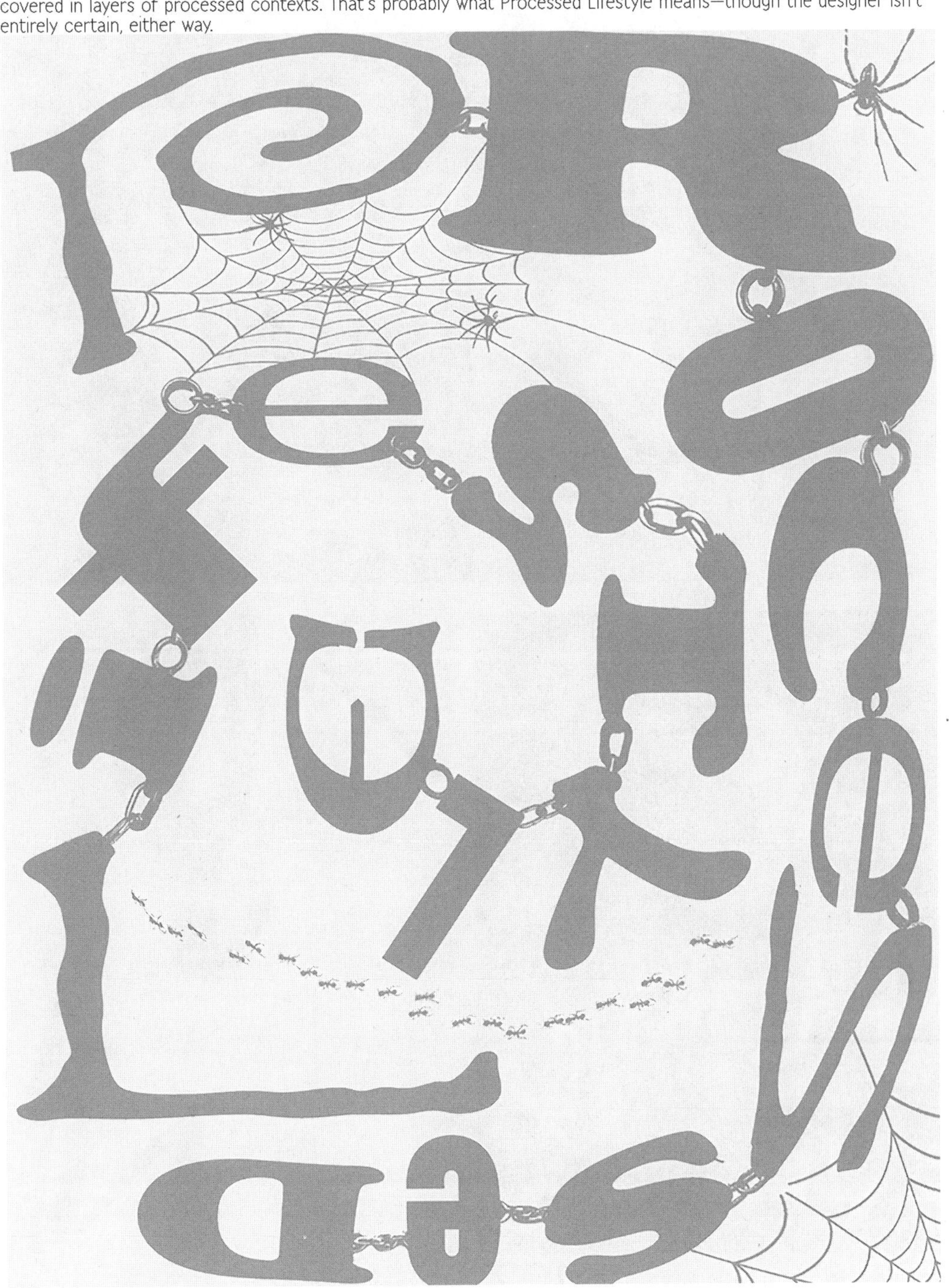

106 Barry Whittaker USA—WHATNOT

Whatnot is an exploration of the peculiarities of the human language. This project explores how an idiom may suggest a geographic region while the term's meaning may remain ambiguous.

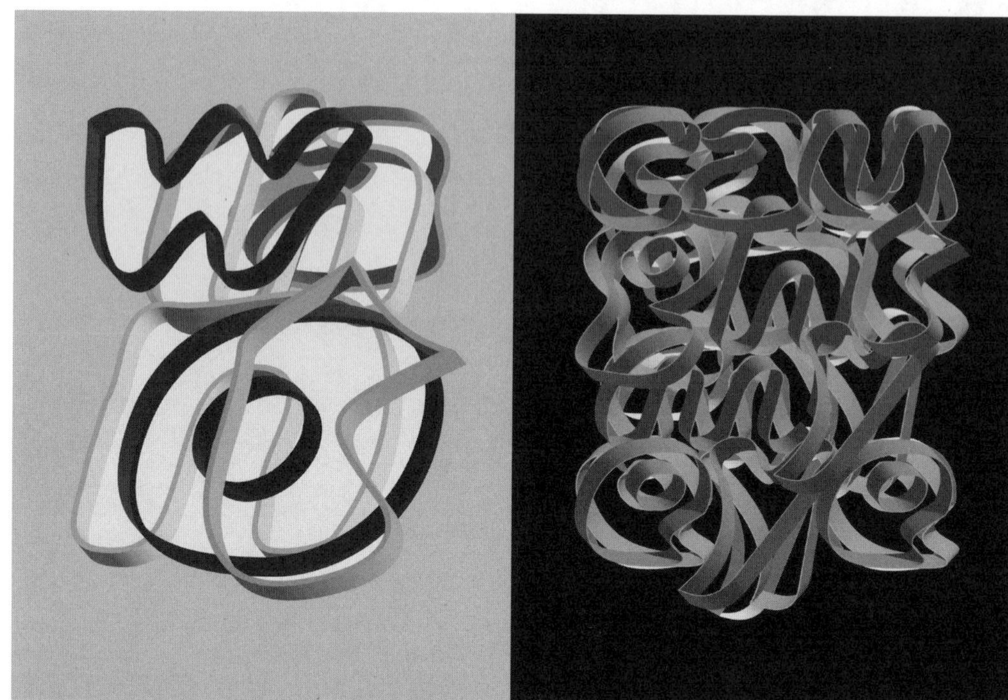

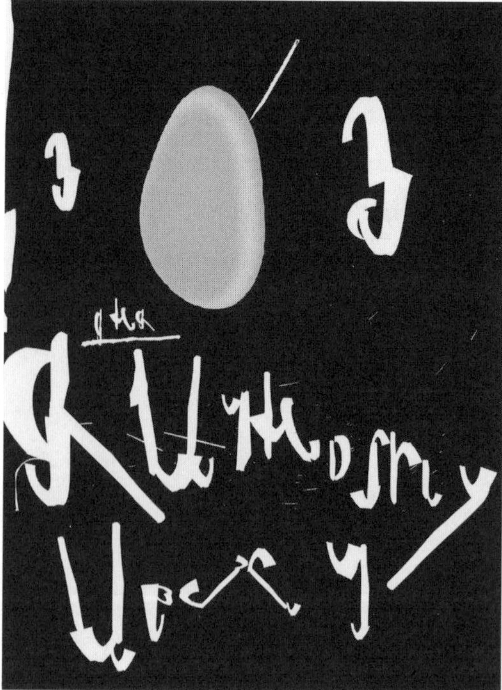

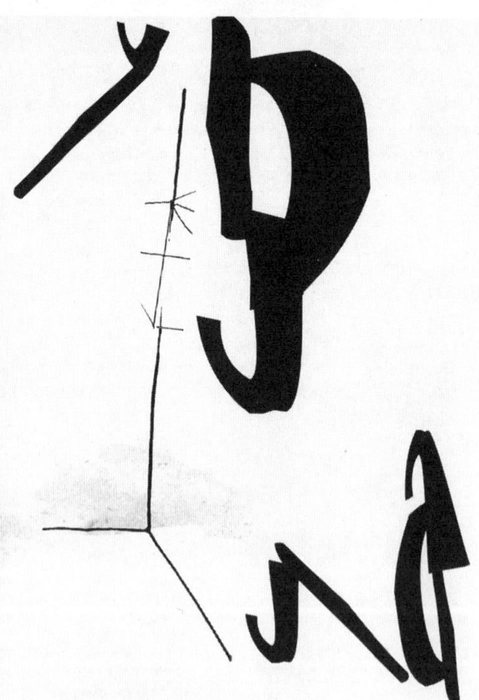

107 Unkke RUS—URLA

Toughest in the infants

108 Ivan Kashlakov BGR—RACHMANINOFF 150

A simplistic approach towards recreating the virtuoso Rachmininoff and his legacy. In the series, the designer explored a typographic approach alongside with symbolic compositions.

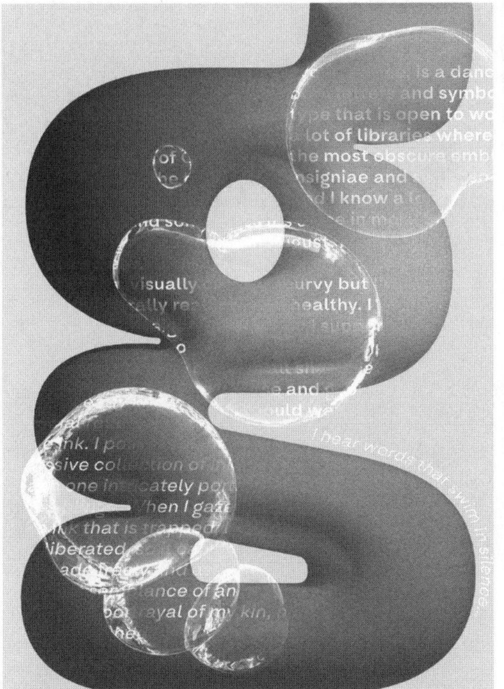

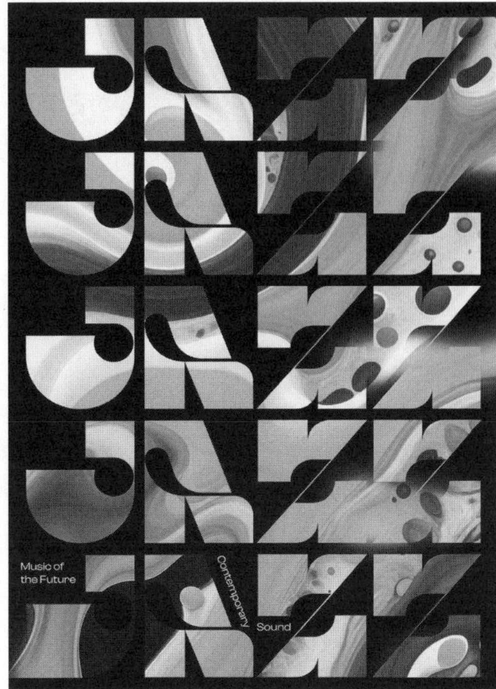

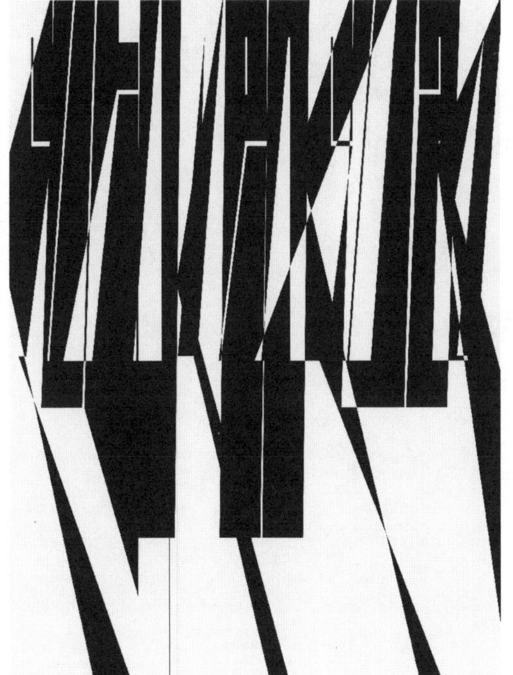

109 Lilli Gölz DEU— FUTURE OF DESTRUCTION

Follow the path. Can you still follow?

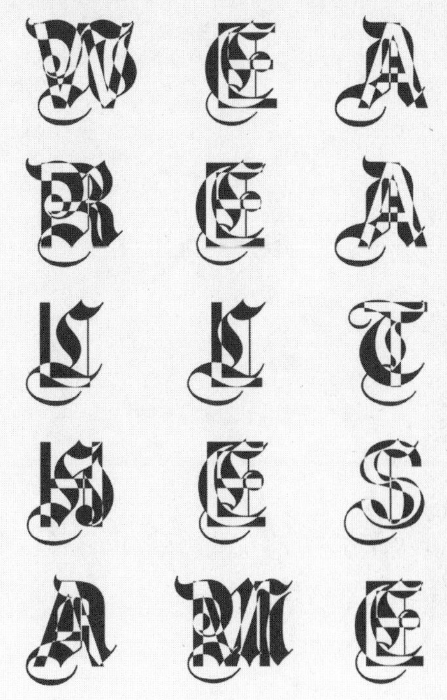

110 Adelisa Ljesnjanin DEU—Layer Type

Experimental letter study.

111 Mark Kokotov EST— TO TEXT TO FORM

Kokotov analyzes how the distinctive, uniform structure of monospaced typefaces shapes the visual and communicative impact of selected posters. By exploring complex design layouts, the author investigates the balance between aesthetic appeal and readability within these font types.

112 Matej Vojtus CZE— MIKROZVUK #17

The experimental poster series MIKROZVUK for LOM space employs brutalist design techniques and unconventional visual elements to capture the essence of the avant-garde nature of sound experiences. Each poster combines abstract composition with bold, modernist-inspired typography, reflecting the client's exploratory vision of music and listening events that are raw and unpolished.

113 Anton Abo UKR— UNTITLED

REC.

NODES REC. IS A MUSIC LABEL FOUNDED IN 2023 BY LEON , MO-SHI, MILAM, AND NINO (FR). IT IS A MUSIC COMMUNITY FOCUSED ON SHOWCASING THE BEST OF ASIA TO THE WORLD.

Typography for various music labels, parties, and brands.

114 Anton Abo UKR—UNTITLED

Typography for various music labels, parties, and brands.

115 Nattapol Rojjanarattanangkool, Khaorong Khaoroi THA—INTACT MAKING THINGS

This graphic explores music notes and graphic notation, using existing elements to create new graphics with the principle of "M"aking to create Things.

116 Wouter Tjeenk Willink / Mr.Nelson Design NLD—YES WE SCAN

The designer created an illustration based on the hand-lettered word "Yes." He then scanned this drawing, printed it, scanned it again, printed it again, and repeated this process multiple times, resulting in very rough textures that give the final piece a raw, analog feel. This process has imbued the artwork with a unique appearance and a great deal of character.

117 Thomas Kühnen DEU—
WHITE NIGHT

Silkscreen printed announcement poster for the Culture Night at the Department of Design of the Folkwang University of the Arts. Printed by hand in jet-black and yellow-green afterglow color (yes, the poster glows in the dark :-)).

118 Matej Vojtus CZE—MIKROZVUK #15

The experimental poster series MIKROZVUK for LOM space employs brutalist design techniques and unconventional visual elements to capture the essence of the avant-garde nature of sound experiences. Each poster combines abstract composition with bold, modernist-inspired typography, reflecting the client's exploratory vision of music and listening events that are raw and unpolished.

KӣR (DRUGSTORE BEOGRAD) | LAURA AGNUSDEI | 11/03/2020 19.30 | LOM, MLYNAROVIČOVA 5, BRATISLAVA-PETRŽALKA | LOM SPACE VSTUPNÉ: 5 EUR

KӣR (Drugstore Beograd) KӣR (Drugstore Beograd)

Laura Agnusdei Laura Agnusdei

KӣR (Drugstore Beograd) KӣR (Drugstore Beograd)

Laura Agnusdei Laura Agnusdei

MIKROZVUK #15 

u. fond na podporu umenia

119 Matej Vojtus CZE— MIKROZVUK #40

The experimental poster series MIKROZVUK for LOM space employs brutalist design techniques and unconventional visual elements to capture the essence of the avant-garde nature of sound experiences. Each poster combines abstract composition with bold, modernist-inspired typography, reflecting the client's exploratory vision of music and listening events that are raw and unpolished.

120 Michiel Schuurman NLD—KAMILĖ ČESNAVIČIŪTĖ

Promotional poster for Kunstruimte BlockC, screenprint by Michiel Schuurman in three fluorescent colors and black. Image by ©The Book Photographer.

121 Jeremy Rieger DEU—CHAOS THEORY

Rendered experimental type in a chrome look.

122 Yannik Schmitt DEU—EXPERITYPE

Photos, taken randomly along the way, served as a template for the letters of the Experitype. The aim was not to recognize individual letters in advance, but rather to consider how type could be created from them when looking through the images. The typeface contains a total of 32 characters, with two variants per letter.

123 Matej Vojtus CZE—MIKROZVUK #13

The experimental poster series MIKROZVUK for LOM space employs brutalist design techniques and unconventional visual elements to capture the essence of the avant-garde nature of sound experiences. Each poster combines abstract composition with bold, modernist-inspired typography, reflecting the client's exploratory vision of music and listening events that are raw and unpolished.

REALITY CHECK

While digital media dominates our lives, the physical world offers limitless opportunities for creative expression. Spatial typefaces and designs create a tangible link between visuals and viewers, while real-world branding strengthens identity. In gaming, connecting vir tual and physical ele ments enhances immer sion. The goal is clear: design should not just exist digi tally but also impact the physical world, encouraging interaction and new experiences.

124 whynotedesign何樂不為設計
CHN—JAZZ TRIO NIGHT MUSIC FESTIVAL VISUAL DESIGN

They key elements of jazz—from melody to swing, to fusion, to improvisation—are cleverly incorporated into the design, forming a visual symphony that reflects the musical tapestry of Jazz Trio Night. These words, rendered in a bold, pixelated font, hint at the digital age while maintaining a retro feel. Each word is strategically placed within the composition, interacting with the geometric shapes and lines, creating a visual dialog that reflects the interplay of different musical elements.

125 Philipp-Mohncke DEU— SEAT COVERS

As Mohncke was sitting on the train and still needed a main topic for the EXPERIMENTAL TYPE course, he looked at the seat covers he was sitting on, which people encounter every day with all kinds of patterns. Perhaps people no longer consciously look at these patterns and only perceive them passively, which Mohncke thought could be changed by replacing the patterns with typography. Because where there is typography, the viewer tries to read it. So he took pictures from buses and trains, created mock-ups, and made new seat covers with humorous references to the whole subject of public transport. But of course not with a classic Futura that is easy for everyone to read at first glance, but in such a way that the viewer may only be able to read the sentence at third glance.

Bercy

126 Mistaker ITA— CARA CATASTROFE

CARA CATASTROFE is a project about the fascination of disasters. It is a data-driven video, where the typography is altered by a selection of data relating to the major catastrophes that have occurred in the last 100 years. It was projected on the wall of the Alto Forno during Videocittà Festival 2023, just behind the stage.

127
Péter Tóth
HUN —
CLOUD BUSTERS

The international exhibition of EKKM Tallinn Cloudbusters: Intensity vs. Intention explores the invisible connections between the human psyche and technology, using the metaphor of natural and data clouds. The designer manually redrew some letters of the word "Cloudbusters" with Kazuhiro Aihara's Sword font, applying them across various formats for the fictional identity.

128 Gökçe Genç TUR—
KAZA, KÖPEK, KAHVALTI VE YUMURTA

In the play *Kaza, Köpek, Kahvaltı ve Yumurta*, the theme of parallel universes and simultaneity is visually expressed on the poster. Typography is placed at the center, with its reflective behavior emphasized as a key feature. This design offers the audience a subtle hint of the parallel world and simultaneity they will encounter in the play.

129 Jim Sutherland, Christian Eves GBR—
NOTATION ROTATION—

The letterforms form the squares of the chessboard themselves. The designers aimed for the typography to be abstract, allowing it to be perceived as squares first and then as the notation. The typefaces were constructed from a grid of 64 pixels, reflecting the number of squares on the board. Two cuts, light and heavy, were designed to create the black and white squares, named Notation Black and Notation Light. The black and white squares are oriented in each direction for each player to read, leading to the name NOTATION ROTATION.

130 Parascolaire CAN— PARASCOLAIRE

These works were created in a workshop, investigating the creation of modular typographic characters inspired by the architectural heritage of the city. The participants had to create a modular grid based on their favorite heritage building in proximity of the workshop, and create a complete alphabet using the grid as the main creation method.

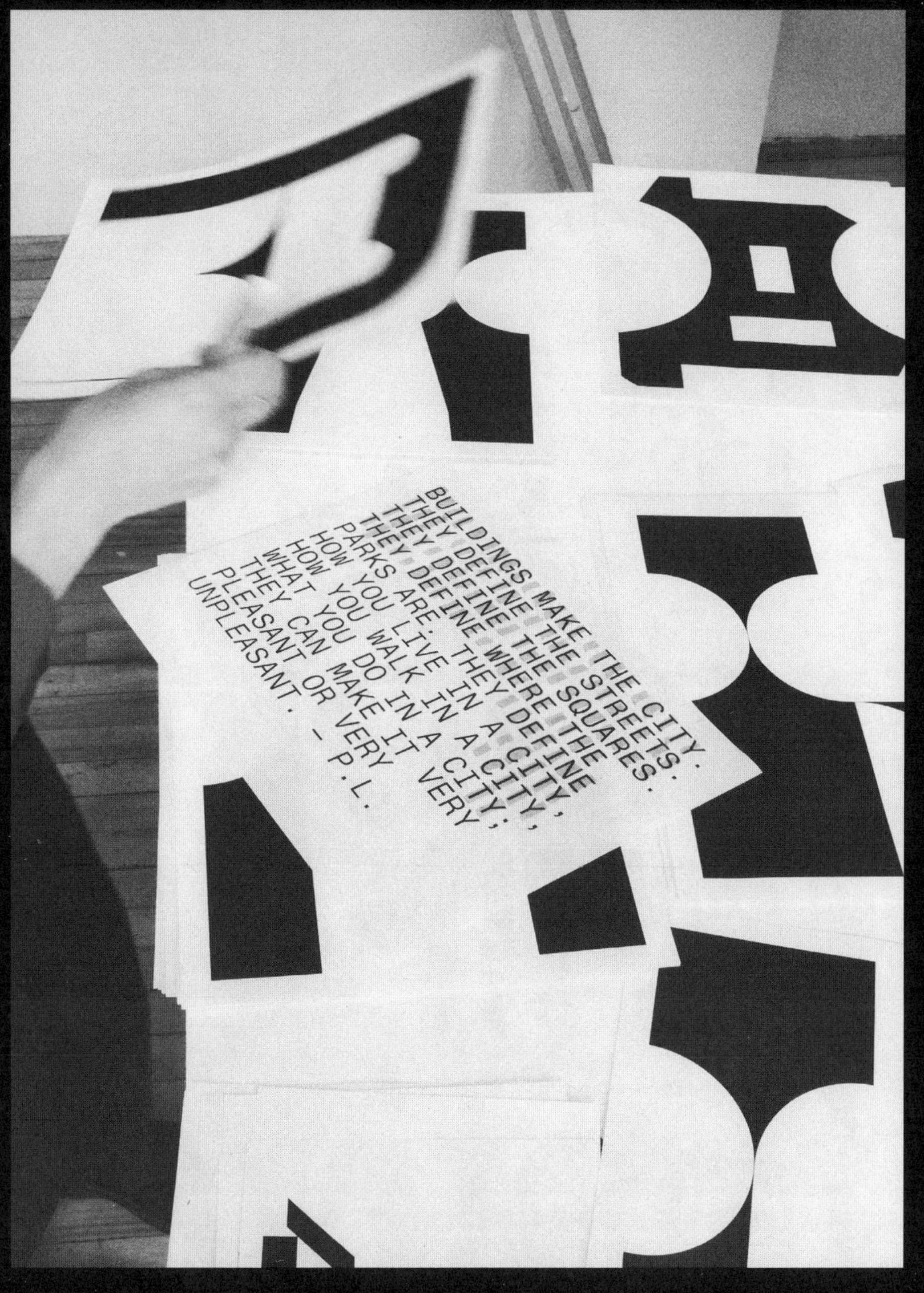
BUILDINGS MAKE THE CITY.
THEY DEFINE THE STREETS.
THEY DEFINE THE SQUARES.
THEY DEFINE WHERE THE
PARKS ARE. THEY DEFINE
HOW YOU LIVE IN A CITY,
HOW YOU WALK IN A CITY;
WHAT YOU DO IN A CITY.
THEY CAN MAKE IT VERY
PLEASANT OR VERY
UNPLEASANT. – P.L.

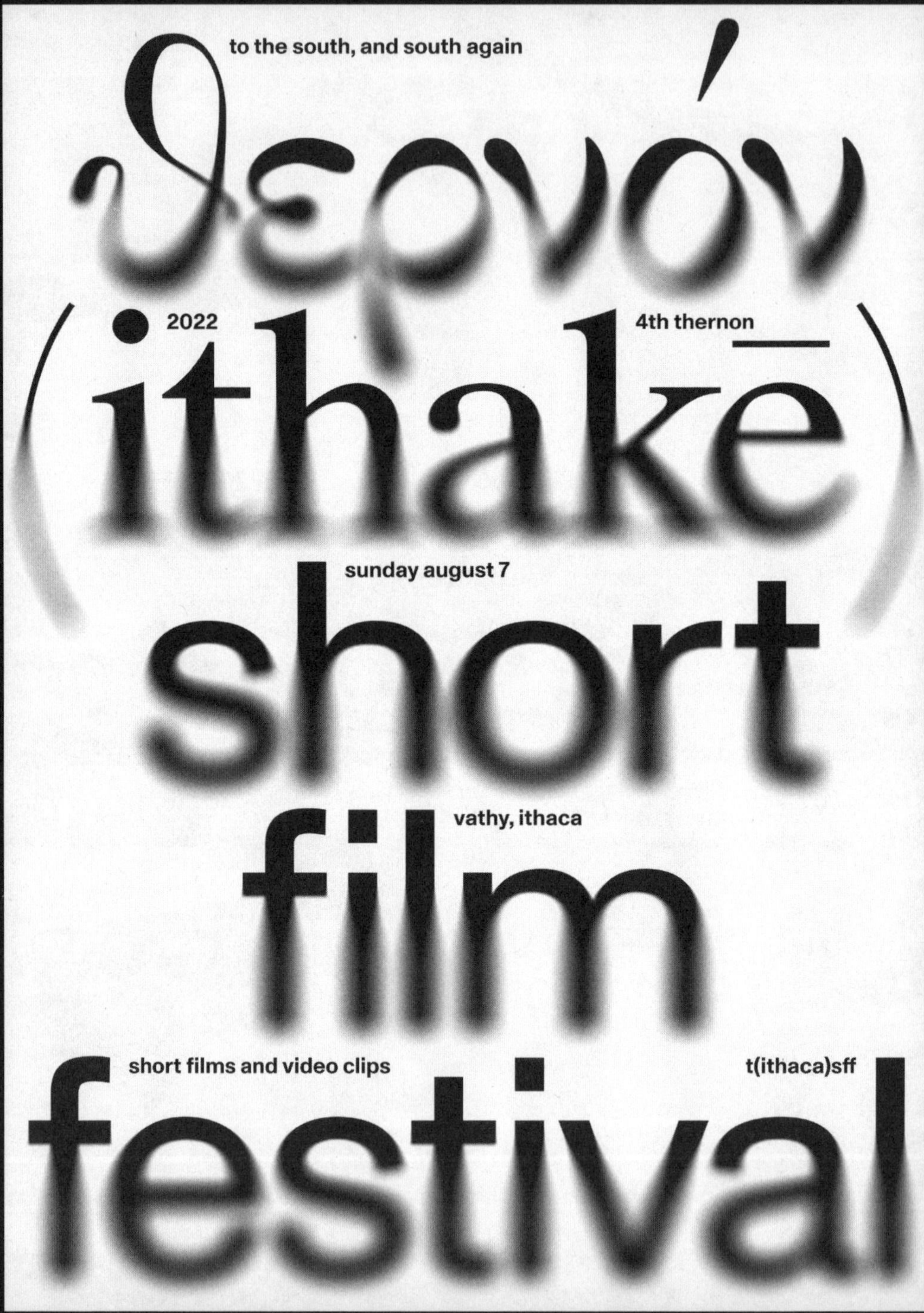

to the south, and south again

θερνόν

(ithakē)

2022

4th thernon

sunday august 7

short

vathy, ithaca

film

short films and video clips

t(ithaca)sff

festival

131 . Dimitris Lelakis, Maria Tsilomitrou GRC— THERNON SHORT FILM FESTIVAL

Thernon is a nomadic short film festival featuring Greek directors, traveling to unique remote locations like small vineyards, ancient ruins, and secret gardens. Inspired by Odysseus' journey, its identity emphasizes topos, the locality. The title uses Apla, an old Greek serif typeface, while Monument Grotesk, a sans serif typeface, highlights the contrast between poetic locality and neutrality. Blurry, noisy typography symbolizes cinema's essence and the festival's constant movement.

132 Veronika Huff DEU—STAR

Veronika Huff's latest project in her Communication Design studies is an exploration of form by delving into the geometry of stars. She has crafted an array of mesmerizing patterns, revealing the hidden visual potential of this celestial shape. Veronika Huff's approach invites viewers to see stars not just as symbols, but as dynamic elements of design.

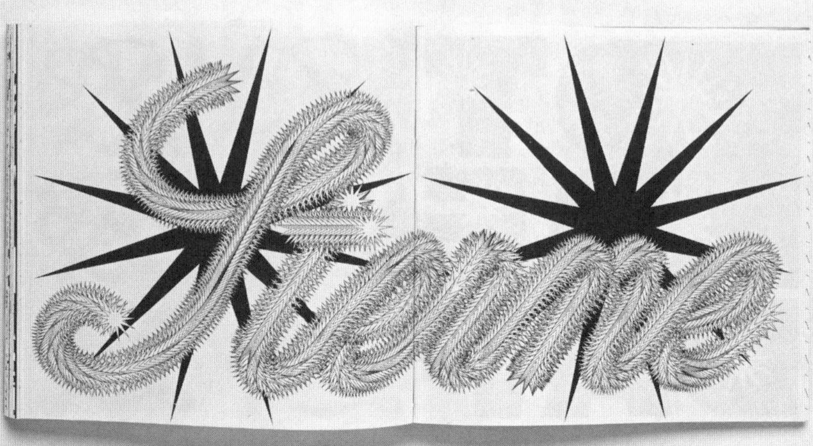

133 Victoria Boyko UKR — REMA

The Factory Street in Lviv gathers many different people around it. Boyko viewed this street as a ready-made identity, collected all its signs, traces of its inhabitants, collected its cracks and smell, and fit it into this identity. Boyko was an observer, she just looked carefully and turned what she saw into an identity.

134 Rhoda Herold DEU— WITHOUT IMAGE: AN ARTISTIC PERSPECTIVE ON APHANTASIA — AN EXHIBITION

In her bachelor exhibition Without Image, Rhoda Herold presents code-based deconstructed type as well as the resulting digital design tool "Image without Image," which translates text into abstract images. The exhibition also shows an endless dot matrix print installation that gradually deconstructs a text about the artist's personal background over a period of five days in order to make APHANTASIA visible.

135 Anna Katalin Szilágyi HUN— NINCS IS KORLÁ

Spatial installation at MOME University Campus in Budapest. The name (which translates to "There is no limit") is a wordplay on the fact that the word "korlát" can mean both a physical barrier and a limit in Hungarian.

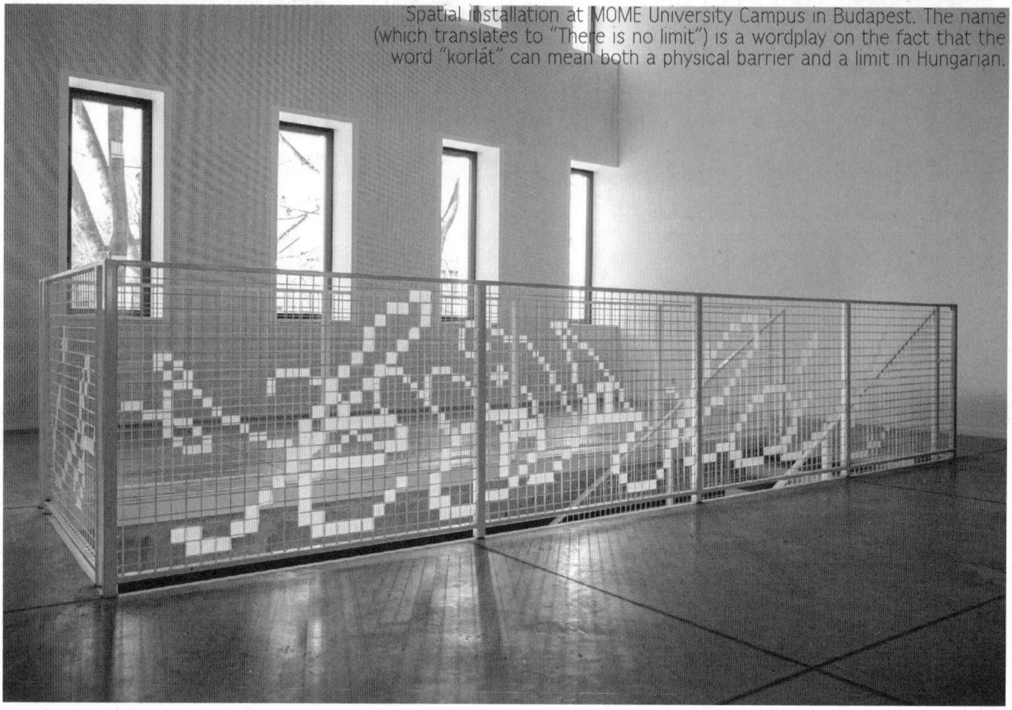

136 Georg Zinsser DEU— KIESELECH

This typeface goes back to the analog world. While much is generated by AI and similar aesthetics may be created there, nature remains an endless resource of inspiration. The stones I collected for this experiment were found in the river right in front of my house. On my journey to becoming a designer, it served not only as a place for relaxation and swimming but also as a source of ideas for my work.

137 Vincent Liu USA— KOI

Modular Display typeface inspired by koi fish patterns on Chinese bowls.

↓ Scan with artivive

138 Studio MOS DEU— LEERSTAND GROTESK

Unused spaces and vacant properties are a growing problem for many cities, which has economic and, above all, social consequences. The project uses a variable font in combination with an AR application to draw attention to this problem. With the constant disappearance of supporting letter elements, the typeface becomes increasingly porous and unstable. Within the AR app, the variable font can be implemented three-dimensionally in spaces to fill them with thematically appropriate messages. App development in cooperation with YNT Studio.

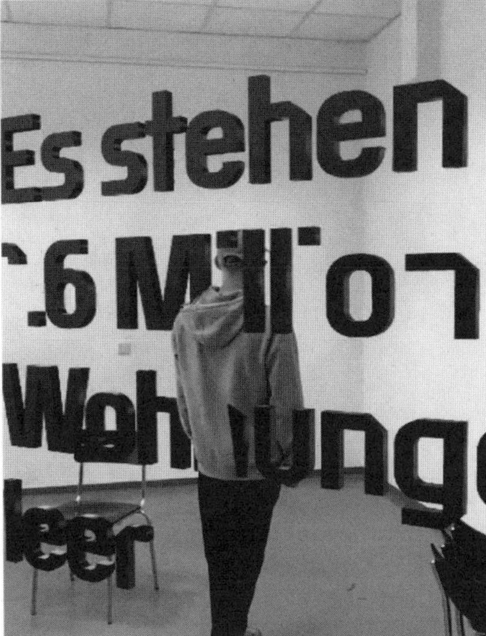

AWAY FROM KEYBOARD

In an age where digital media dominates, it is important to recognize the value of physical materials and craft techniques. Material works bring design to life, creating a tangible connection between concept and execution. Incorporating traditional craftsmanship enhances visual impact and celebrates the tactile processes that enrich the final creation.

139 Morgane Vantorre FRA —PIXELS ENGRAVED IN STONE

Vantorre's intention was to experiment by engraving lettering inspired by embroidery and bitmap language, composed solely of the same unit. The gesture of the process is entirely dependent on light, which makes the approach to "drawing" the letter interesting.

140 Til Lohmeyer DEU—SUNBURN

Experimenting with typography burned onto light-sensitive paper, much like a sunburn on skin.

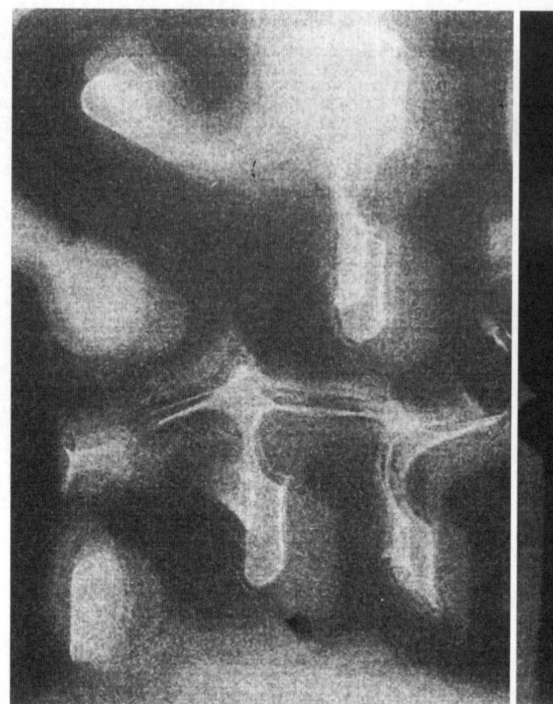

141 Rus Khasanov RUS—FLAME TYPE

FLAME TYPE is an experimental font created using fire. The creation process involved applying flammable liquid to a surface in the shape of letters, which was then ignited. The fire gave the font a unique, organic look, with the flames "dancing" under the influence of Khasanov's breath, whimsically distorting the original shape of the letters.

142 Patrekur Björgvinsson ISL — I CUT MY HAIR NOW I DON'T REMEMBER ANYTHING

Type made with locks of hair from the designer, assembled in hand and scanned. The text says "I cut my hair now I don't remember anything" in Icelandic, playing with the idea of hair holding its owners memories.

143 Ole Freytag DEU— WAKE UP – MARCUS AURELIUS

Brush calligraphy with a double negative space, achieved by cutting out the background with a scalpell.

144 Druckwerkstätten der FH Aachen, Robert Franke DEU—HOFMANN GRID TYPE TOOL

THE HOFMANN GRID TYPE TOOL is based on a grid system by Armin Hofmann and the digital Display font Hofmann by Hoang Nguyen and David Gobber. It enables the analog printing of graphic shapes and outline letters in a calligraphic style on the printing press. The tool was developed in the printing workshops of the University of Applied Sciences Aachen as part of Robert Franke's Type Tool seminar. A modern rebellion.

145 Aysel Kopuz DEU — EAT ME

Experimental typography on the human object.

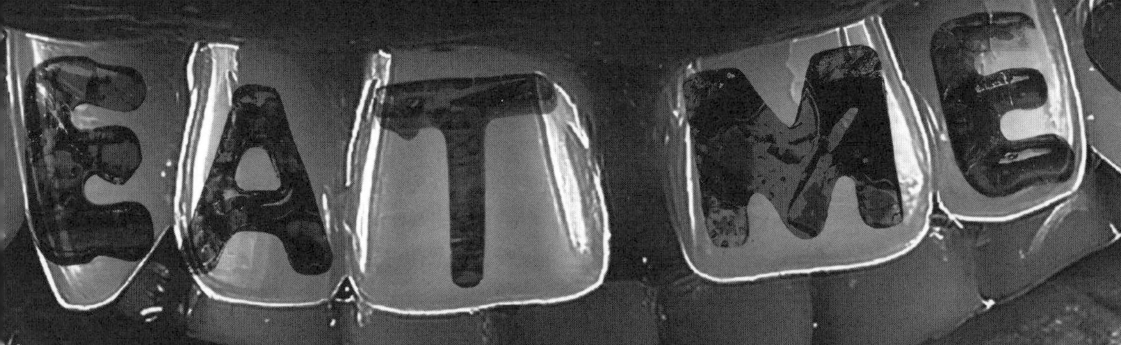

146 Alec Vivier-Reynaud FRA—MYCOGRAPHIÆ: FUNGAL AND TYPE MATTER SYMBIOSIS

MYCOGRAPHIÆ proposes typography as living beings through a bio-printing process with biological inks made of molds and yeasts. Like micro-fungi that permeate the layers of life, new forms of symbiotic writings come to life to redefine the experience of an image/letter: a letter that's now cultivated. In this act, the fungus no longer reproduces a sign; it digests its form, seizing it to redefine its structure and vitality : the sign gradually gains an organic autonomy that escapes the designer.

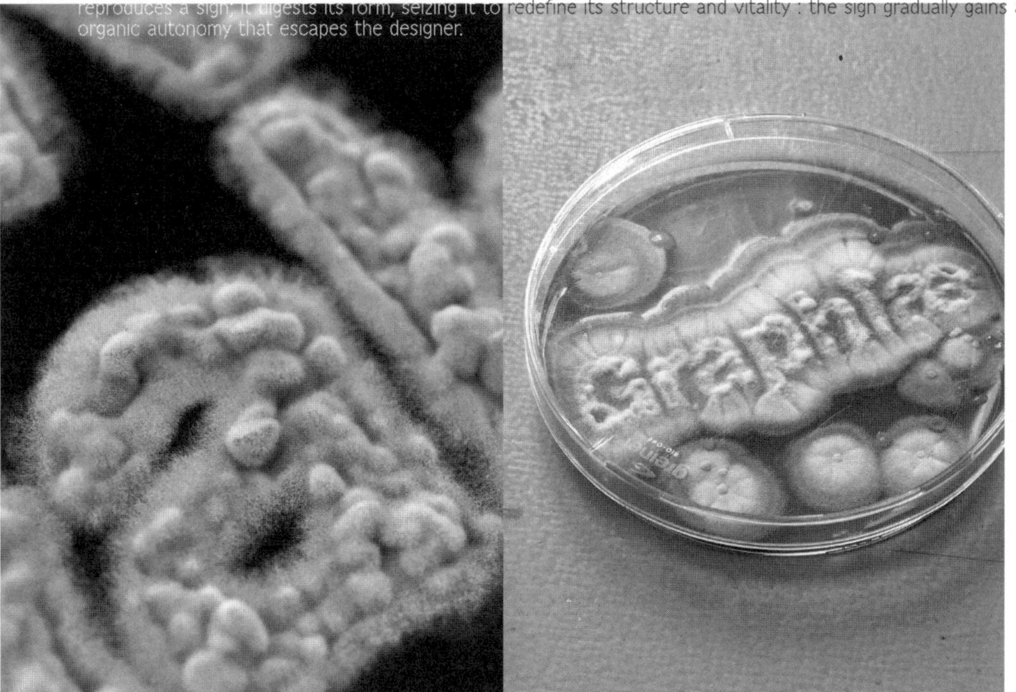

147 Hares Bassil FIN—OVERWHELMED

OVERWHELMED visualizes thought triggers in an oversaturated medium/mental state. A modular, dot-based letter system was created with sodium acetate crystals. The crystals expand from single points and merge with others until the basic letter shape is completely engulfed/consumed in the crystalline structures, depicting rising intrusive thoughts taking over an oversaturated mind, the Petri dish. The chemical reaction creates arbitrary forms within the characters, a feature this project embraces.

148 Parco Studio ITA— LETTERING FOR MILANO ARCH WEEK 2024

Parco Studio designed a campaign focused on the word "weak," that, spreading like a tag on walls, quickly invaded urban spaces—almost like a temporary graffiti. The lettering has a handmade and rough character, in order to give an organic and human feeling to the communication. The visual project is inspired by the importance of vocabulary in conveying messages and the communication is based on key words presented on a large scale to create a provocative shouting effect.

149 Clara Wendt DEU—
WERKSCHAU DESIGN 2024 FH POTSDAM

This work is a ubmission for the visual identity of the design department exhibition: the design includes various digital and analog formats. The typography focused on an experimental approach, using analog materials to create different letters. These were combined with existing display fonts, reflecting the department's strong practical and interdisciplinary teaching approach. The type design was developed in the workshop Typographic Playground by Laura Hilbert, in the class of Susanne Stahl.

150 Svitlana Korniienko UKR—EXPLORING ACCIDENTS

Korniienko explores the influence of various analog mediums on the character of letters. She works spontaneously and intuitively, embracing failed, accidental, and imperfect shapes as the foundation of her letterforms.

151 Christian Stifani, Sofia Cambiaggio ITA—
ARRIVEDERCI E GRAZIE—THERMAL TRACES

This experimental lettering is one of the results of visual experiments conducted for the ARRIVEDERCI E GRAZIE publishing project. It is a letterset created by blackening receipts, exploring the thermal paper properties. Many letters show residues of other words contained in the receipts themselves. This practice is inspired by the work of M. Duchamp who used ready-mades to create art by giving them a second life. Following the same principle, even the receipts can reveal something unexpected. A modern rebellion.

152 Sascha Simm DEU—
FROZEN LETTERS

Analog experimentation with frozen letters.

153 Sascha Simm DEU—THE PRESERVE TYPE

With the series Kinky, Glossy, Candy aka THE PRESERVE TYPE, Sascha Simm absolutely took the cake. For the 10th anniversary of 36DaysOfType, he wanted to create something very special, with the idea of not investing too much time, as his second son had been born a few weeks earlier. But when he brought Kris Rampmaier on board, this project became something really big. Typeporn 2 the fullest.

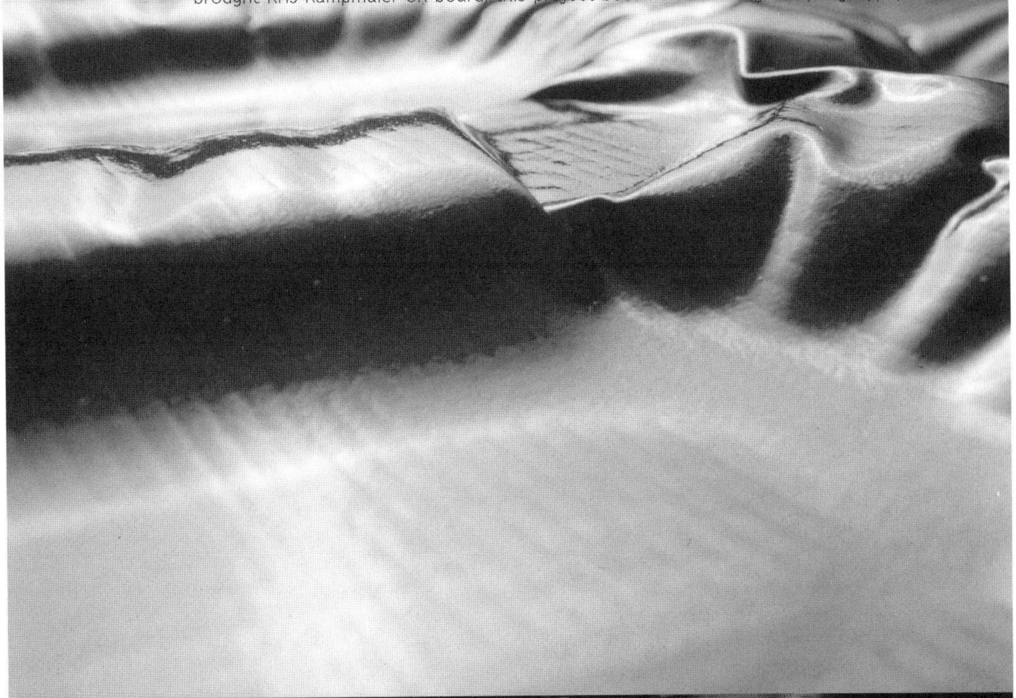

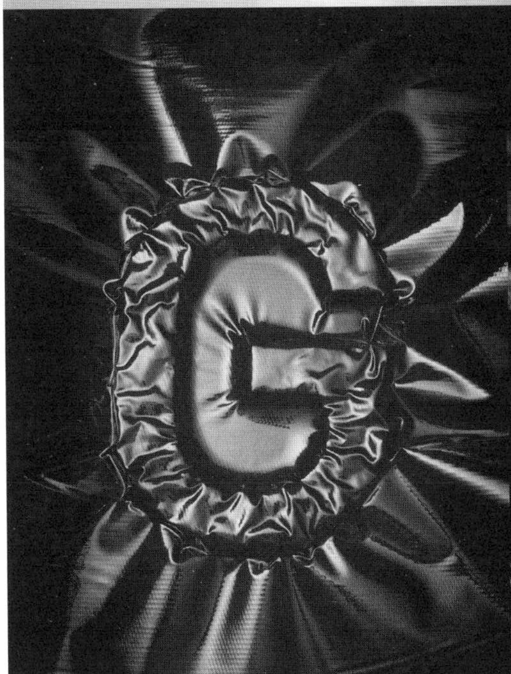

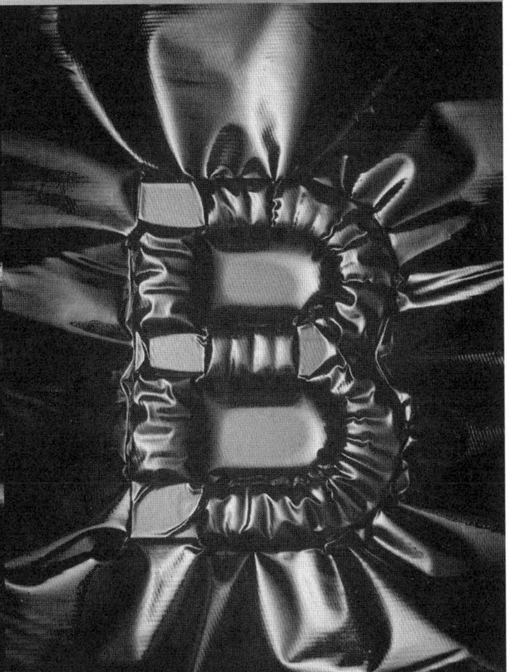

154 Sumire Yoshida GBR—IN PRAISE OF DISTORTION

In contemporary Japan, the appreciation of imperfection is fading. Geert Hofstede's (2016) studies highlight Japan's high value on perfection and success, seen even in design. Growing up in Japan, Yoshida felt the suffocating nature of strict societal expectations. The project explores "distortion" in typography, inspired by Okakura's *The Book of Tea* (1961) and the Shino Tea Bowl, celebrated for its imperfect beauty. The *Yugami* typeface, with its bumpy forms, aims to revive Japan's historical aesthetic that this project embraces.

155 Vera van de Seyp NL—MORE FORM

MORE FORM is a knitted type animation piece.

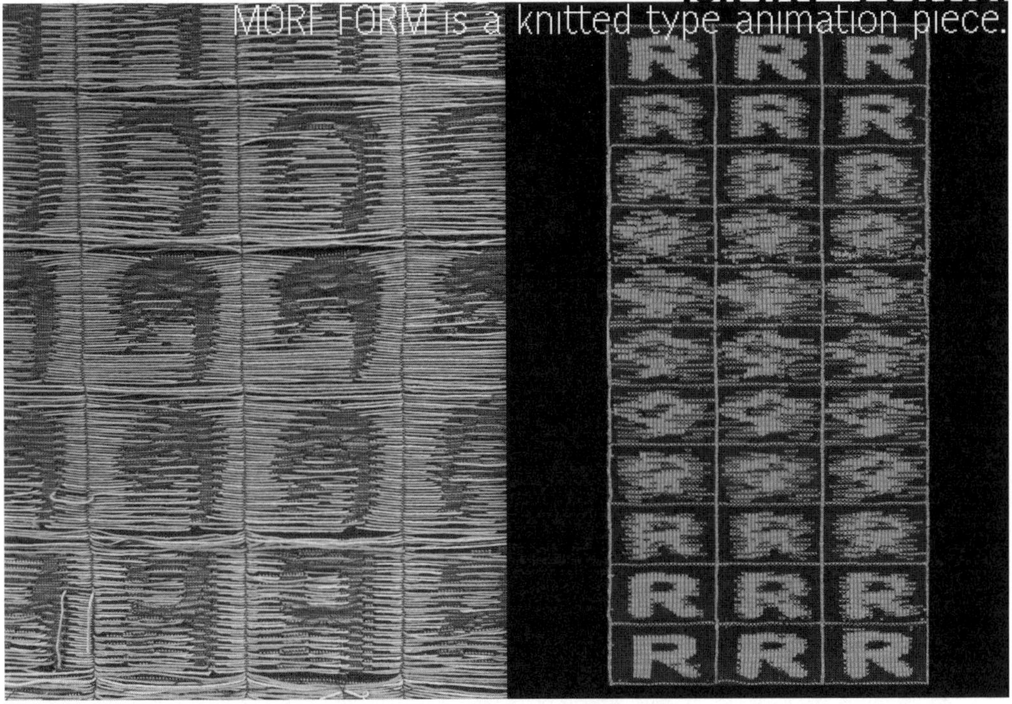

156 Kitti Bakonyi HUN—SNITCHES GET STITCHES TYPEFACE

This experimental typeface was inspired and shaped by cross-stitch embroidery. The aim was to use this traditional method and integrate it into the contemporary art world. The design is implemented within a grid system, thus mixing embroidery and pixel-based techniques. Embroidery is an old art form that carries values from the past, while the pixel-based approach and the irregular lettering are kind of a modern rebellion.

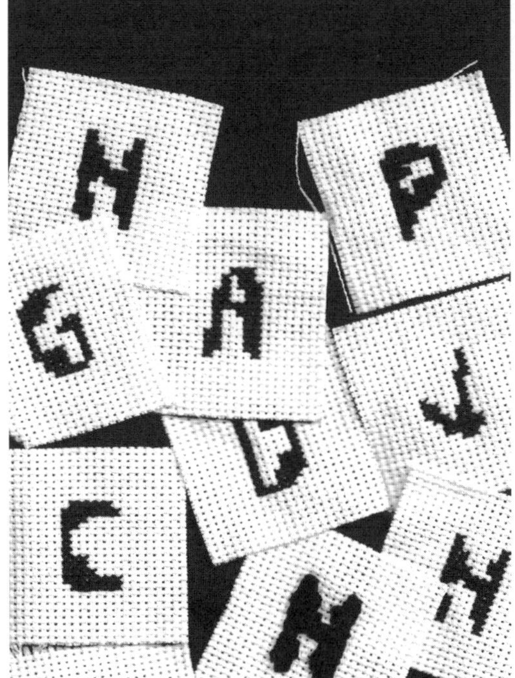

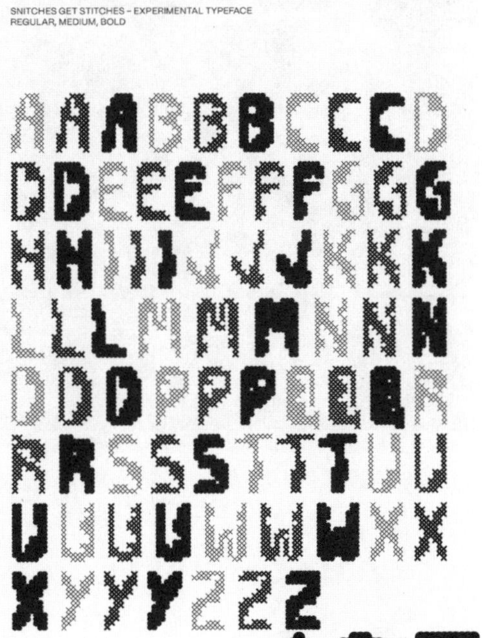

SNITCHES GET STITCHES – EXPERIMENTAL TYPEFACE
REGULAR, MEDIUM, BOLD

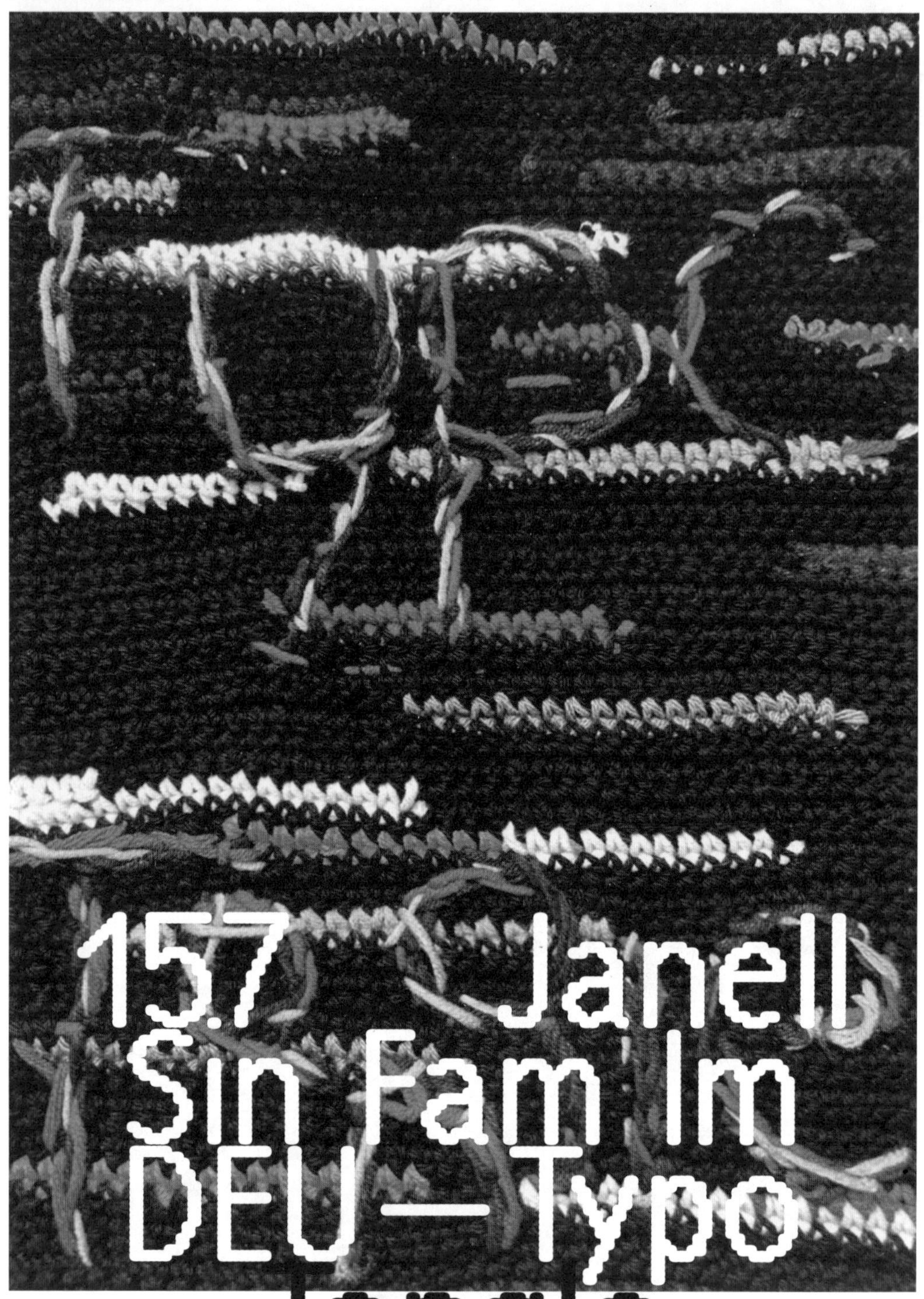

15.7 Janell Sin Fam Im DEU — Typo Tangle

Analog type exploration with yarn.

158 Rüdiger Schlömer CHE—KNIT HELLO INFINITE VARIATION SCARF

KNIT HELLO is the second Typeknitting Font by Rüdiger Schlömer made especially for hand knitting. KNIT HELLO is for beginners: knitters with little knowledge in typography, and graphic designers who have just picked up the needles. The KNIT HELLO INFINITE VARIATION SCARF is a wearable protocol of your exploration process in typographic knitting. Starting with simple layout grids, it invites you to bring your Typeknitting skills to a next level, segment by segment, stitch by stitch.

159 Cecily Li USA— FOLDED ALPHABETS

The ordinariness of paper as an object introduces complexity in content, material, and format. The 26 paper-folded alphabets challenge the relationship between the ephemeral and the ethereal, demonstrating how a mundane object can be transformed into a meaningful state. The folding technique serves a dual purpose: it embodies conceptual duplicity and allows modulation to dominate the realm of paper-based thought. Engaging with the fold reconnects us with the fundamental tactility of paper.

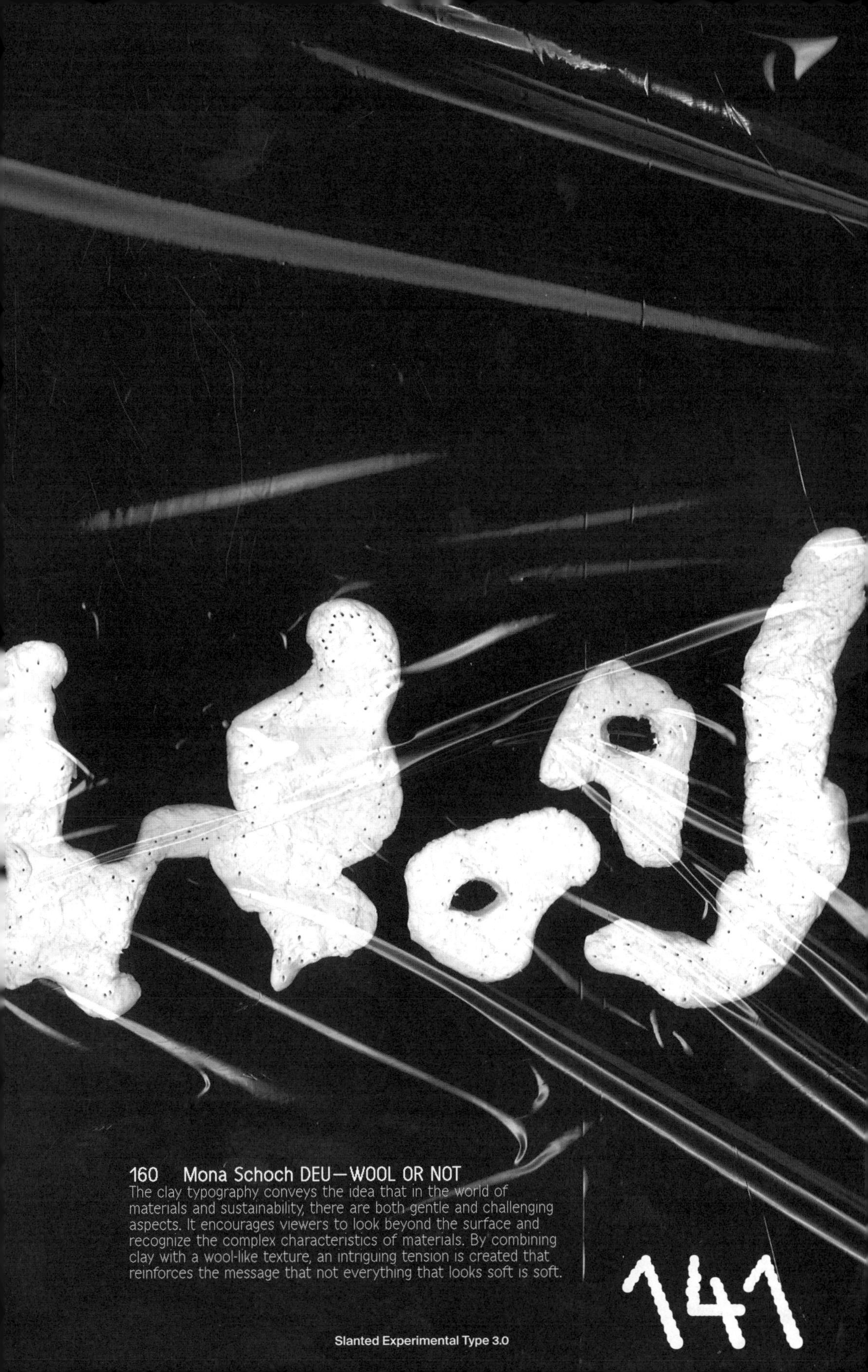

160 Mona Schoch DEU—WOOL OR NOT
The clay typography conveys the idea that in the world of materials and sustainability, there are both gentle and challenging aspects. It encourages viewers to look beyond the surface and recognize the complex characteristics of materials. By combining clay with a wool-like texture, an intriguing tension is created that reinforces the message that not everything that looks soft is soft.

161 Pati Olszowka BEL—ABOUT PUBLICATIONS

This student publication features several interviews and essays about graphic design. The cover was made by experimenting with 3D printed type that was vacuum sealed under a transparent sheet to create a flat cover with relief typography.

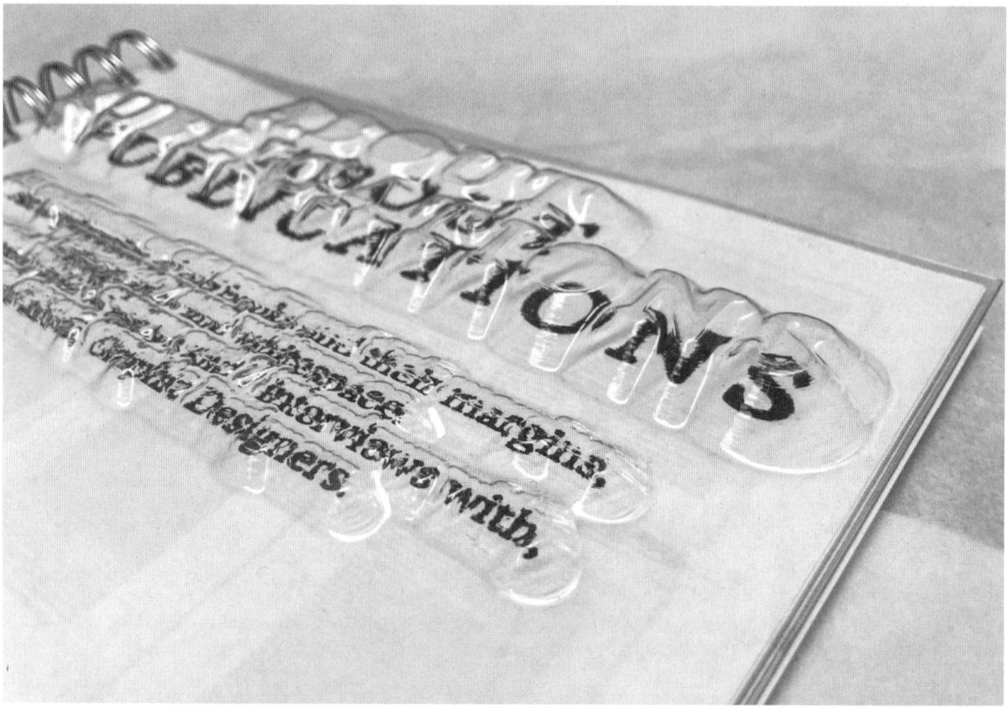

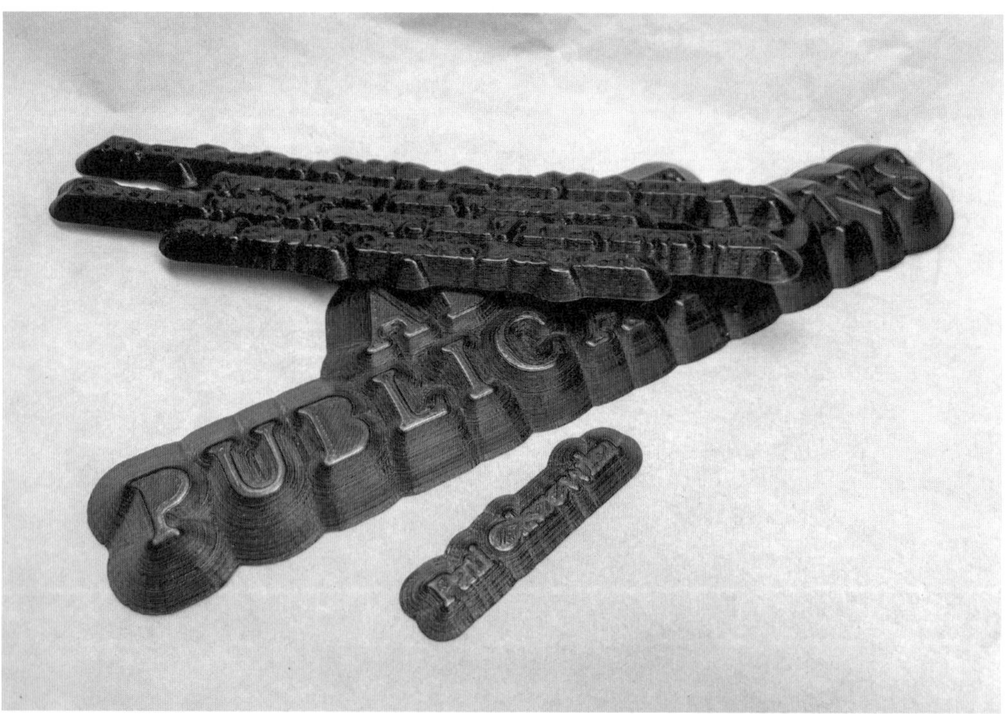

Andreas Panayi CYP—SAME STORY—MULTIPLEÂ ITERATION

How can type, layout, and shape add additional meaning to a piece of text? This is an object with new formal connotations.

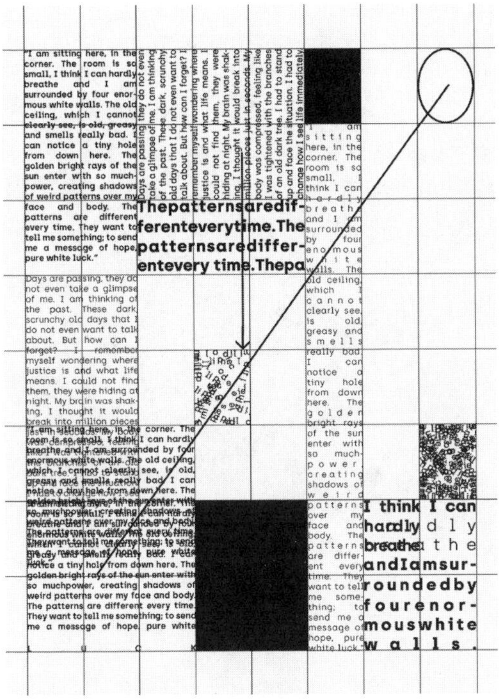

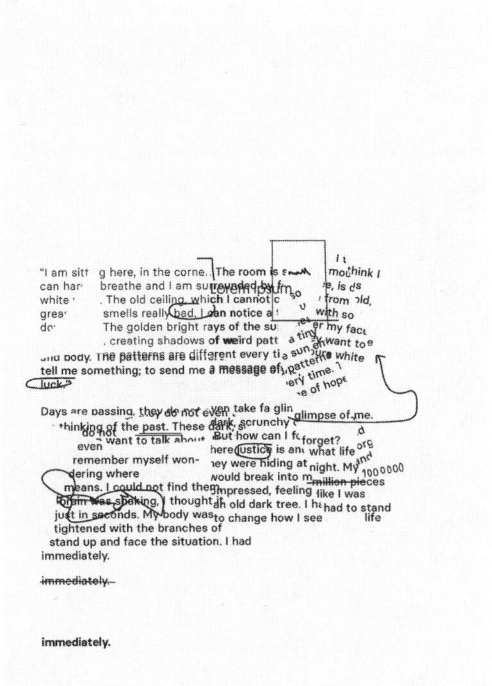

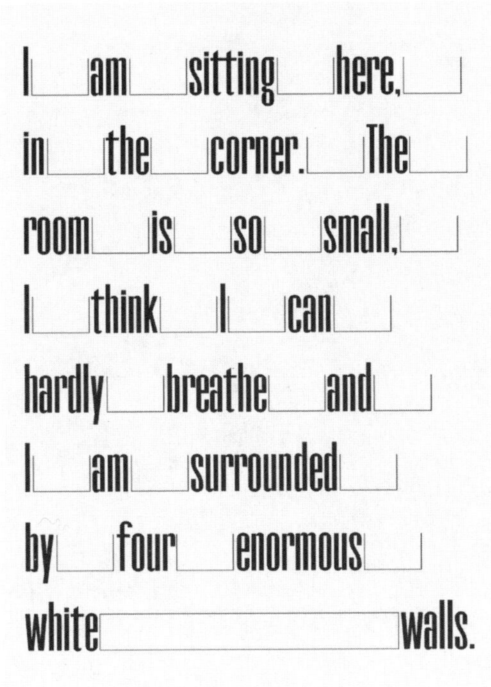

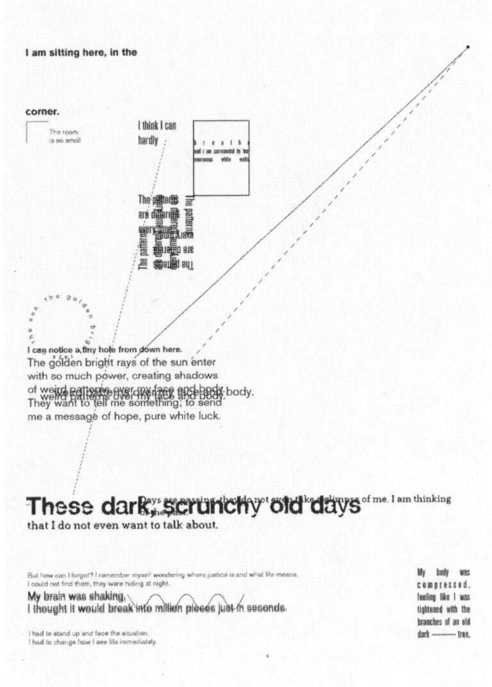

"I am sitting here, in the corner. The room is so small, I think I can hardly breathe and I am surrounded by four enormous white walls. The old ceiling, which I cannot clearly see, is old, greasy and smells really bad. I can notice a tiny hole from down here. The golden bright rays of the sun enter with so much power, creating shadows of weird patterns over my face and body. The patterns are different every time. They want to tell me something; to send me a message of hope, pure white luck."

Thepatternsaredifferenteverytime.Thepatternsaredifferentevery time.Thepa

I think I can hardly breathe and I am surrounded by four enormous white walls.

immediately.

I am sitting here, in the corner. The room is so small, I think I can hardly breathe and I am surrounded by four enormous white walls.

These dark, scrunchy old days that I do not even want to talk about.

My brain was shaking, I thought it would break into million pieces just in seconds.

My body was compressed, feeling like I was tightened with the branches of an old dark —— tree.

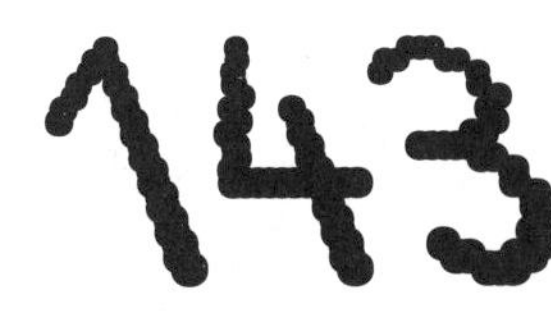

163 Alexandra Sagalow DEU—PIXEL

For her experimental type, Sagalow used her iPad and a hair-gel-water mixture. Sagalow wrote the sentences "I miss my pre-internet brain," and "the downside of being connected is that you're connected" with the mixture on a pixel background. The letters have a 3D effect and enlarge the pixels. With the claims and the technique she wanted to reflect the problem of excessive phone and media use, which many of us know.

164 Taekyeom Lee USA—CAN IT BE TYPOGRAPHY?!

In the process of experimenting with punched and folded paper using a 3D-printed gadget, the long paper strip could be turned into a letterform. The study of the letterform, material, and process ended in a series of explorations.

165 Matilda Greiner DEU— YOUR WORDS CHOKE ME

Though written words are merely letters strung together, they possess immense power over our emotions. this typographic necklace made out of sheet metal represents a feeling of suffocation. "CTRGFS" is the chaotic result of smashing your head on the keyboard in frustration.

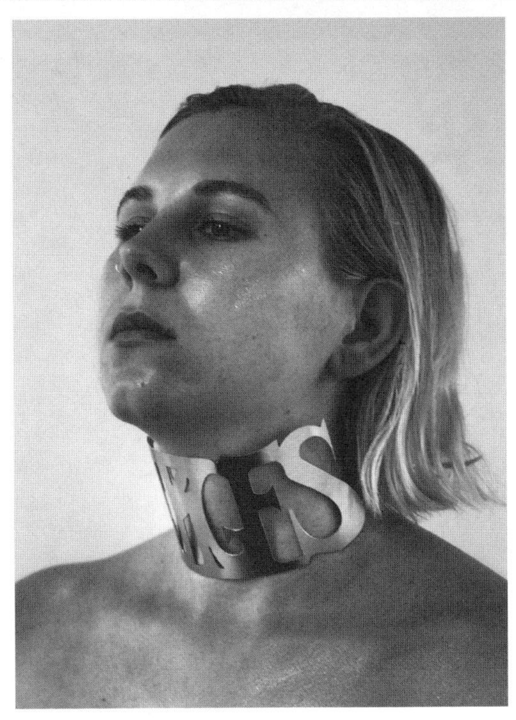

166 Hiral Bhagat IND— IN SEARCH OF POIESIS

This work represents contemporary form of calligraphy, never attempted before with Gujarati script. This extensive repertoire illustrates how stereotypical typographically-composed texts from poetry are transformed and detached to present a pictorial representation of form. This adds an extended, personalized level of meaning to the expression by methodology: considerations regarding text content, rhythm, and depth of language, graphic contrast, and coordination of color and gray values.

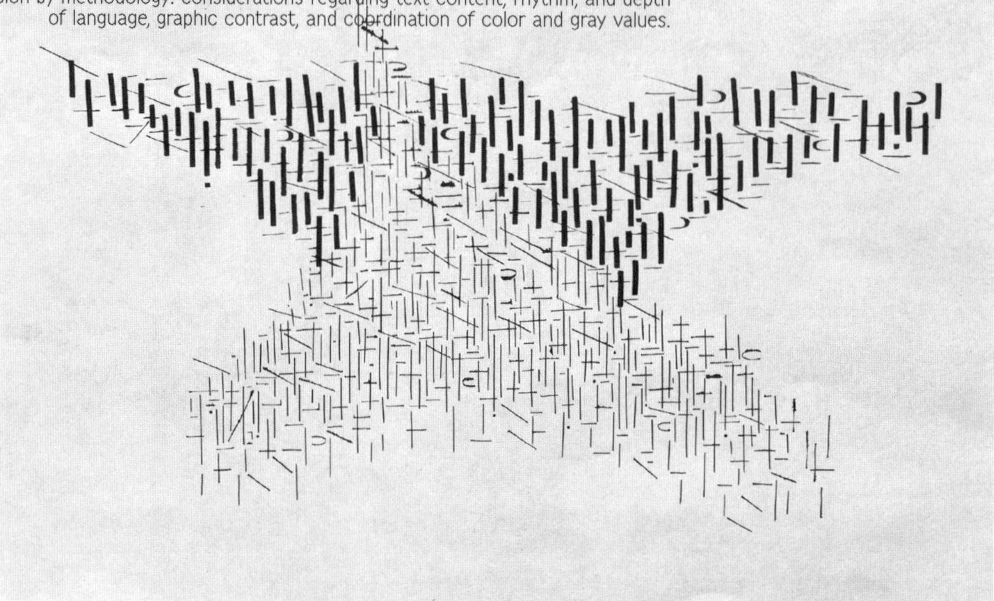

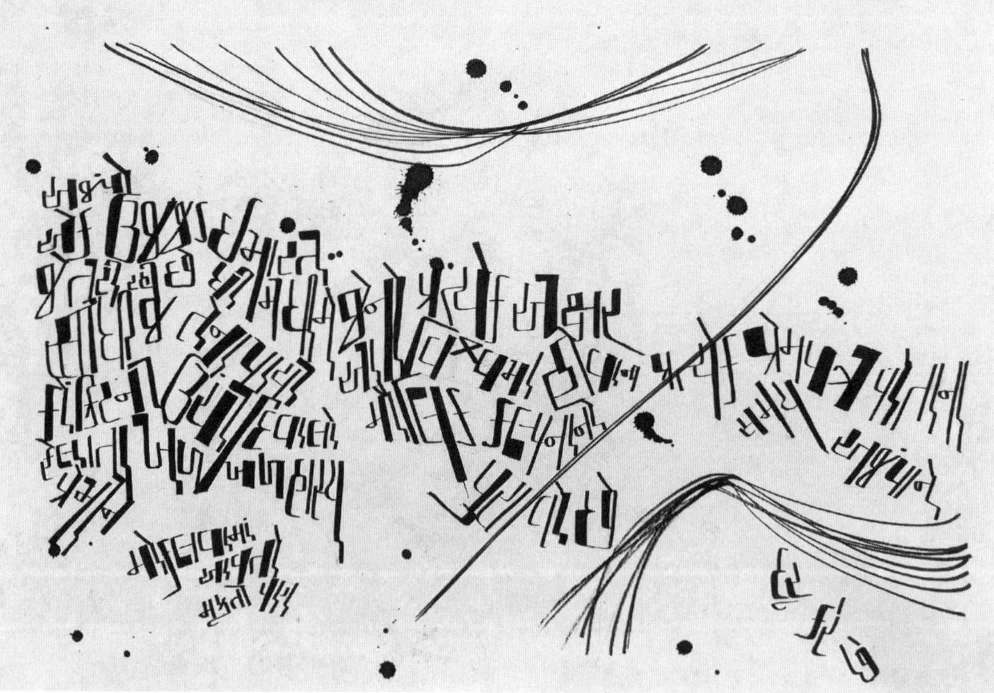

167 Andreas Panayi CYP—BREAK DOWN THE WALLS

Visual study that employs the grid and typography to convey and illustrate the transgression of social boundaries.

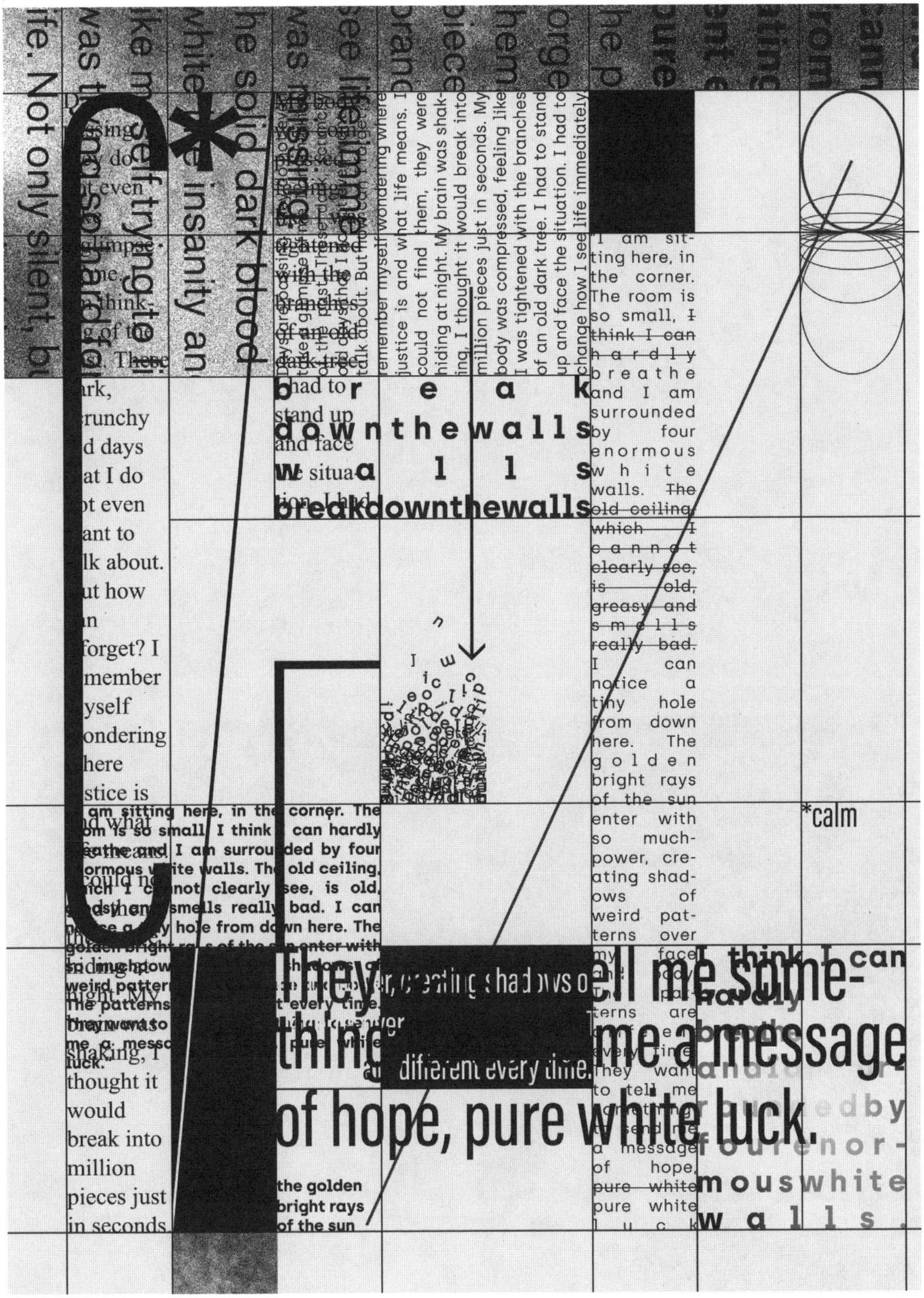

168 Taekyeom Lee USA—PHYSICAL TYPOGRAPHY USING 3D

A 3D-printed embosser can cut and score paper. In the process of experimenting with paper and 3D-printed embossers, Lee noticed that when embossing was a little too strong—it could even rip the paper. The designer then wanted to use this for something beyond printing or folding. The study of the letterform, material, and process ended in a series of typographic explorations.

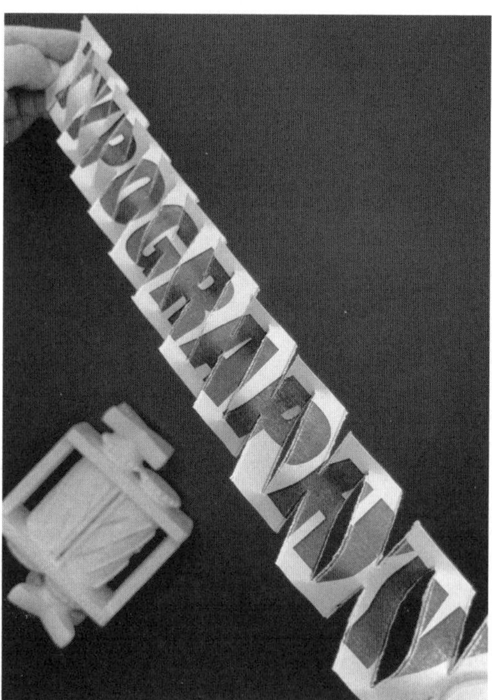

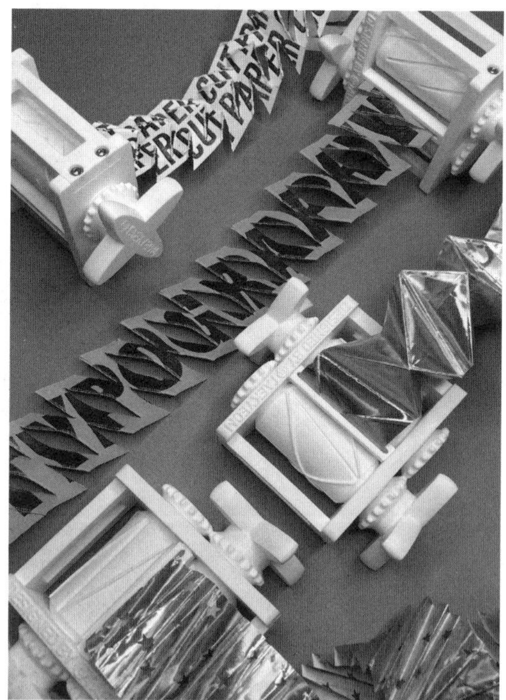

169 Regina Vitanyi
HUN—IPS TYPOGRAPHUS

This project presents a non-human perspective on typography: the featured text was found in the wild, and it was carefully created by IPS TYPOGRAPHUS, an insect which got its latin name from its calligraphic approach to altering its environment.

it is a
magn
ifica
tion

112 μm

170 Moritz Stolz DEU—IT'S A MAGNIFICATION

Stolz experimented with the microscopic enlargement of printed letters on various papers and materials in order to gain a new perspective on type. This work is a hundredfold magnification of an embossing with letters on aluminum foil.

171 Charlotte Wächter DEU—LANGSAM SCHREIBEN DANN KATZE

These AI generated poems experiment with the visuality of letters and writing as a sort of painting with language. The poetic and visual compositions are based on the ideas of concrete poetry. They try to use language as a material to question its underlying structures.

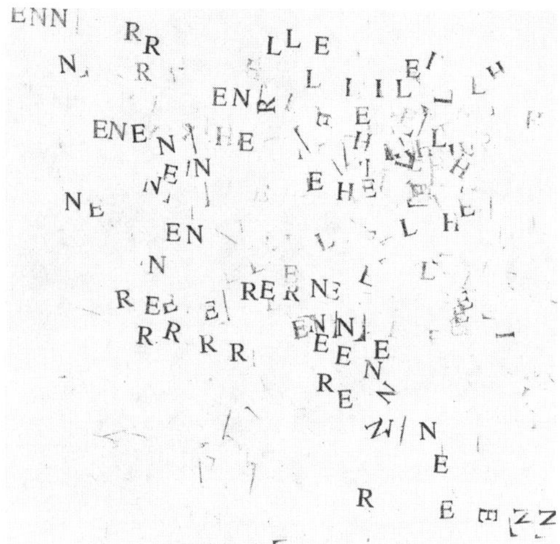

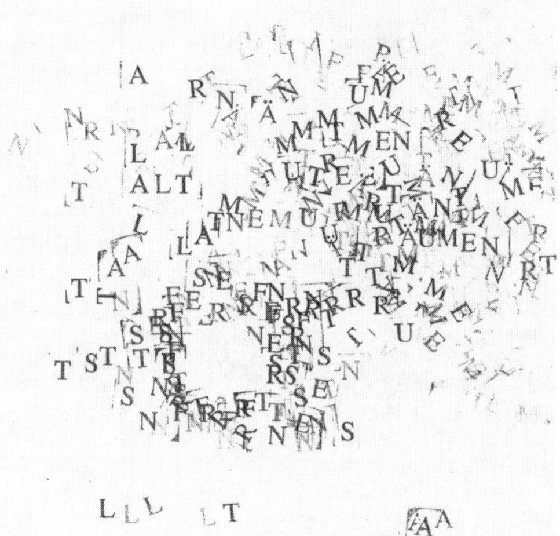

172 Eva Schlotzhauer
DEU—GEOPUM

Experimental typographic exploration with construction foam.

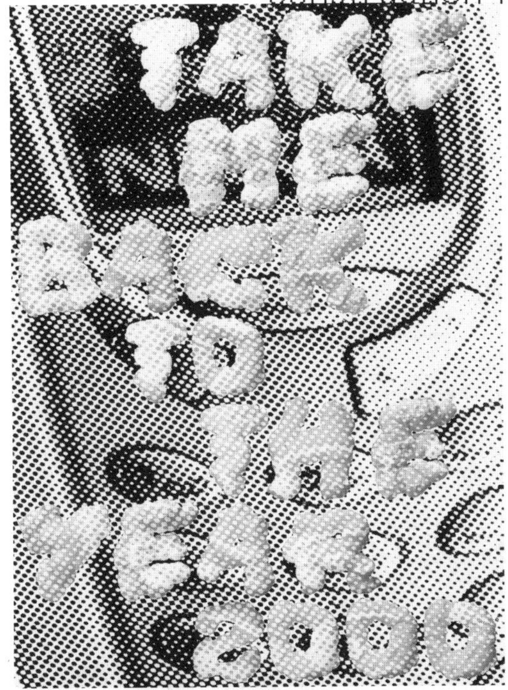

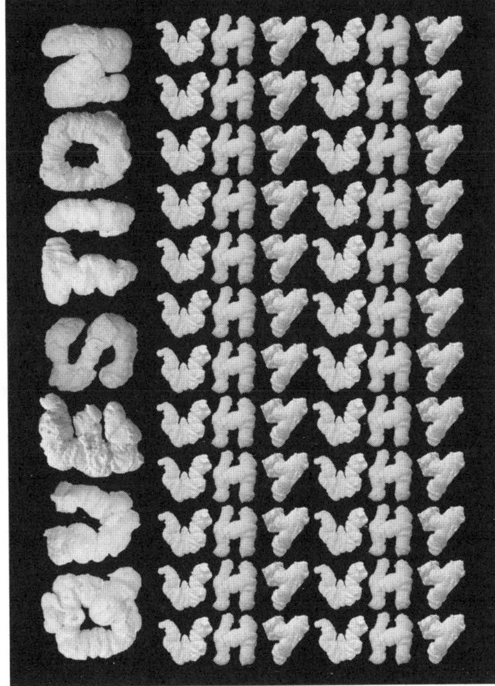

173 Hannah Baumann DEU— TYPOGRAPHIC GRID DISTORTIONS

As part of her experimental type project, Baumann chose a physical approach. To achieve this, she worked with three DIN A2 boards: one made of wood, one made of mirrored acrylic glass, and one made of transparent acrylic glass. The plates were machined with a laser to create a grid of holes. Through this grid, she threaded different materials to create writing. The writing clearly breaks away from the grid on the plates, exploring the limits of readability. This process results in interesting, abstract shapes. The respective materials are closely connected to the concept of the claims.

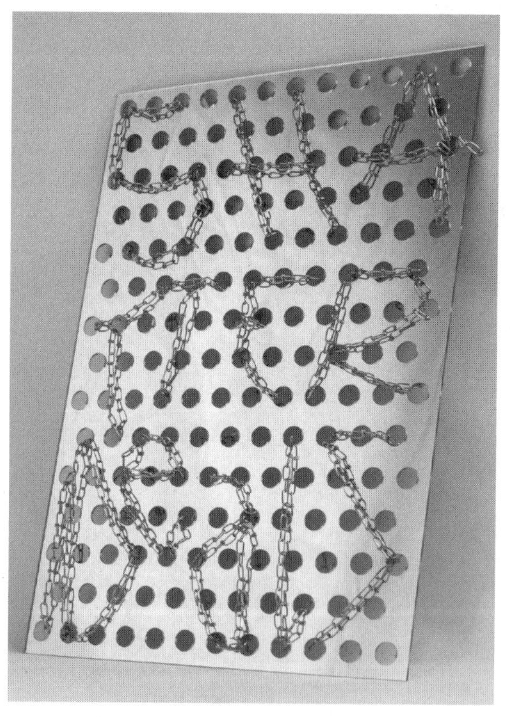

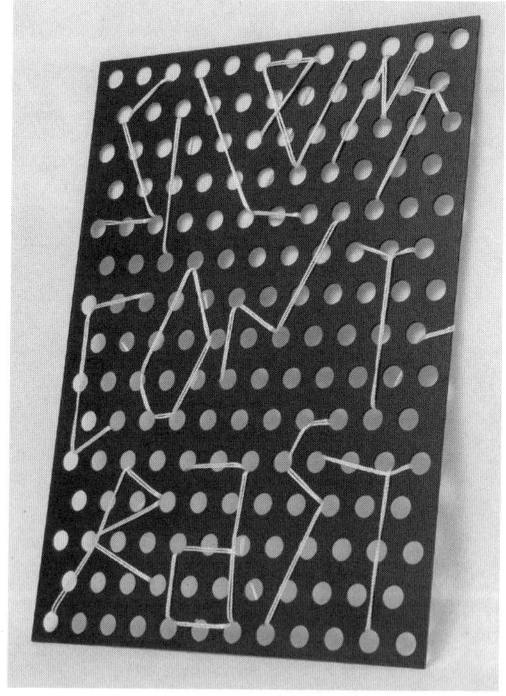

174 Janett Jakubow DEU—BURN BOOK

Crocheting and sewing are one of Jakubow's hobbies that she likes to pursue in her free time. The aim of this project was to challenge the legibility of letters through stitching. The project was also bound into a book and contains a single word.

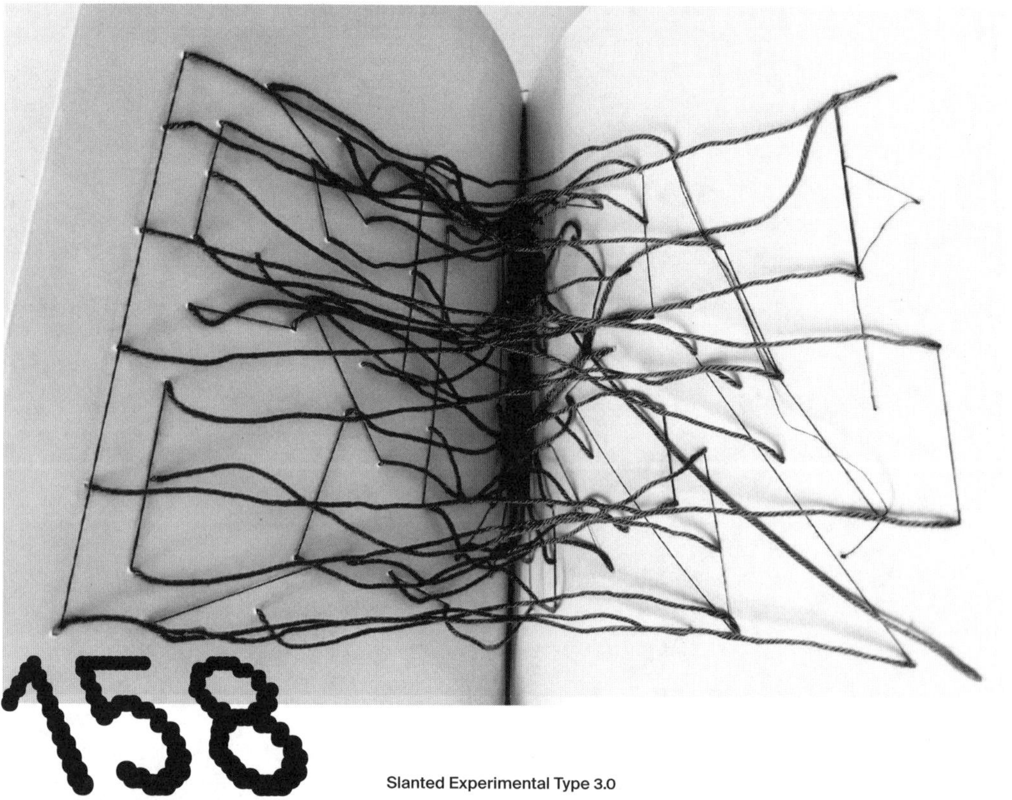

175 Alina Jungclaus, Lena Galitsch DEU—UNRULY SCRIPT

Take an unbalanced motor/Glue it to the cap of a spray can/ape some markers to it/Attach four strings to control the device/Find a partner to operate the device together/Power it.

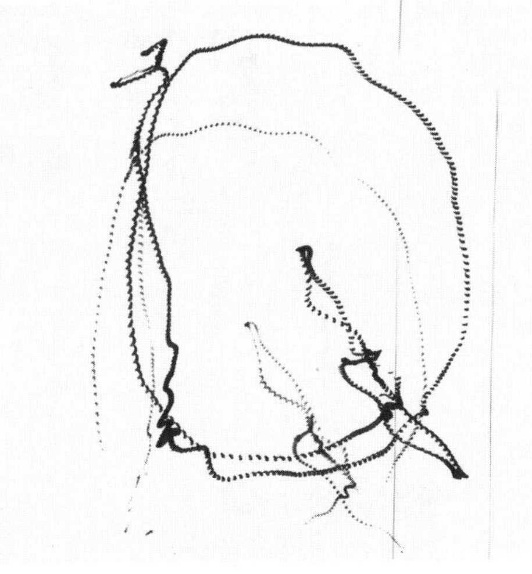

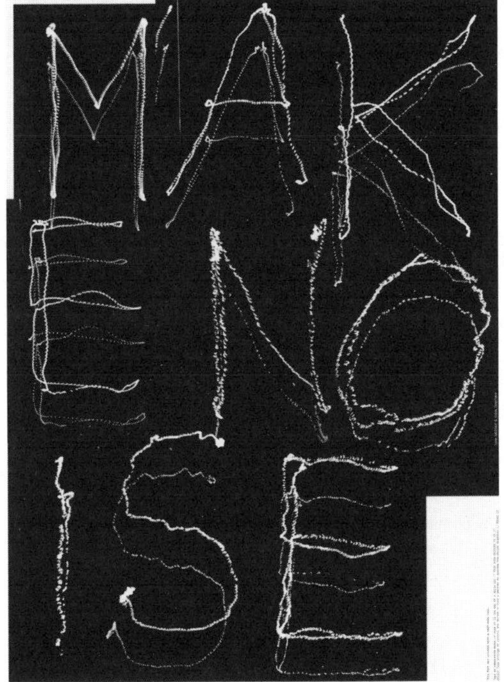

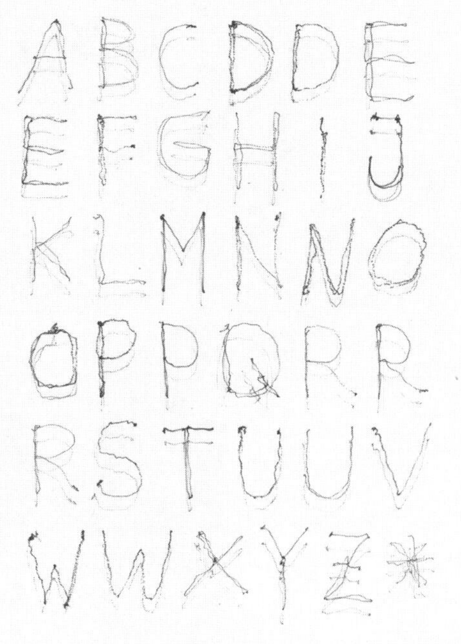

176 Vianne Brugger DEU— IT'S OK!

Brugger's experimental typography series explores various feelings. Each feeling shows its weight, its interweaving and its strength. The typography is created with beads by hand.

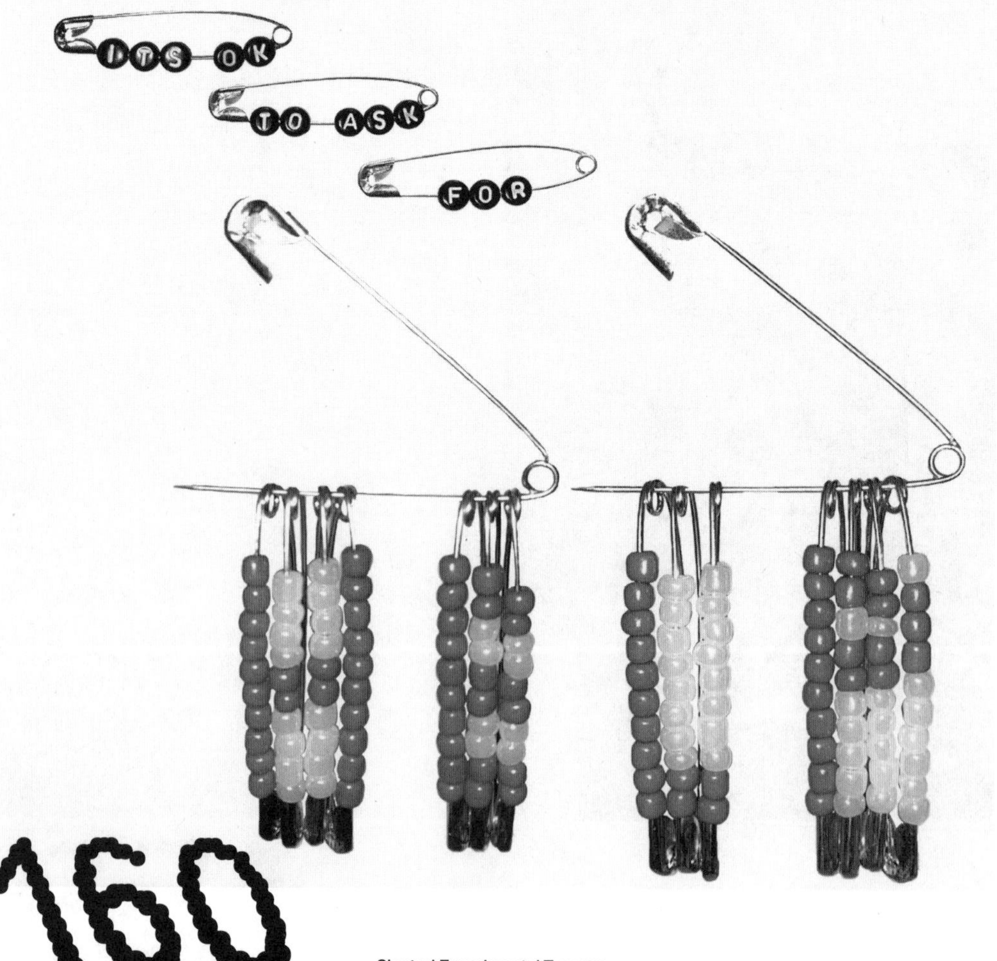

177 Victoria Hohage DEU—EARTH IS CANCELED

These posters use an experimental technique where ink is applied to wet paper, causing the letters to warp and flow. The interaction between the ink and water creates a sense of movement, with the typography taking on organic, fluid forms, blurring the boundaries between control and chance.

In today's digital era, Hoffman is experiencing a renaissance in typography that challenges traditional rules and explores new aesthetic dimensions. With his project XTASE, he aims to combine traditional and digital techniques to create unique typefaces. By creatively using stamp systems and modern digital tools, Hoffmann creates new, fascinating forms and textures. This approach allows him to present typography as a living and dynamic art form that constantly opens up new horizons. In his experimental typography, Hoffmann strives to transform the familiar and make the unknown visible

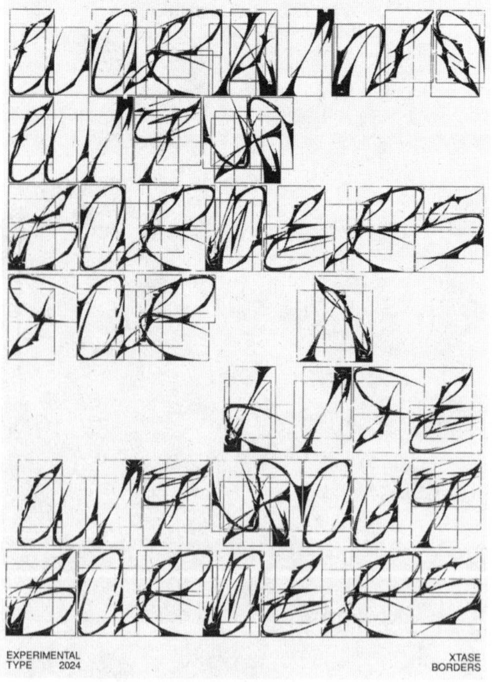

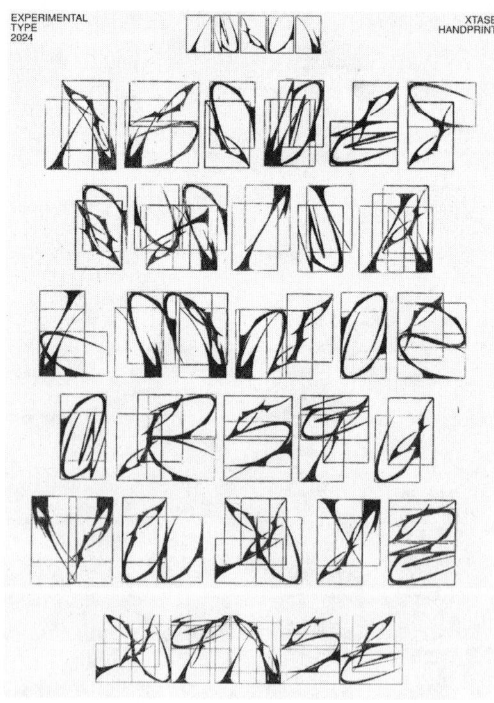

179 Pelin Yapici DEU— TIME MELTS AWAY

The project addresses the transience of time, visualized through melting candle letters. Two techniques were used: dripping wax forms diffuse, flowing letters, while precise letters were created from cast wax. Both approaches symbolize the passage of time, similar to a candle slowly melting away. The concept TIME MELTS AWAY is also featured in the poster designs, where the melting letters represent the steady and unstoppable flow of time.

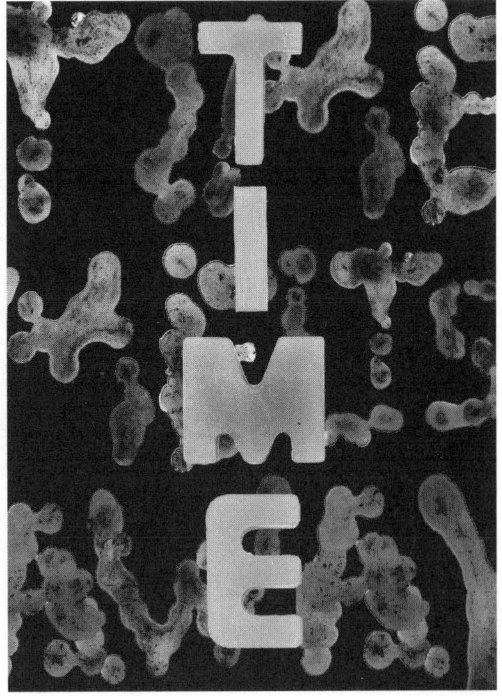

180 Lena Windisch
CHE—UNDER PRESSURE

This experimental setup is a playful commentary on the 3D, glossy, blubbery, chrome-type aesthetics increasingly produced by designers using the latest software. In UNDER PRESSURE, the shapes are created by applying welding wire to a metal printing plate, which ultimately serves as a stamp to emboss letters into anodized aluminum sheets. It is a process where imperfection, spontaneity, and openness to results are key, leading to a unique visual language.

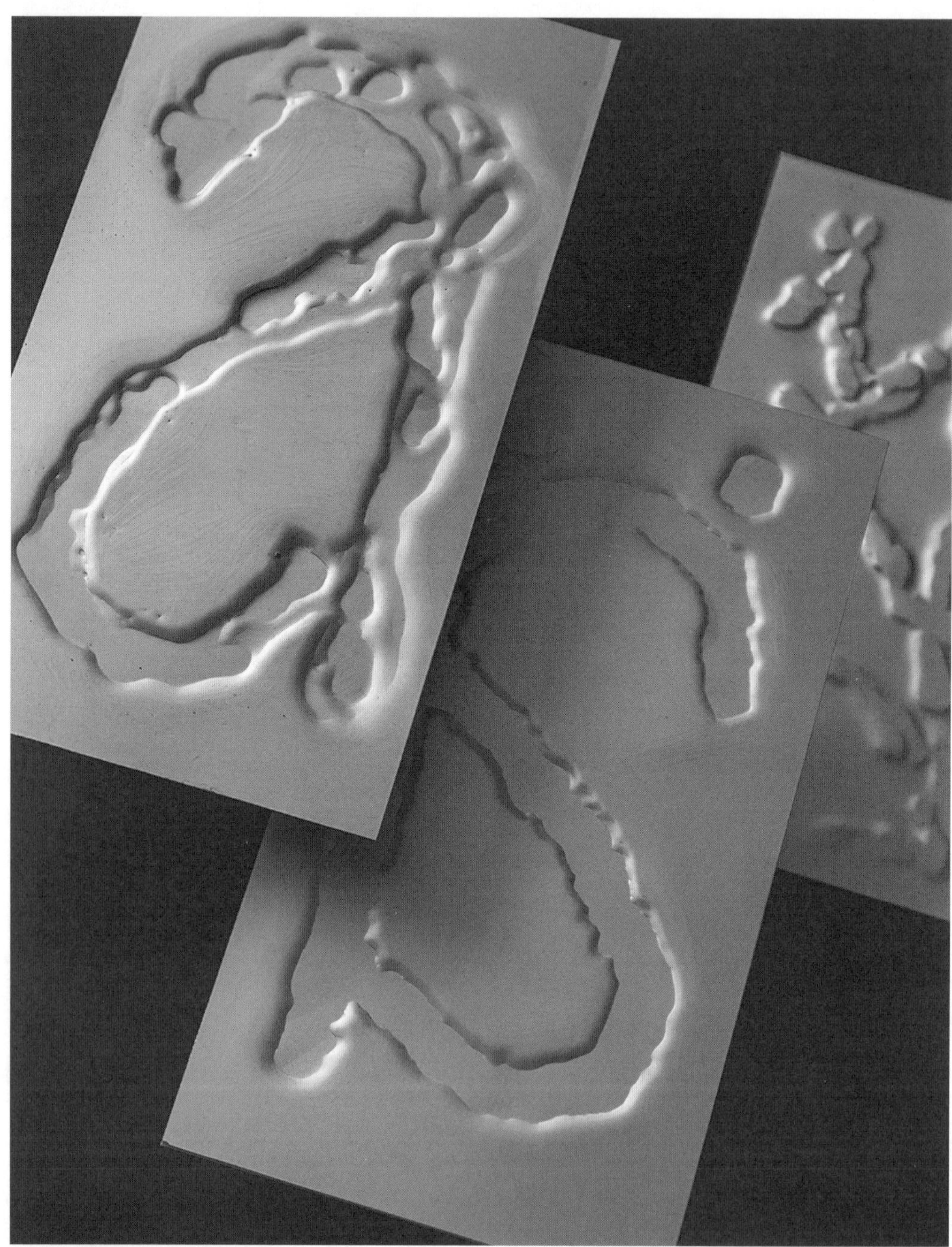

181 Stefan Lüdemann DEU—AFF. (1 + 2)

AFFECTION (1) is a sculpture. It is made out of wire, concrete, plaster, acrylic paint and a reflective stainless steel plate, measuring approx. 300 × 400 × 600 mm (D × W × H). It needs a wall to lean on. AFFECTION (2) is a state of mind and body. It is the coming together of two different beings or forces under good will and tenderness. AFF. (1 + 2) is the sum of AFFECTION (1) and (2). It also is the realization, that one half is leaning on a reflection, that is leaning on something else.

182 Guillaume Tourscher FRA—RETRACER

RETRACER is a master's degree project created at ÉSAD d'Amiens, 2022.

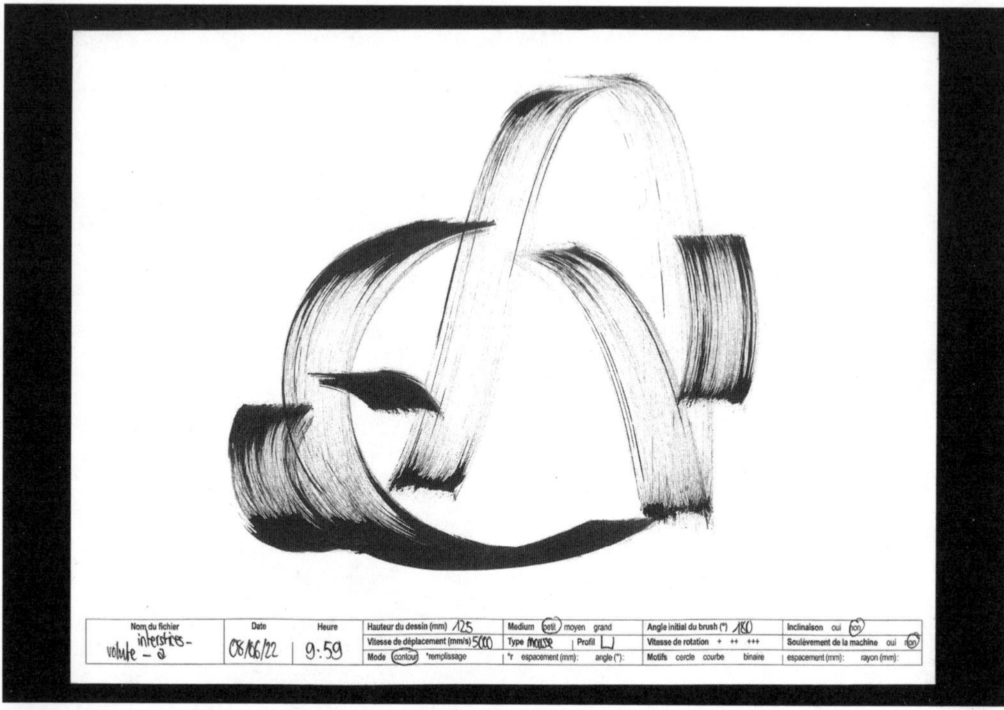

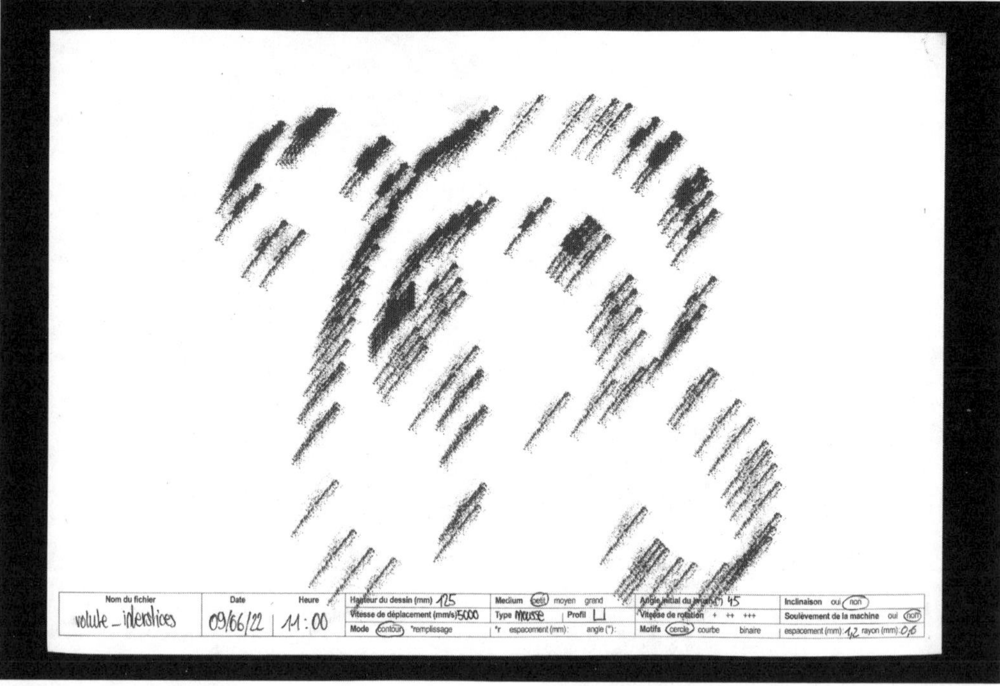

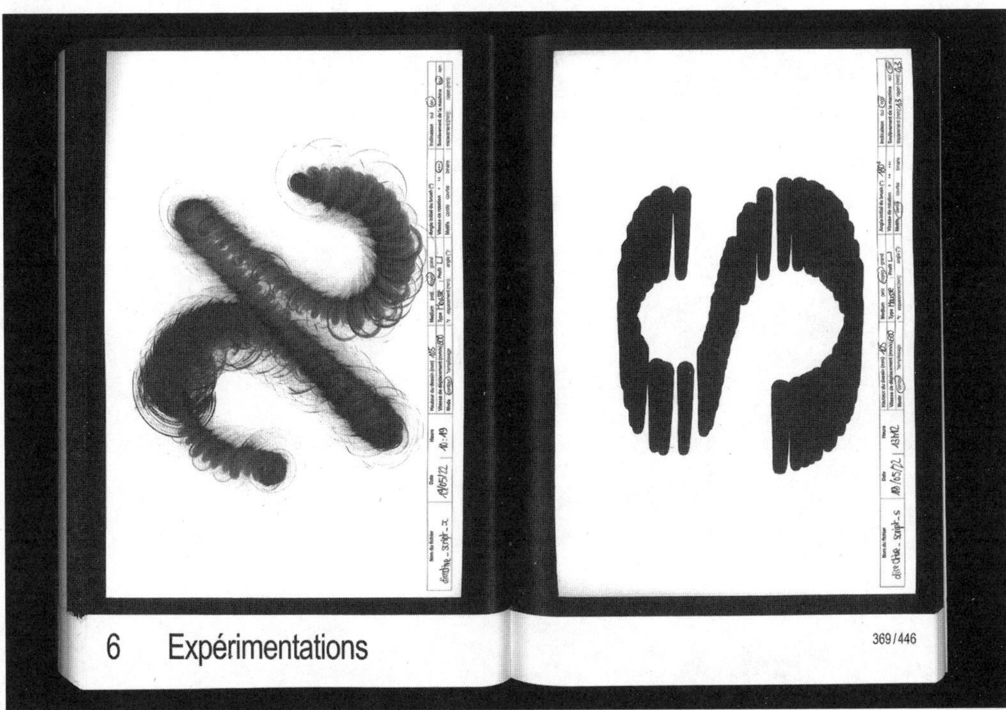
6 Expérimentations
369/446

Nom du fichier
directive_script_x
Date
19/05/22
Heure
10:00
Hauteur du dessin (mm) 105
Vitesse de déplacement (mm/s) 4000
Mode contour *remplissage
Medium
Type MOUSSE
Profil
*r espacement (mm): angle (°):
initial du brush (°) 90
Vitesse de rotation + ++ +++
Motifs cercle courbe binaire
Inclinaison oui non
Soulèvement de la machine oui non
espacement (mm): rayon (mm):

183 Marie Nieddu

DEU—FLORA & FONT

Typographic experimentation.

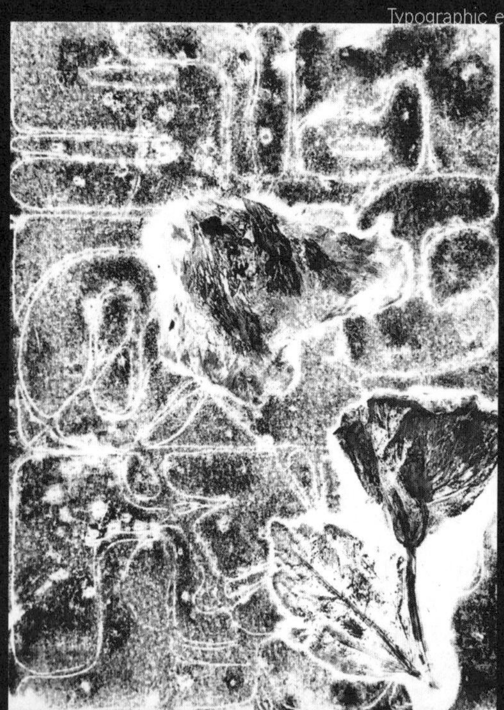

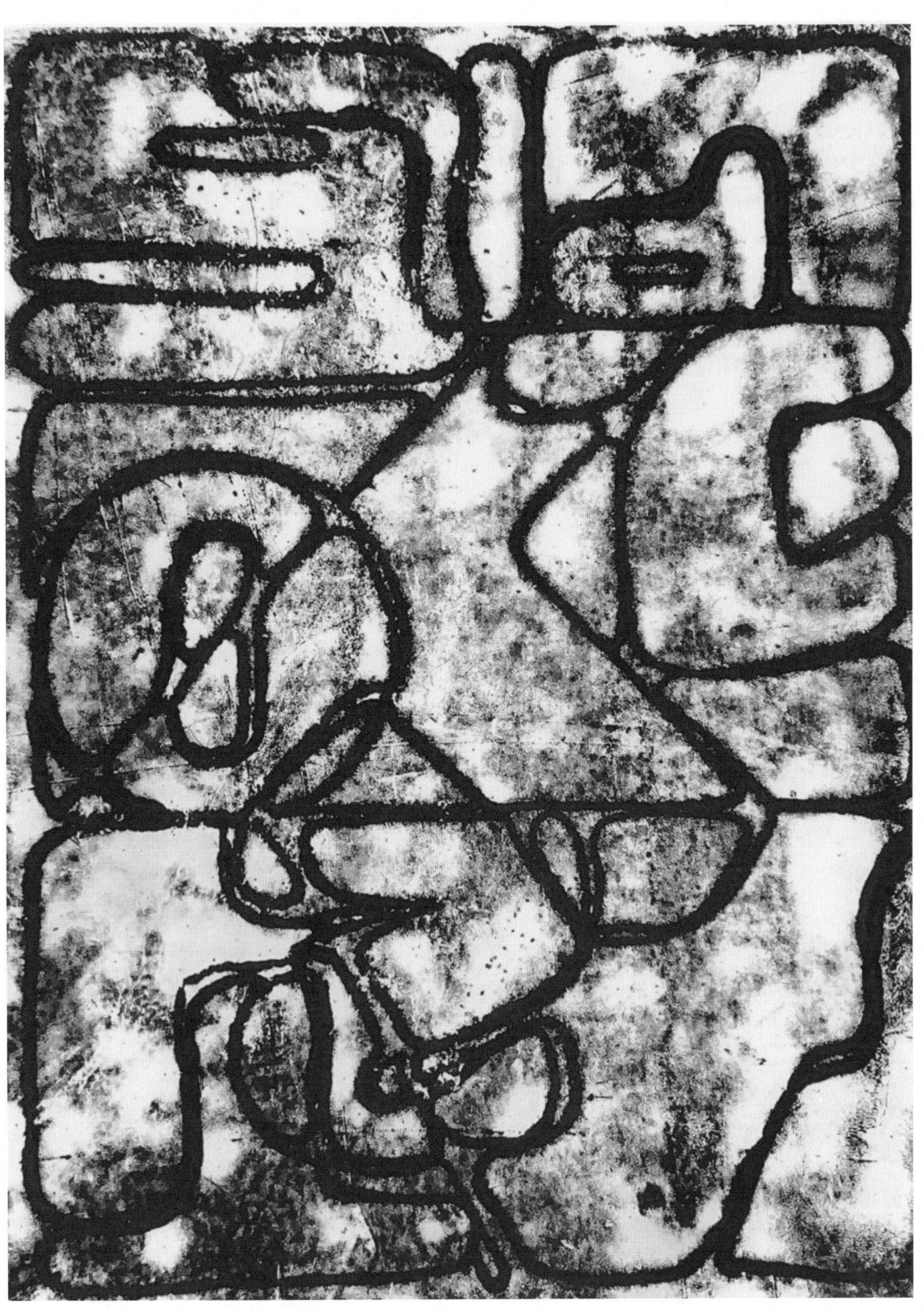

184 Shahed Al Suleiman

ARE—BUBBLE TYPE

BUBBLE TYPE is a bilingual legibility spectrum exploring the transformation of letters from a liquid state to bubbles, pushing visibility and legibility boundaries. Beginning with fluid, formless letters, it emphasizes motion and abstraction. As they solidify into defined bubbles, the design tests manipulation limits while maintaining recognition. This spectrum challenges traditional typographic notions and examines legibility across languages, creating a unique bilingual visual experiment.

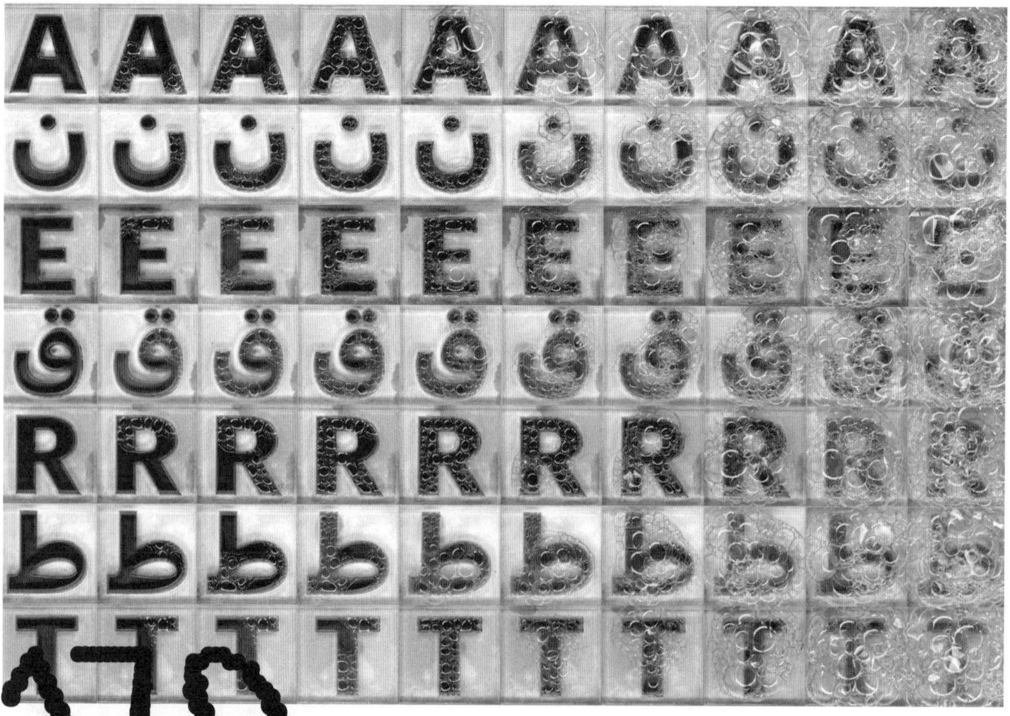

185 Janette Bartkowiak DEU—(NOT) SO CUTE

The (NOT) SO CUTE project examines the disconnect between aesthetics and reality using ribbon shaped into letters spelling "so cute." These seemingly charming letters and the ribbon, normally associated with gifts, celebrations and positive associations, are juxtaposed with unpleasant settings like construction sites, creating ironic tension. The choice of the word "so cute" reinforces this irony, as it is often used in modern pop culture to describe something particularly cute or attractive. By placing the ribbon in these environments, the project critiques superficial descriptions and questions how easily appearances deceive. It challenges viewers to reconsider the meaning and impact of aesthetics in contrasting contexts.

186 Linda Hallstan
SWE — TIME-WASTERS

Lettering hand-embossed on reused aluminum. This time-consuming and inefficient process is intentionally integrated into the design workflow. It serves as an experiment and speculation on whether the slowness of craft can encourage a reevaluation of time and imperfections, rather than prioritizing efficiency and optimization in design and production.

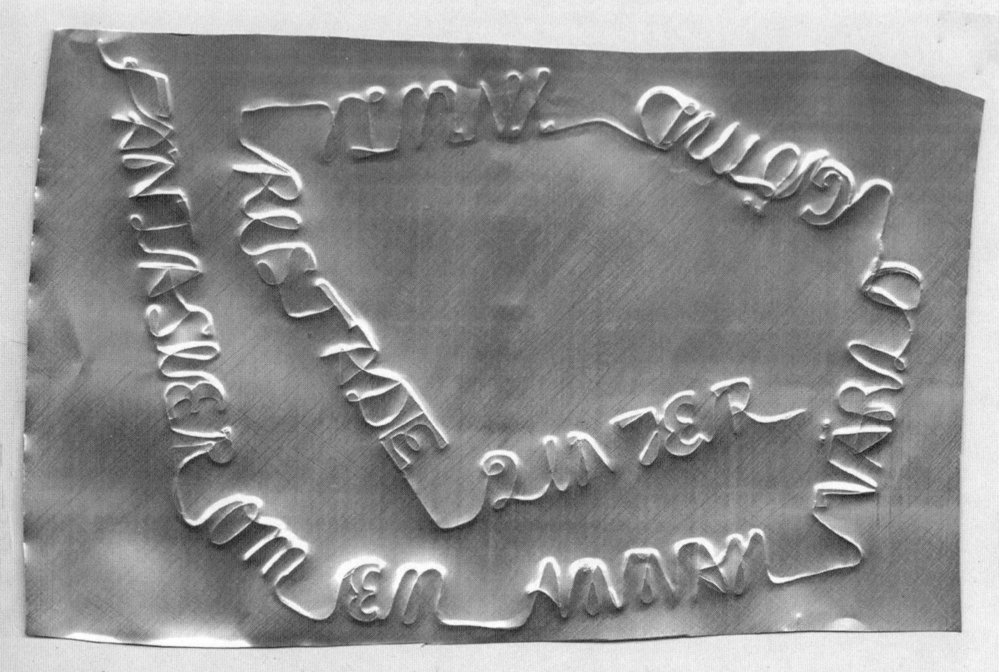

187 Viktoria Hermanenko DEU—UKR TOTEM IS DICHOTOMIES

The letter "I" represents the concept that one's totem is oneself. The designer's totem is dichotomy: destruction, which brings suffering but also intensifies the experience of life. The form of the letter was derived from an impulsive sketch, shaped and refined to reflect these emotions.

188 Youri Precht DEU— CREATE DON'T HATE
Analog typographic exploration.

189 Youri Precht DEU— KILL YOUR IDOLS
Analog typographic exploration.

190 Youri Precht DEU— SEX IS ANALOG PORN IS DIGITAL
Analog typographic exploration.

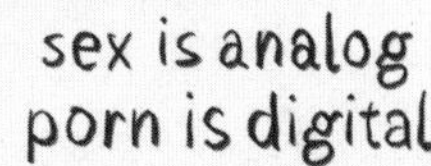

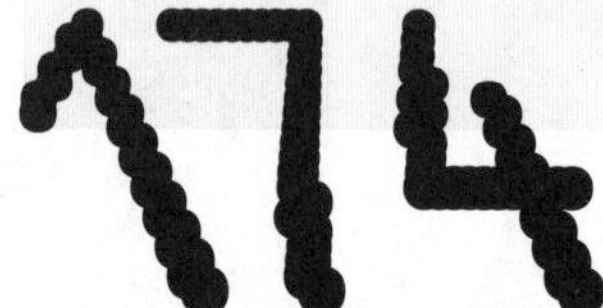

191 Zakentiy Horobyov UKR—TRANSFORMATION

A series of works created from repurposed materials, such as boards and plywood, that were previously used and discarded. The project highlights the importance of discovering new qualities within oneself and viewing them as strengths. It encourages rethinking past experiences, recognizing both their positive and negative aspects, and learning from mistakes.

STAY IN THE GRID

The grid has been essential to typographic design, providing structure and clarity. In experimental typography, grids become starting points for innovation. This chapter explores how designers reinterpret and decon- struct grids to create striking com positions, blending tra ditional order with creative freedom. Join us to see how today's design ers transform grids into dynam ic canvases for typographic expression.

192 A.Müller, V.Dinsing DEU— POV CUBE

Letters, like society, are constructs that require specific perspectives and tools to be understood. The POV CUBE introduces a modular typeface designed to challenge conventional reading by forcing the viewer to adjust their perspective. The letters are formed using six modules that, when arranged correctly, reveal recognizable letterforms. Each module spans two to three sides of the cube—two around a corner and one on the top or bottom—creating a dynamic interaction between structure and perception within the grid.

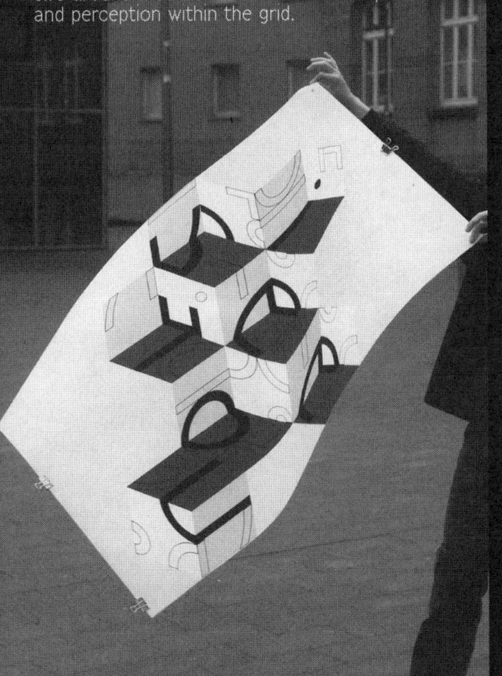

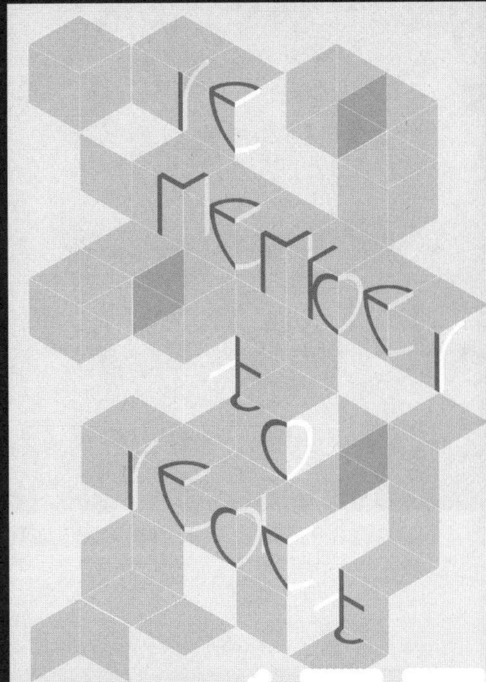

193 Christine Rudi DEU—INDEX MONO

Censorship is the withholding of information and happens in two extreme ways: by blackening, and by disappearing. INDEX MONO is an experimental font that combines these two extremes of censorship. As a variable font, it shows censorship not as a binary but as a gradual process. The font aims to draw attention to the ways censorship alienates us from reality, as it causes us to lose the links through which we interpret the world.

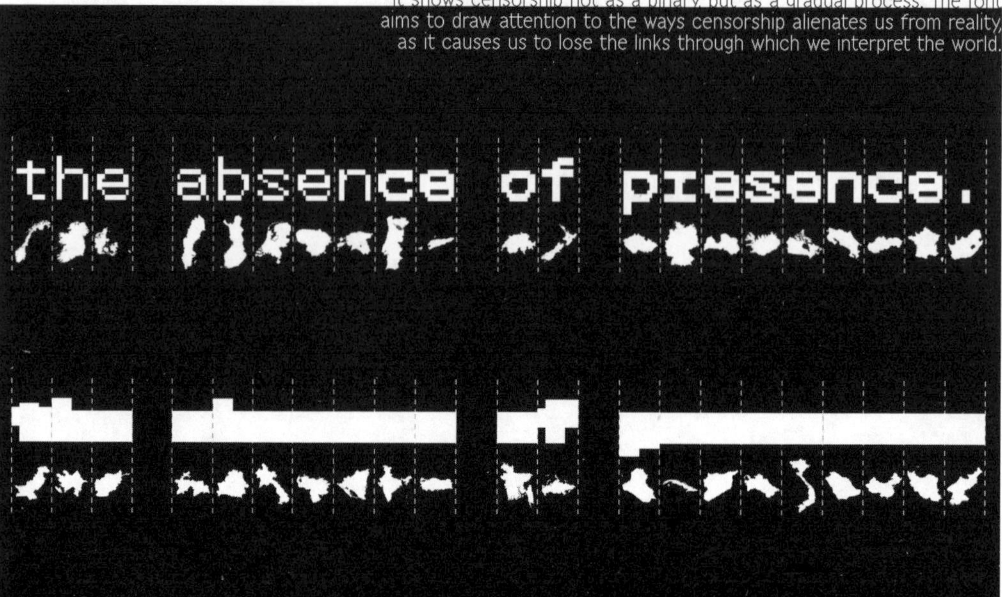

194 Merle Michaelis DEU—SPACE_FIRSTTRY_02-SPACE_V01

In this type design project the boundaries between result and process are fluid. Inspired by a lettering piece by Hans Findling, the creation of a complete alphabet was initiated. The project explores the process of designing a font using both analog and digital tools alternately, from which an independent visual language emerged. Through editing and layering in various image editing programs, new, sometimes abstract image layers emerge, opening up new compositions and spaces.

195 Mikhail Lychkovskiy
GEO—TEN LOST YEARS

Conceptual poster for the theatrical show Ten Lost Years held in the Domino Theatre in Kingston, created at a workshop of Peter Bankov. Fonts in use: Eurocat by Giliane Cachin (Maxitype), Resist Sans by Groteskly Yours Studio.

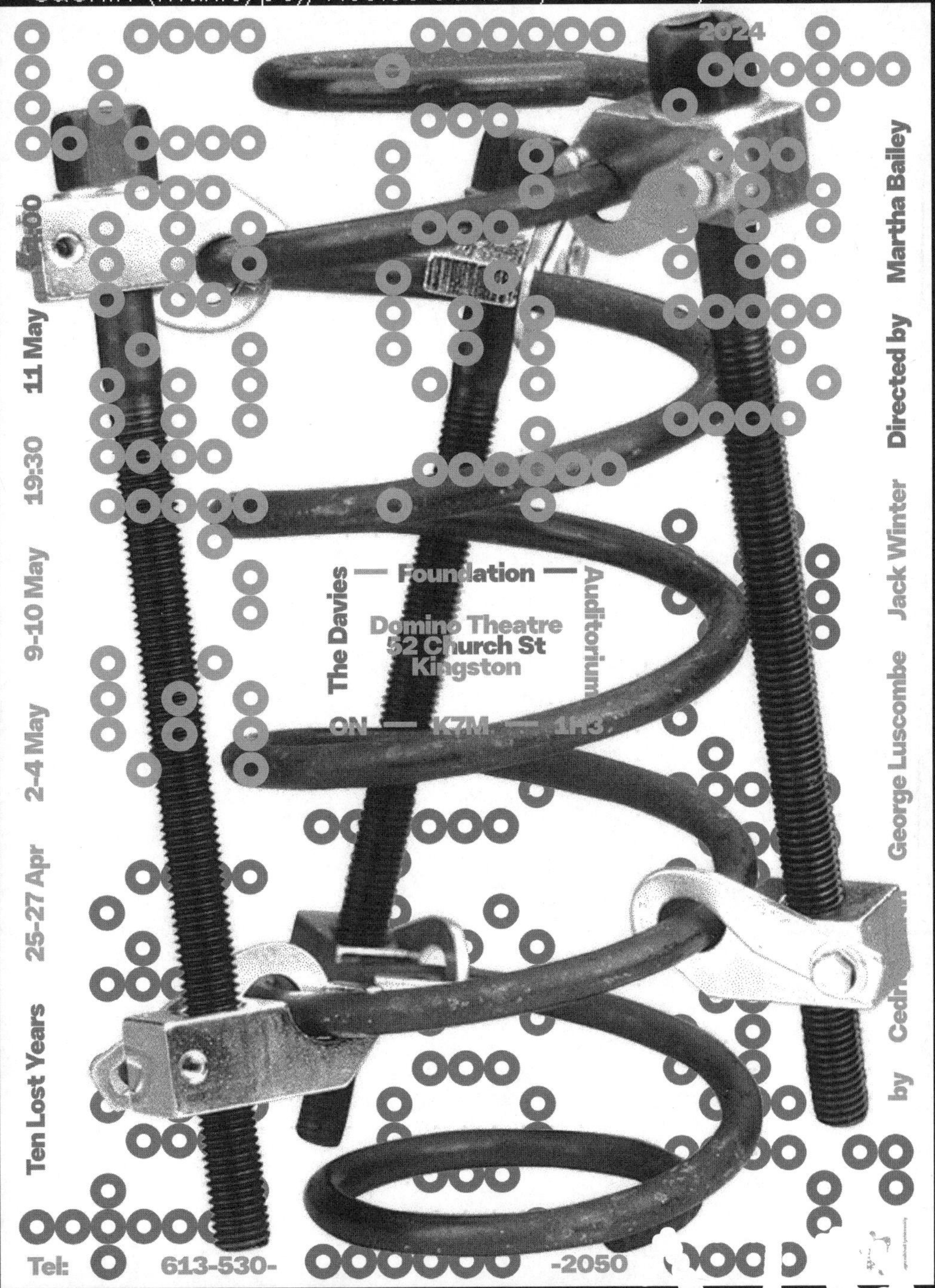

196 Daniela Vogel DEU— EXPLODE FONT

The font captures the essence of fireworks, radiating from a central point and becoming increasingly intricate as they expand. Much like fireworks, it offers an experience that demands patience and perseverance from the viewer. By engaging with the graphical forms, the hidden information gradually reveals itself, all while delighting the viewer with its captivating visual display.

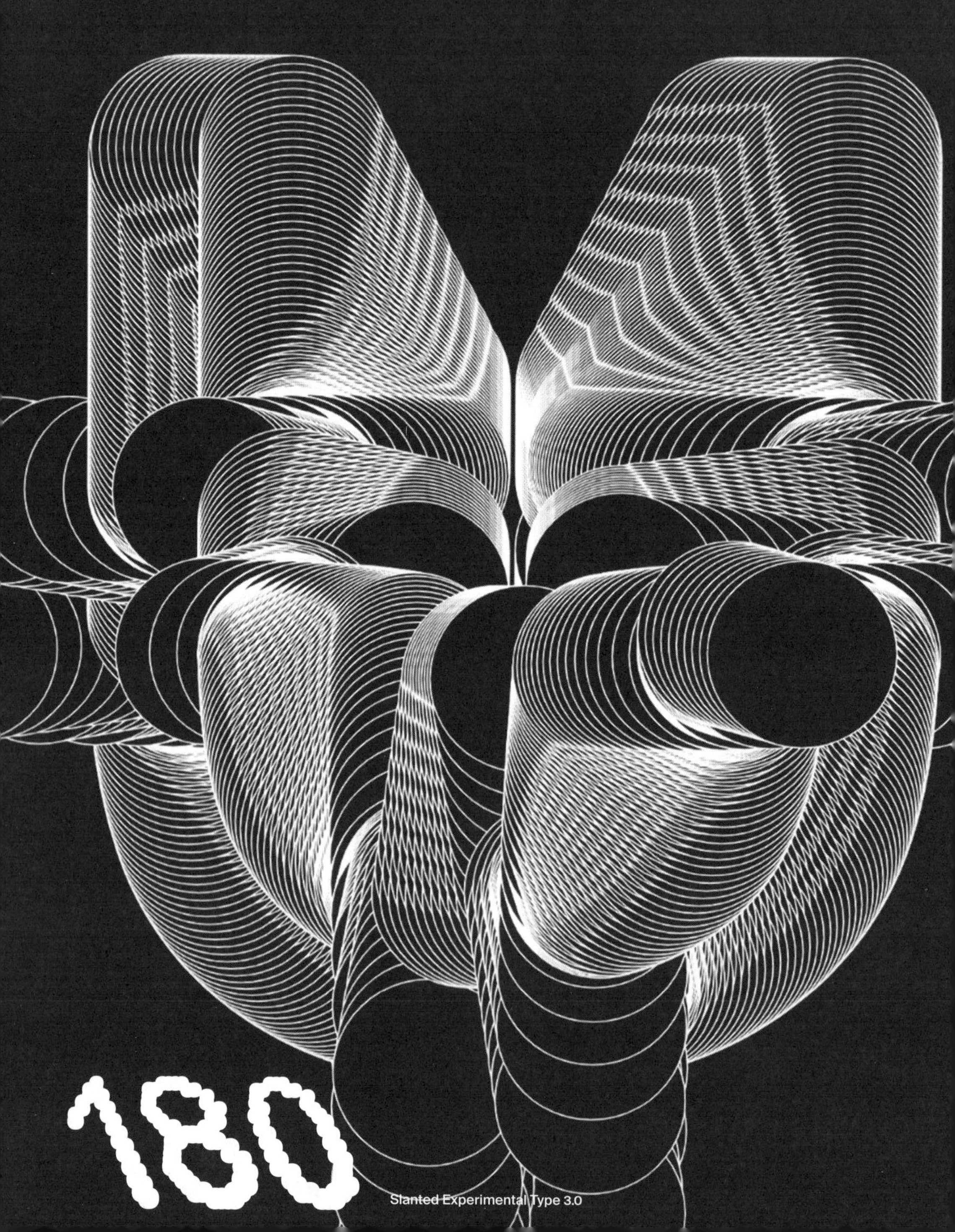

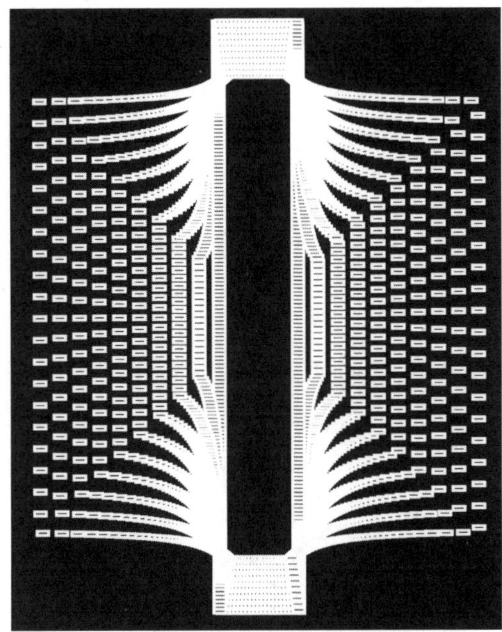

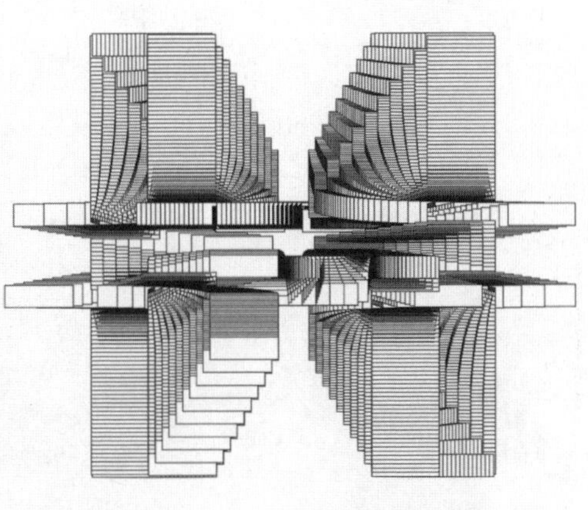

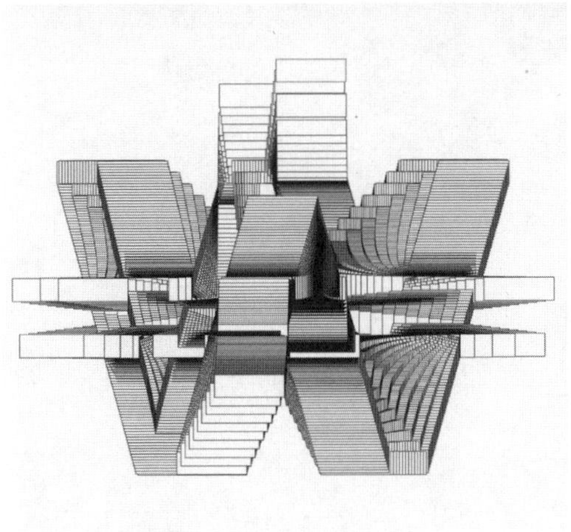

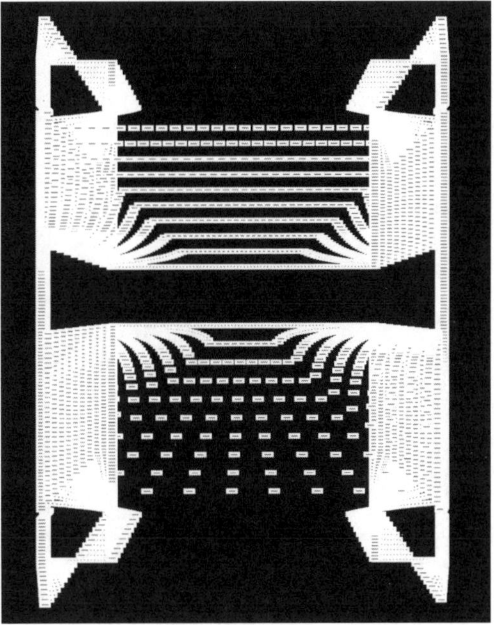

197 Atypography SRB— ATYPOGRAPHY: A NEW ART MOVEMENT

This approach transforms conventional typography into abstract yet readable forms, providing a new visual language that challenges the perception and interpretation of letters. In other words, it is possible to create an abstract painting resembling Piet Mondrian's work, but instead of random shapes, it is composed of legible text. Patience is crucial in understanding ATYPOGRAPHY. What initially appears as difficult legibility is, in fact, a fundamental aspect of this art movement—encryption.

Example text:
"SCAM"

↓

↓

↳

198 Adna Tučić, Maja Schuster DEU—ARTIFICIAL TYPE ARCHIVE

The ARTIFICIAL TYPE ARCHIVE showcases the synergy between human creativity and AI, fostering a dynamic dialog between the two. It serves as a platform for designers seeking inspiration and understanding AI's creative potential. By leveraging AI to generate letters through three distinct models and prompts, it unveils uncharted typographic possibilities. This project highlights technology's role in inspiring creativity and chronicles the advancements in AI's typographic capabilities.

199 Andréa Bouin FRA—NOTDEF

Scattered among our folders and hard drives, often unnoticed, are pretty glyphs. This specimen has been conceived and designed as a collection of attractive characters. Beyond the usual typographic signs, it deploys a constellation of heterogeneous signs that tell stories. It's a question of taking the time to observe these decals, out of fascination, obsession, and adoration. Let their original meanings disappear and turn them into independent entities among which one can now navigate.

200 Hannah Friedrich DEU—BUBBLE BATH

BUBBLE BATH is a variable font that ranges from bold, round shapes to their star-like reversal. With the aim to combine type design and creative coding, the grid on which the typeface is based, as well as the individual design of each letter, was created using JavaScript.

201 Giulio Galli / CAST—Cooperativa Anonima Servizi Tipografici ITA—SCATTERPLOT

SCATTERPLOT is a variable slab serif typeface composed of dots arranged on a geometric structure. The result is a font with a weight axis that is distinctly brutalist, featuring dots that increase in diameter without optical corrections. Additionally, a randomness axis scatters the dots across the bounding box, making the letters perfectly legible at one end while becoming increasingly illegible at the other extreme.

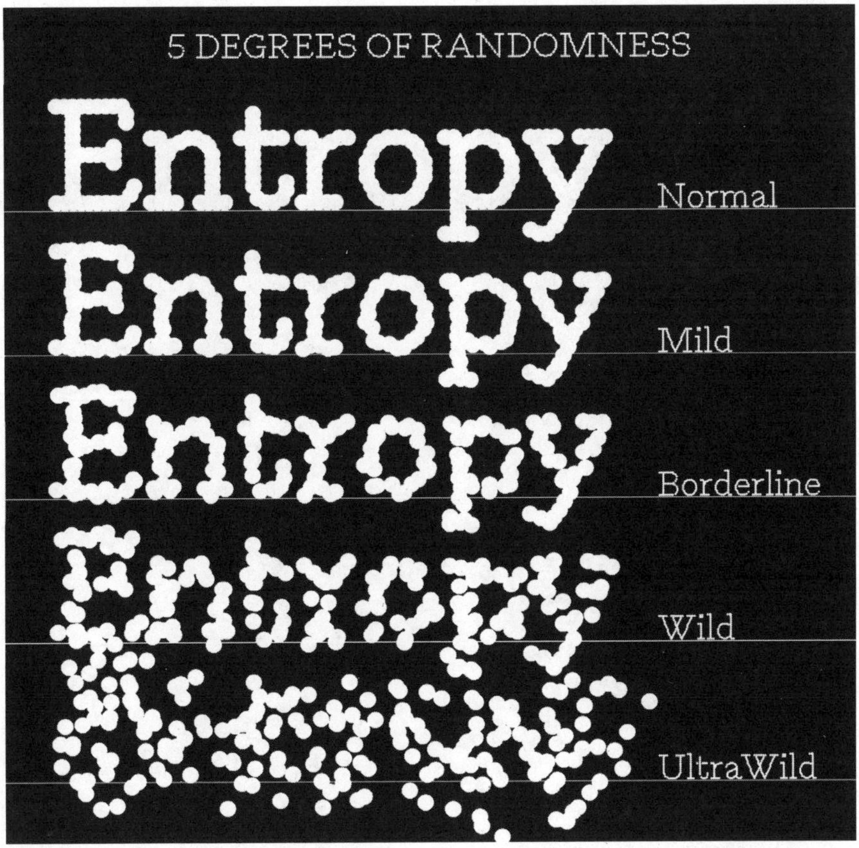

5 DEGREES OF RANDOMNESS

Entropy Normal

Entropy Mild

Entropy Borderline

Entropy Wild

UltraWild

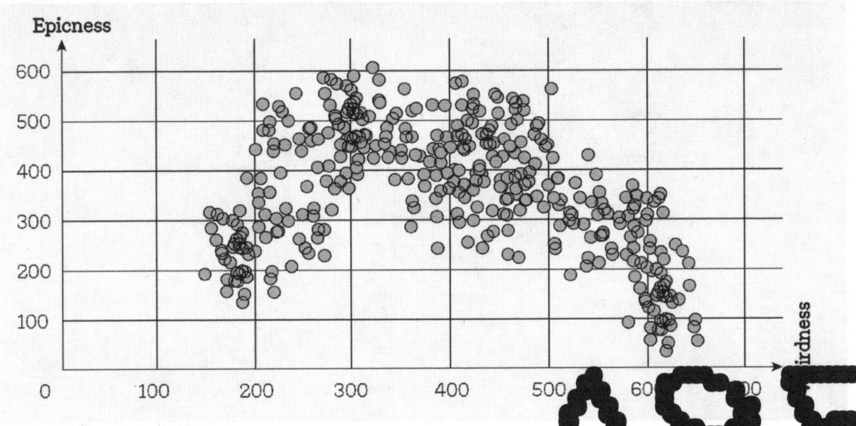

202 Seywan Hosseinpour DEU—

ARABIC TYPE DESIGN, A GEOMETRIC APPROACH

This project aims to design a simplified, modular Arabic typeface, inspired by the simplification reforms of the 1930s and 1960s, as well as Linotype's Simplified Arabic from the 1950s. Developed in a master's seminar at University of Applied Sciences Aachen, it seeks to ease learning of Arabic script by reducing standard letter forms from four to two per glyph. The goal is to create simpler forms while retaining essential features of Arabic script. Geo Kufi is designed as a display font suitable for headlines or short texts.

جيوكوفي
Geo Kufi, A geometric approach
Juli 2024
Type Specimen
Geo Kufi

203 Dorottya Nagy HUN —SCROLL

SCROLL is a manually created experimental typographic book that reflects the amount of time we spend on social media platforms every day. The book reflects on this act of scrolling. The total time spent is represented by the weight and thickness of the book. The momentary attention is represented by the fact that one can "read" this book, scroll through it, in 5–10 seconds—just like people do with an Instagram reel.

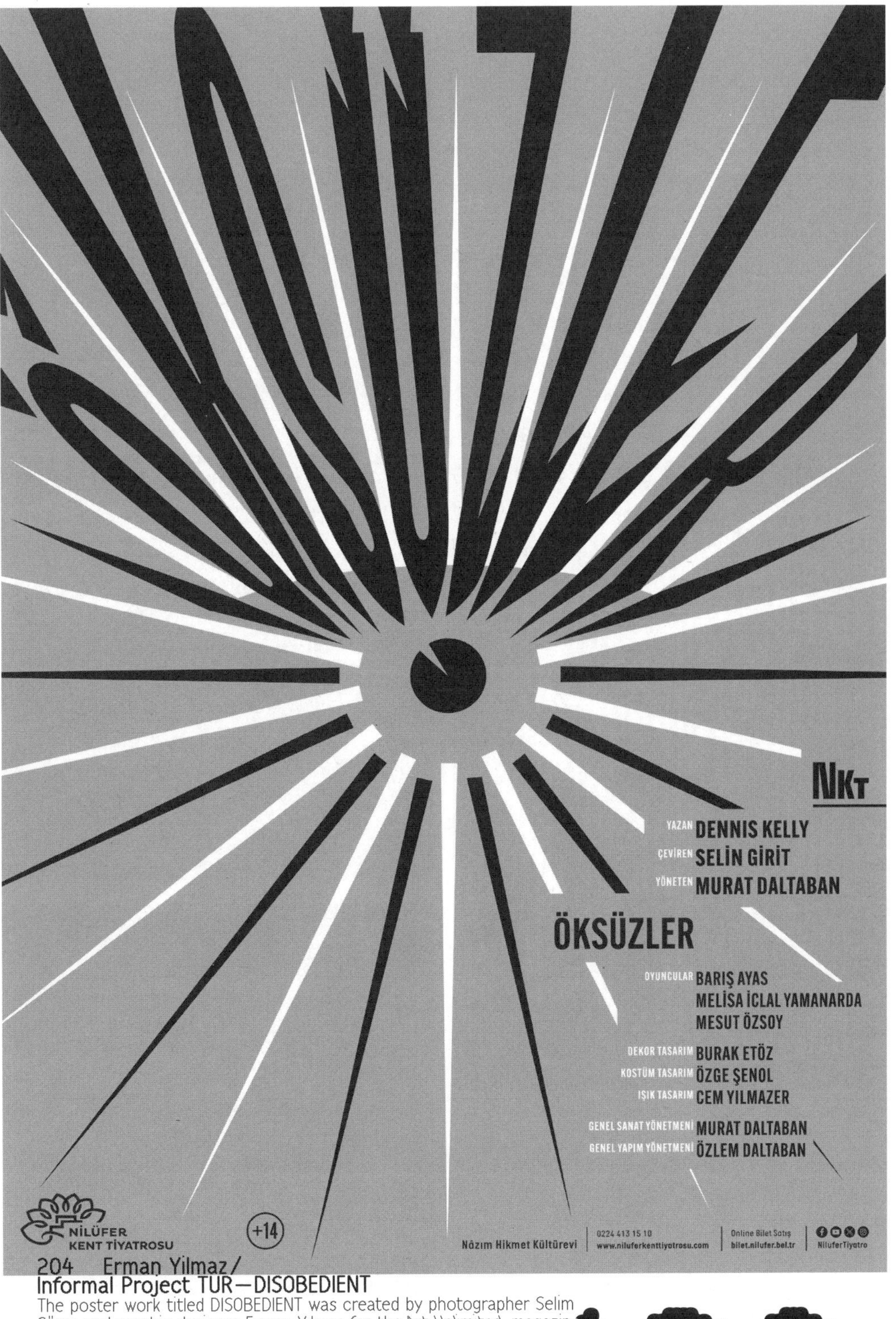

204 Erman Yilmaz/
Informal Project TUR—DISOBEDIENT
The poster work titled DISOBEDIENT was created by photographer Selim Süme and graphic designer Erman Yılmaz for the Art Unlimited magazine. What is disobedience in typography and photography? This work is not an answer, it is just an experiment.

205 Iryna Baranova / liistva UKR— 9:09 PM

9:09 PM is a rhythmic, brutal, and retro-futuristic exploration of motion, with a nod to the iconic drum machine.

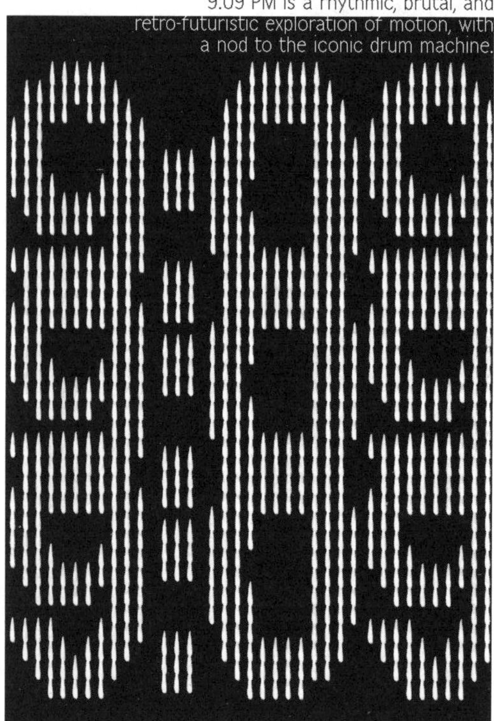

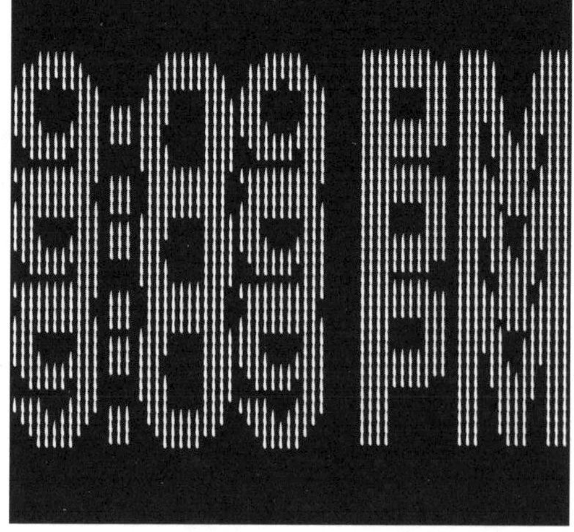

206 Long Nguyen DEU— ICH SEHE NICHTS

"I SEE NOTHING." The poster questions the inability or failure to perceive certain societal or cultural phenomena.

207 David Archiv
LTU — MIRAGE

This is a personal project for an exhibition series called Mirage—the Disappearing Line between Reality & Fiction. The typography captures the physical essence of a mirage. When you view it from a distance, you see one thing, but as you get closer, the mirage disappears and you start to read between the lines. In addition, the details of the letters create a visual connection to the New Museum, where the exhibition takes place.

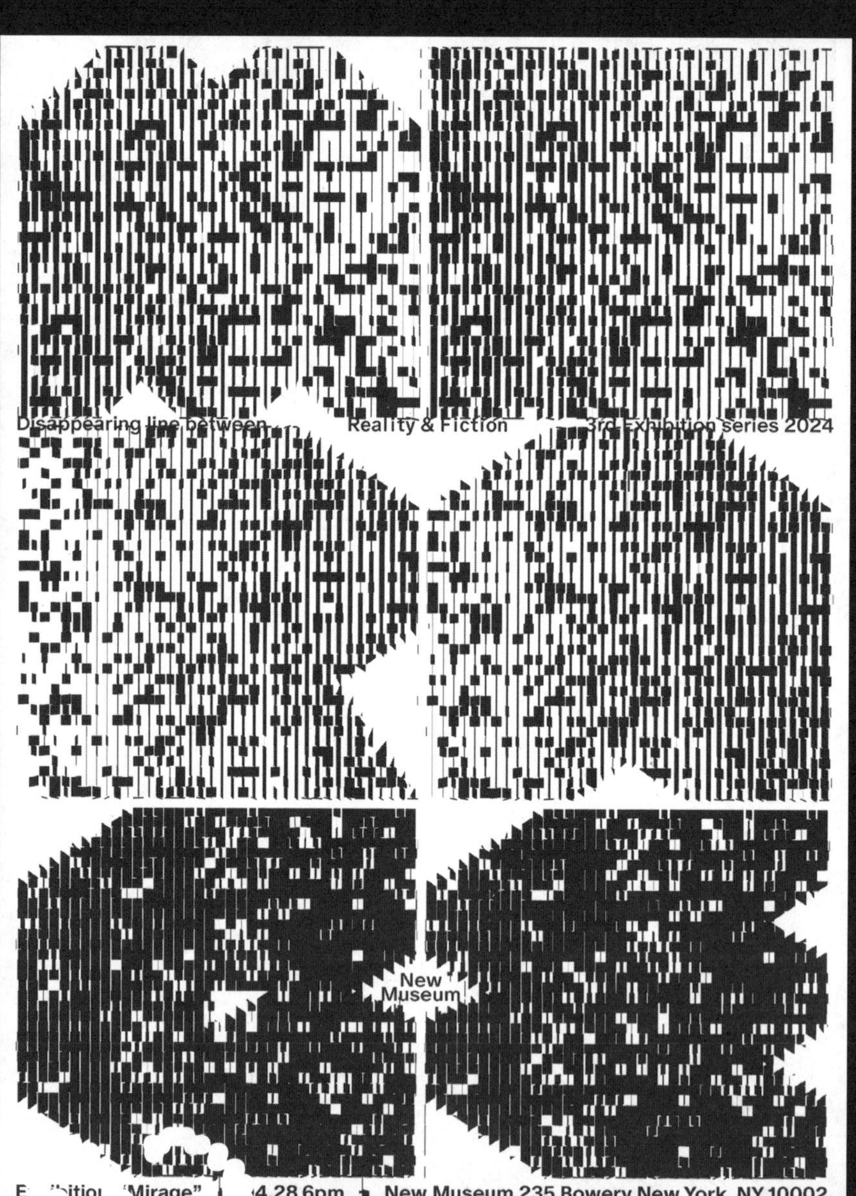

208 Dora Balla / Dora Balla Design HUN— HV 100 FONT REDESIGN I.

HV 100 FONT REDESIGN glitch experiments. Balla's aim is to transform their rigid geometric digital typeface into a unique and unrepeatable version.

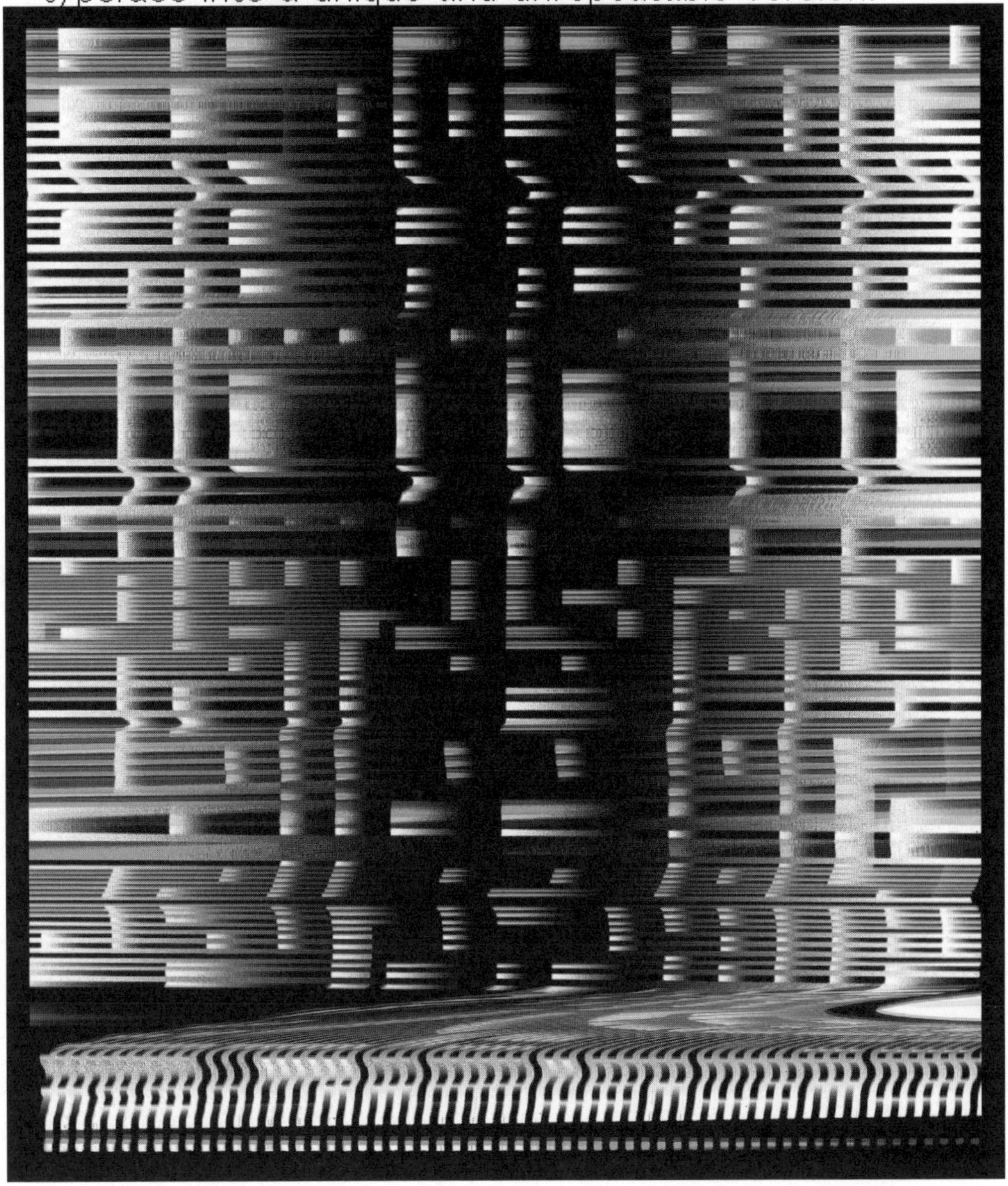

209 Haocheng Zhang AUS— BODY EXPERIMENTAL TYPE POSTER

The BODY EXPERIMENTAL typeface focuses on body movement. This project aims to explore not only the physical body but also the visual body. The body can take the form of text design, type design, and other experimental visual directions. It seeks to explore the dynamic visual qualities of type, capture the structural relationships between letterforms, and convey the emotional essence of typography. The project also encourages experimental designs and aims to foster cross-disciplinary collaborations.

210 Yuliya Ratnikova GBR— MUSIC IN THE ANSWER

Poster design for the Tea Break Collective × Yuliya Ra party and exhibition that took place in July at an arcade bar in Peckham, London. The idea for the poster and experimental typography was inspired by the 3D Tetris game that the designer used to play as a kid.

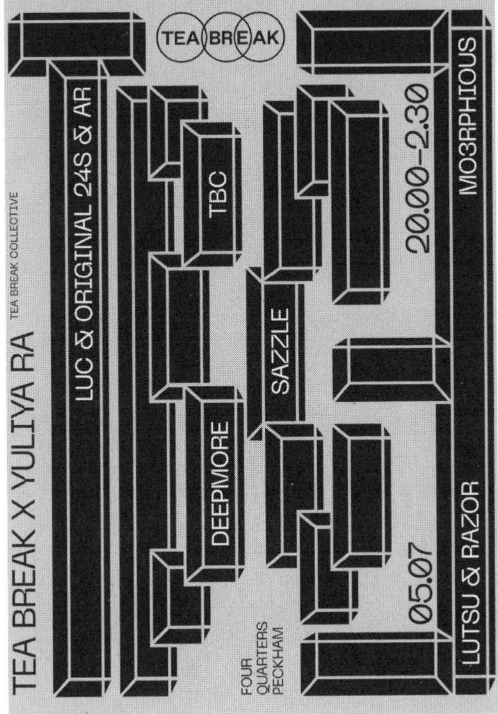

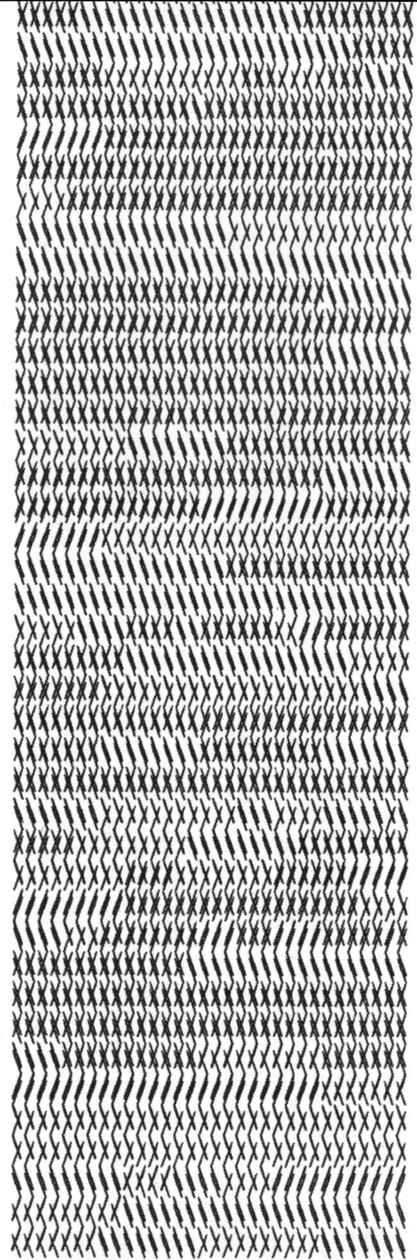

211 Sasha Bychenko, Kultura Studio UKR—THERMAL PRINTER CONCRETE POETRY

We, as designers, constantly strive to improve our skills, tools, materials, and workflow. This is a normal part of our work in the capitalist market. But what if we consciously downgrade our own tools? This visual poetry was created on a simple thermal printer using only two non-letter symbols from its limited basic glyph set. By abandoning content and message, the observer gain the opportunity to focus more on sensations and form creation.

Pola Małaczewska

POL—ELEKTOR PATTERN SYSTEM

ELEKTOR PATTERN SYSTEM is an experimental tool in the form of a font. ELEKTOR functions as a pattern language that originated from a deconstructed image-processing experiment. Its foundation consists of various illustrations of digital circuits recovered from hobbyist magazines from the 70s to 90s rotting in the digital archives. Małaczewska pixelated them and set together as a font. The font comes in two styles: Regular & Round. This way they become a language that may be used as a system for creating pixel patterns.

213 Noémie Erb FRA—URSULA—TYPOGRAPHY INSPIRED BY SMALL LIVING BEINGS

URSULA is master's degree project created at Esad d'Amiens. URSULA is a single width, variable, and random typography. The typography is inspired by various forms offered by nature and by small living beings, such as ants, termites, or bacteria. Ursula is composed of characters close to the Latin alphabet and other abstract characters called "traces." The typeface consists of six weights, representing different levels of snacking. The typeface name is a nod to the author Ursula Le Guin.

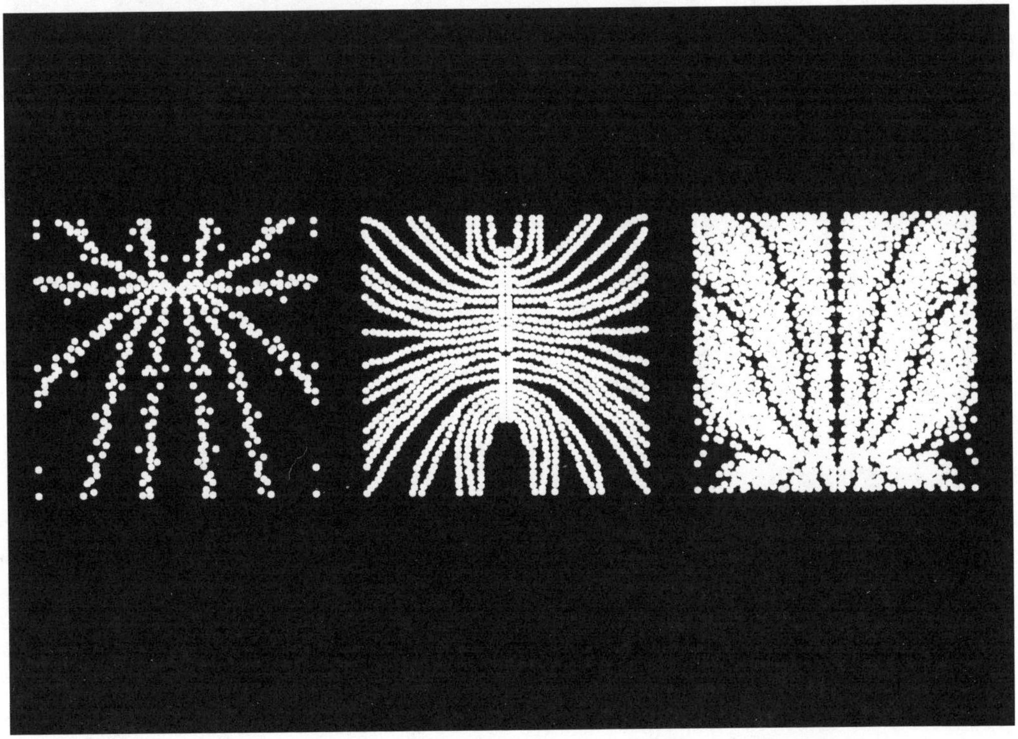

Brian Heffernan
IRL—PARTS

PARTS is a modular typeface. The letterforms were created from a combination of eight elements.

Coming together
is a beginning,
staying together
is progress, and
working together
is success.
Henry Ford

Light Parts
Medium Parts
Heavy Parts

215 Hanna Hartwig, Miriam Winter DEU—SWAY PROJECT

With the SWAY PROJECT, Hanna Hartwig and Miriam Winter have developed an analog, playful approach in order to break away from learned design and to develop an unusual design language. The monospace font plays with legibility by constantly alternating between letterforms and spaces.

TRIAL AND ERROR

Trial and Error is the opposite from aiming for perfection on the first attempt—this approach views failure and mistakes as essential learning tools. Each misstep becomes an opportunity to gain insight, adjust, and improve. This process values the lessons of the real-world. Recognizing that growth of ten does not come from getting it right the first time.

216 Julian Ratay DEU—
OUT OF PLACE

OUT OF
PLACE
PLACE

Christian Tkaczuk DEU—
WHEREISMYMIND

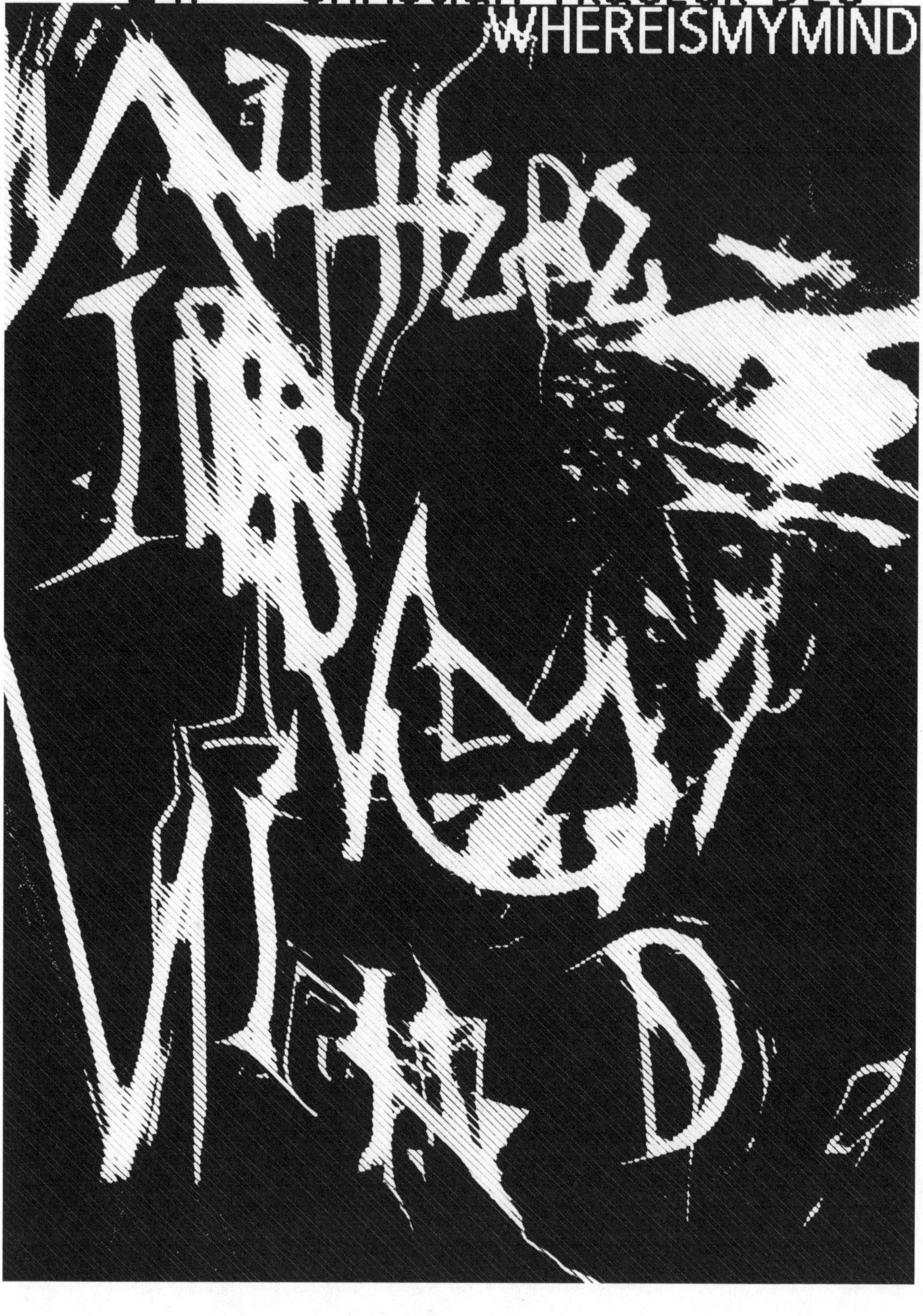

218 Christoph Reinicke DEU—UNTITLED

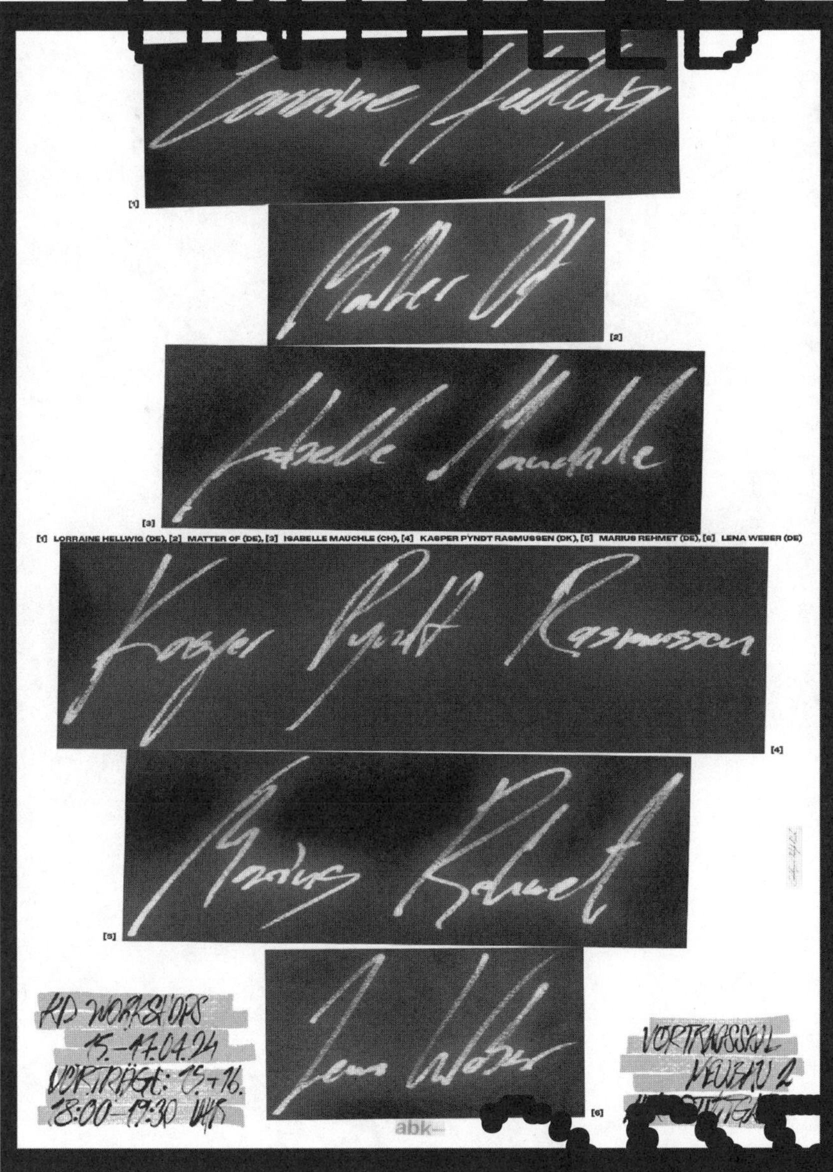

219 Mirjam Goldschmidt DEU—
DON'T FOLLOW ME AT NIGHT

220 Nele Kreuger DEU—
ES IST EIN
SCHMALER GRAD

221 Julian Tillmann
DEU—VERSTECKT

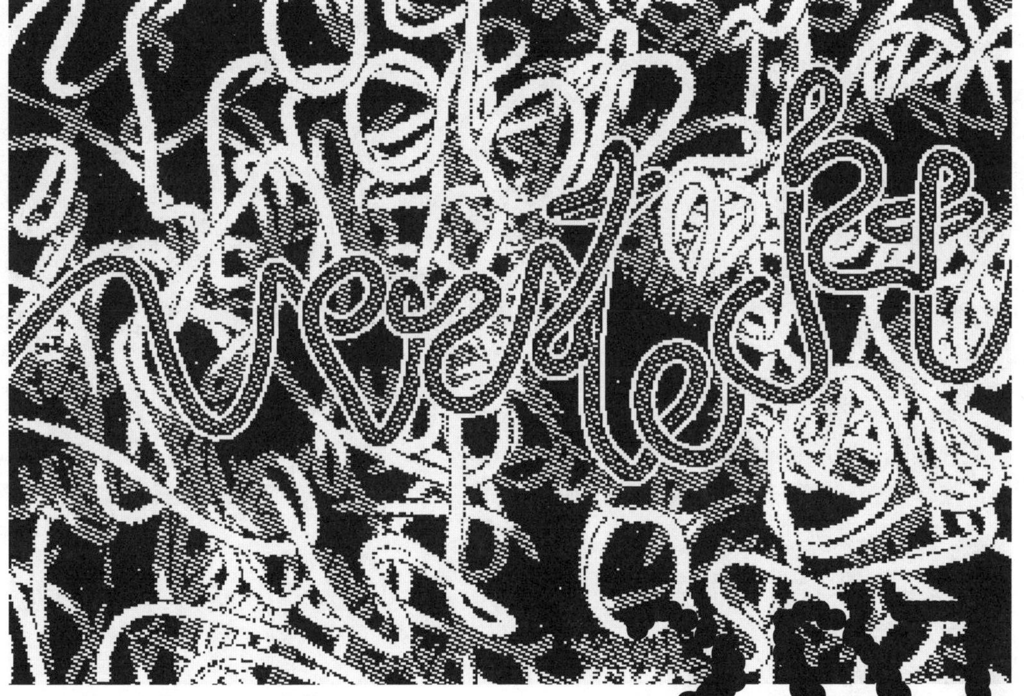

222
Tim Stange
DEU—
CHROME
CONSTRUCTION

223
Fabian Meyer
DEU—
UNTITLED

224 Marie Sadlo DEU—
UNTITLED

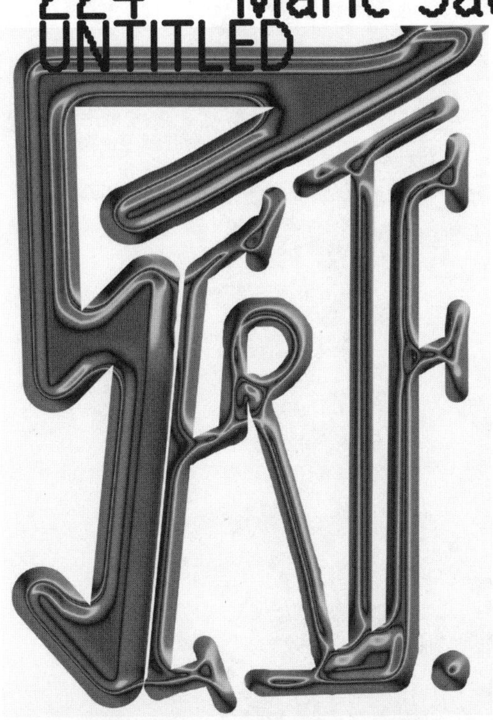

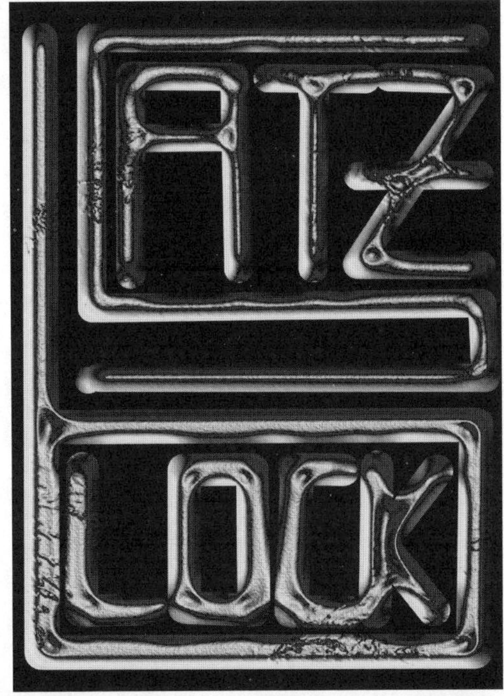

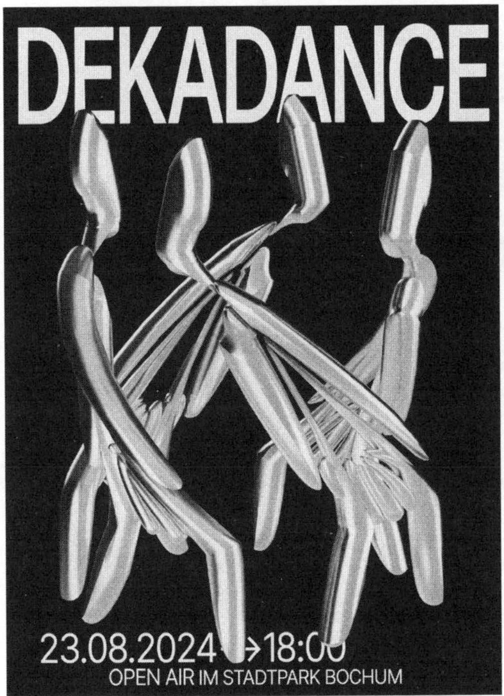

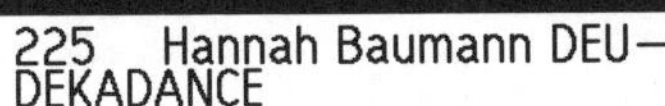

225 Hannah Baumann DEU—
DEKADANCE

226 Hannah Baumann DEU—
NO WAY OUT

227 Fabian Hoffmann
DEU — GLOW UP

228 Fabian Hoffmann DEU—
NEO NEO ARCHITECTURE
Slanted Experimental Type 3.0

229 Anja Bolender DEU—
REFLECTION

230 Franziska Prüsener
DEU—MONOCULTURES

231 Beyza Duyuran
DEU—A&S

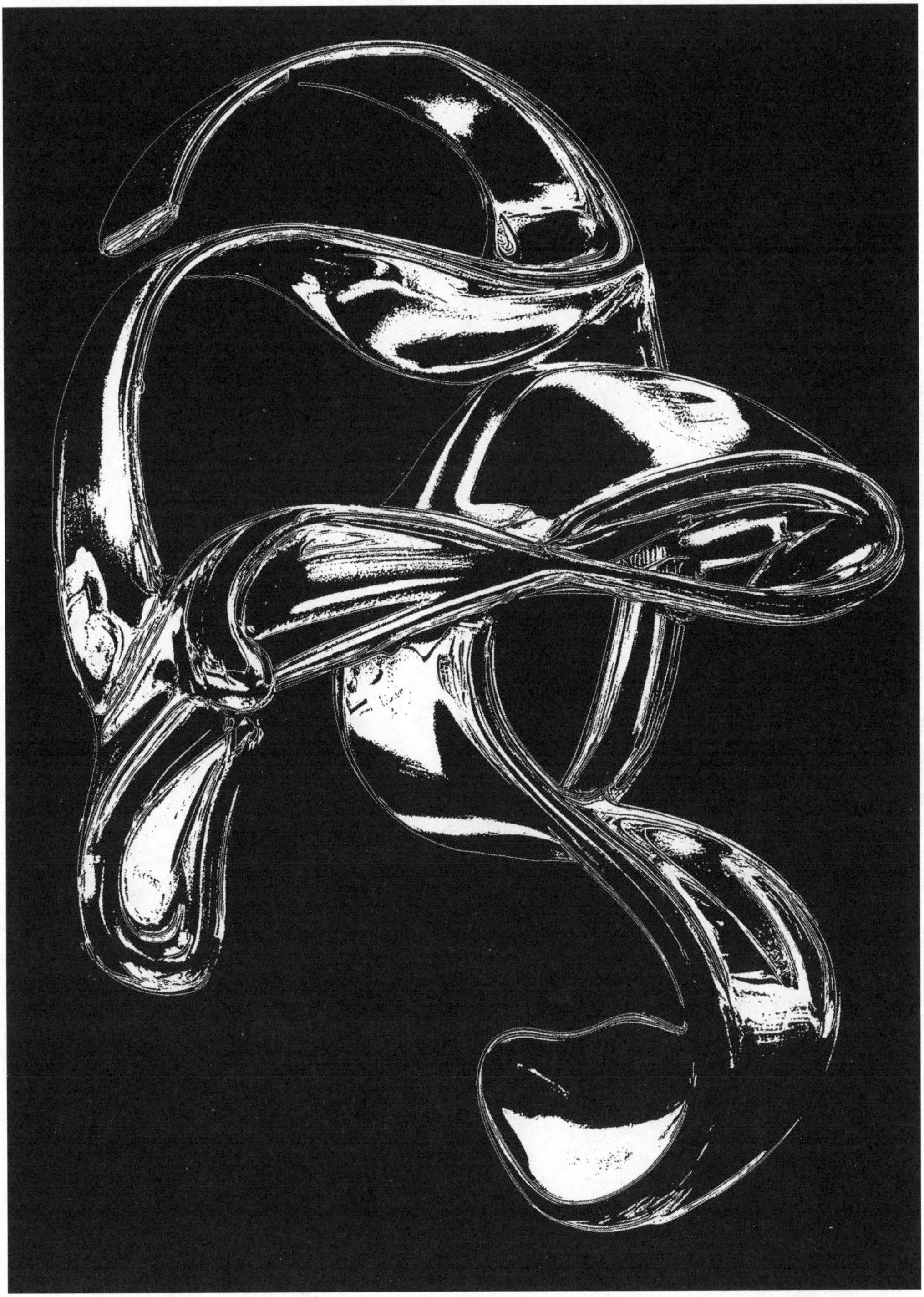

232 Nathalie Knappik DEU— THE ANATOMY OF THE ICONIC LOOP

Slanted Experimental Type 3.0
217

233

Yavuz Sahin
DEU —
TYPESHITYS

TYPESHITYS

234 Nassim Mokarami DEU—SPIKED "O"

235 Aysel Kopuz DEU—BLOOM

236 Kandir Özkan DEU—ZEBRA

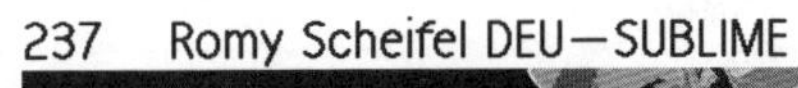

237 Romy Scheifel DEU—SUBLIME

238 Monica Sharoubime DEU—UNTITLED

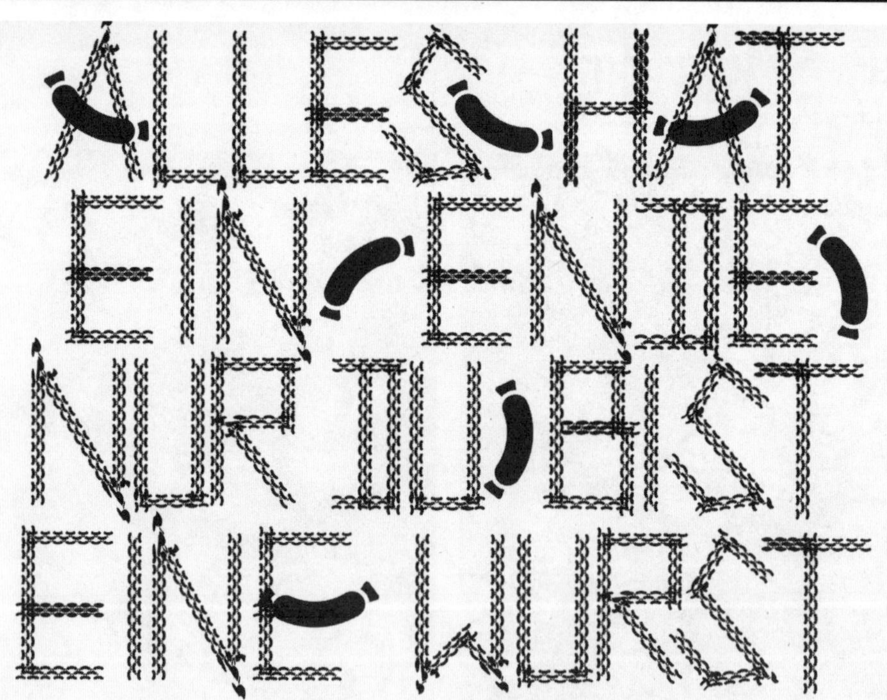

239 Philipp Mohncke DEU—ALLES HAT EIN ENDE NUR DU BIST EINE WURST

240 Nihal Türkyilmaz DEU—HANNIBAL

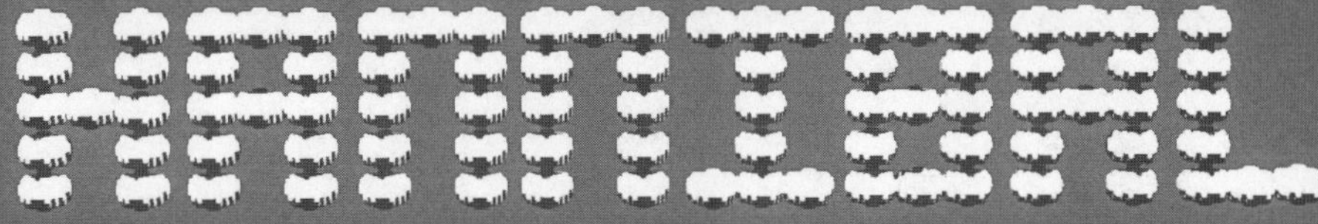

241 Abdulhadi Aldarwich DEU—
MONOLINE ABSTRAKT

242 Chanel Wloka DEU—
WEBBED WORDS

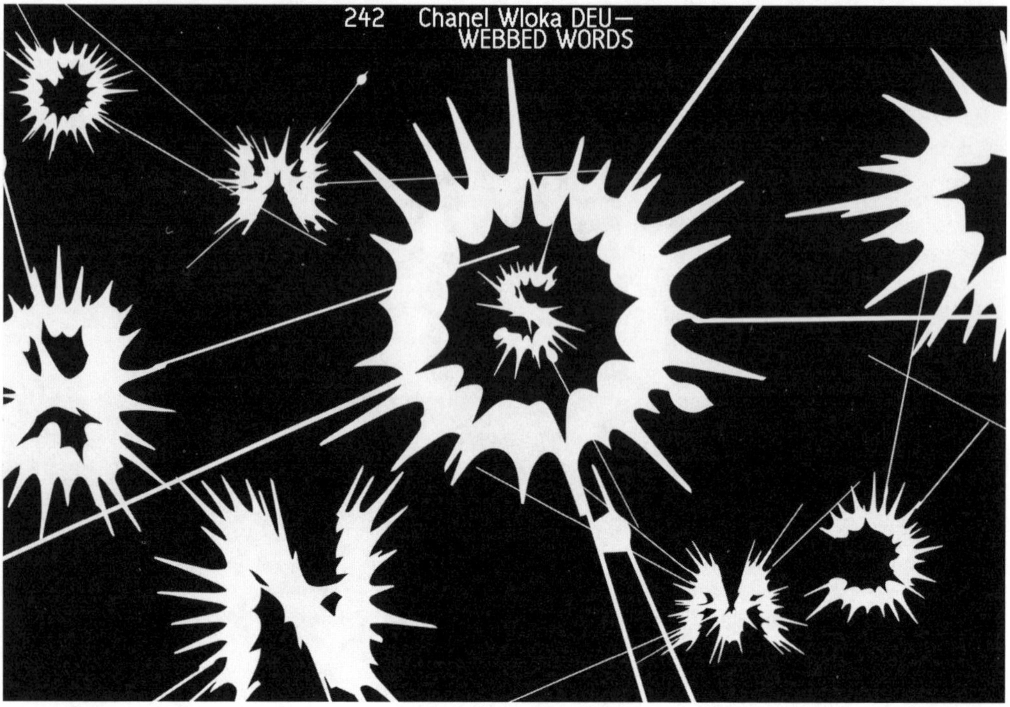

243 Eva Schlotzhauer DEU—
꽃 (PRONOUNCED "KKOT")

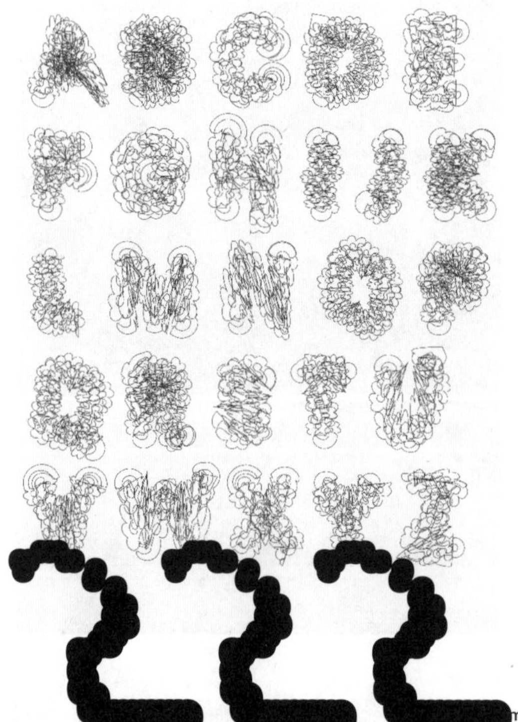

244 Elena
Byalaya USA—
ADHD FONT

245 Muriel Labadi
DEU — DISAGREEMENT

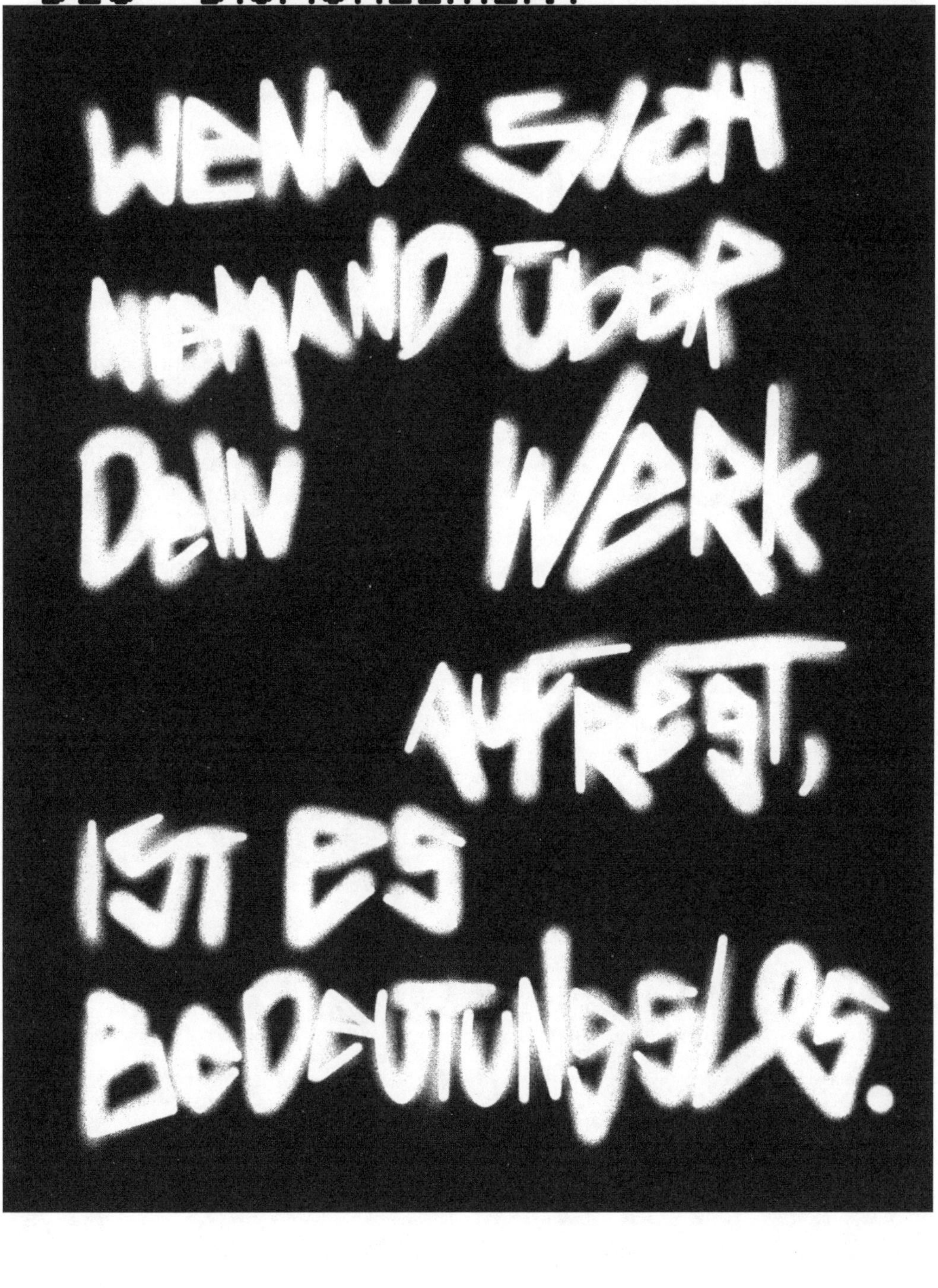

WENN SICH NIEMAND ÜBER DEIN WERK AUFREGT, IST ES BEDEUTUNGSLOS.

246 Jona Kranzusch DEU—SHINE

247 Jannette Bartkowiak DEU—CONNECTED

248 Melissa Smajic DEU—STUCK IN ONE LINE

249 Alexandra Sagalow DEU—MONOLINE

250 Janett Jakubow DEU—UNTITLED

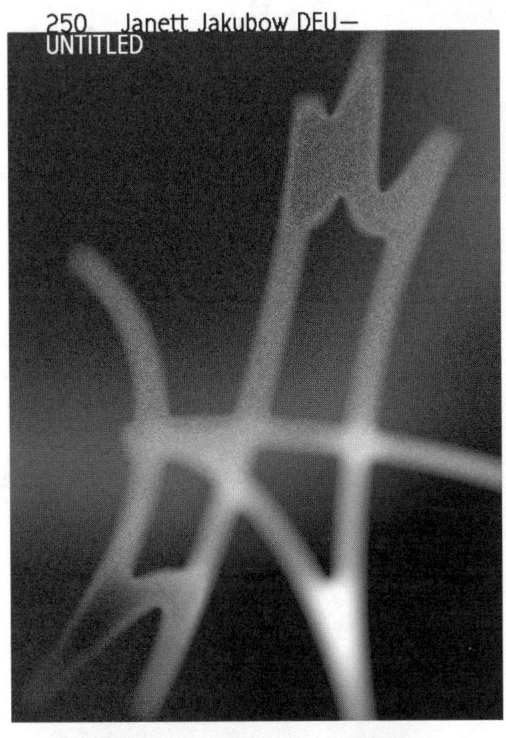

251 Janell Sin Fan Im DEU—UNTITLED

252 Philip Popek DEU—POINT

253 Matilda Greiner DEU—STFU

254 Niclas Kötting DEU—SPLINTER

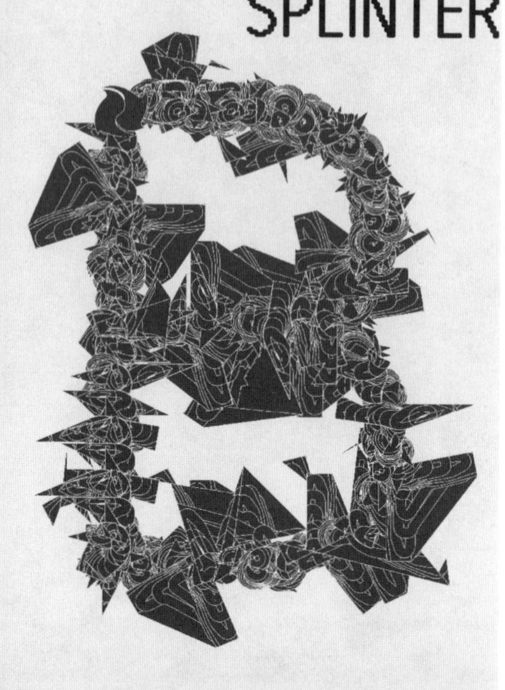

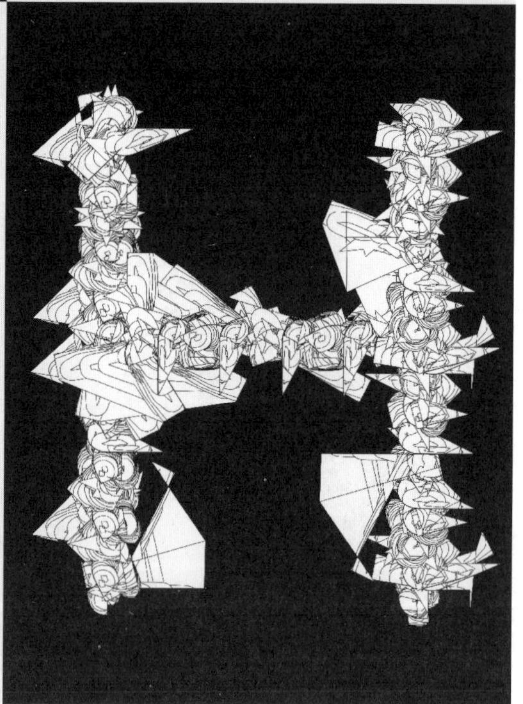

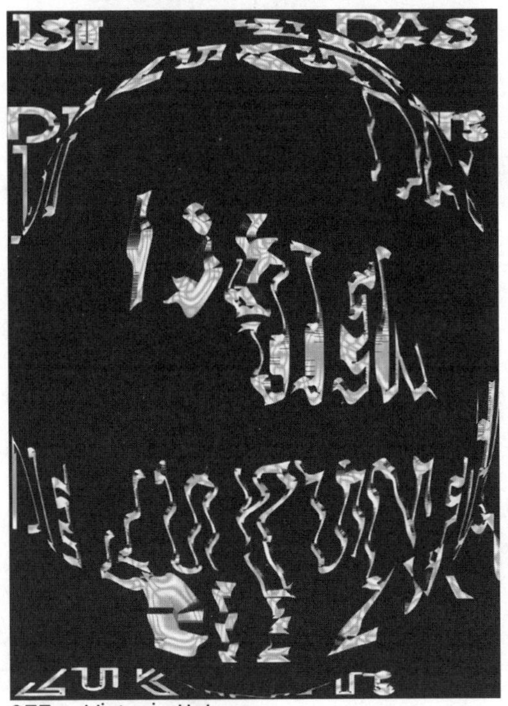

255 Victoria Hohage
DEU—IST DAS DIE ZUKUNFT?

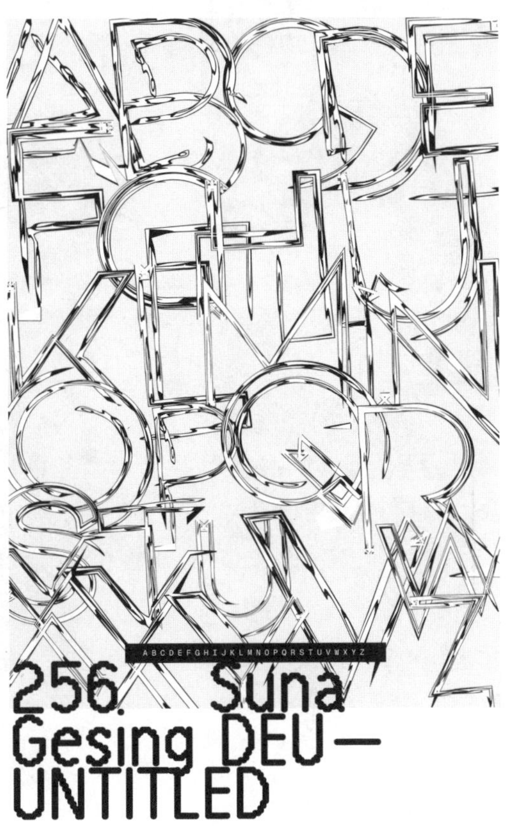

256 Suna Gesing DEU—UNTITLED

257 Lilith Dolch
DEU—TEXT IS SUPPOSED TO BE READ

text is supposed to be read

258 Tim von Bischopinck
DEU—GENERATE ME

Generate Sans is a typeface based on a single generated line. The line loosely follows a template using creative code to generate two messy-looking typefaces. In 3D, a new dimension is added to create large, sculptural letter forms.

259 Moritz Stolz DEU—FLUID

260 Pelin Yapici DEU—LABYRINTH

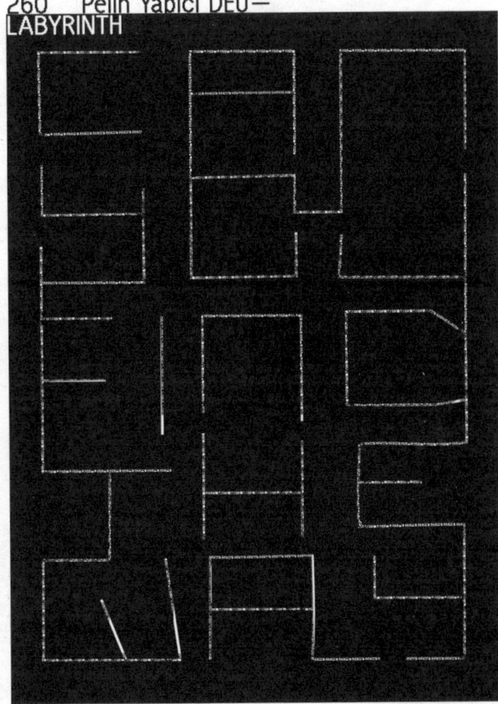

261 Romain Granai BEL—UNTILTED

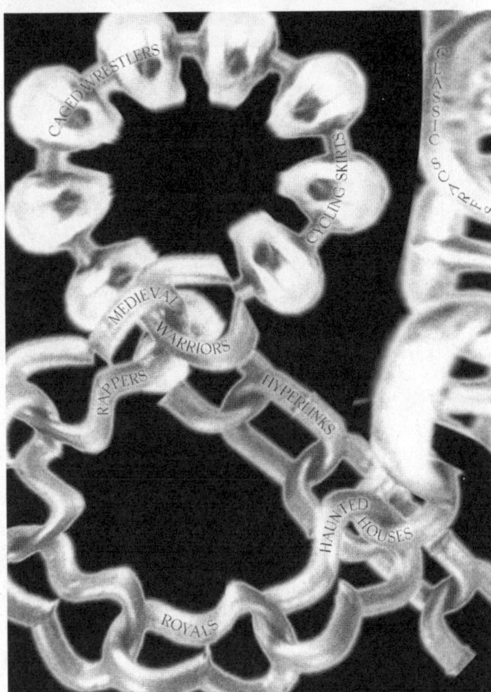

262 Jule Orlik DEU—RAPPERS AND ROYALS

We are

CSTM Fonts

CSTM
Xprmntl 03
Medium

@cstmfonts

Backslanted Regular

and we love

creating *wicked,*

CSTM Xprmntl 02 Italic

peculiar,

CSTM Xprmntl 02 Bold

Backslanted Super

and

Maregraphe Mega Compressed

especially

custom ones

Custom Typeface for Sila Sveta

BERGHALL

Existentialist
…le Hairline

Astrologically
…ine Plus Clair Italic

AFKAIENNES
…ette ExtraLight

Objectivation
Astronef Base ExtraLight

SOLIDARITY
…onqueror Inline Regular

Gratuitement
…a Light

TURQUOISE
…onqueror Sans Regular

ONSTRUCTIONS
…k Bold

Perfectionist
…n Regular

PÂTISSERIE
…onqueror Carved One + Two + Three + Four

ISTINGUISHED IMAGINATION
…ria Compress Demi

KIMONO
…ni Extended Inline Black 48a

Käsefondue
…aic ExtraBold Italic

agliatelle alla Milanaise
Astronef Super Compressed

GEMINI SOCIABLE
…ria Compress Black

NIGHTCLUB
…ette Black

Métro Champs-Élysées
Arbitre Narrow Thin

Abstract Paintings
Altesse 38pt

Distilled from 27 Botanicals
Alyssa Light

Grande Vadrouilles
Alembert

Fall Collection
Aukio

Inspirations
Zingiber

Une Boutique Parisienne
Ambroise François Regular

RAVISHINGLY
Retiro 24pt

Brainstormed
Deréon Italic 32pt

MULTICOLORS
Retiro 24pt

L'Illustration
Le Monde Journal Bold Italic

Systematize
Caslonian S Heavy

ORIGINALLY
Mencken Heavy Italic

Newsletters
PS Fournier Black Italic

PACKAGER
Arsen Display He…

GROUNDWORKS
Arbitre Condensed…

234

American Grotesk® klim.co.nz

ESSAYS

CARLOTTA KRÄMER
ROB STOLTE
ROOSJE VAN DER KAMP
IAN LYNAM
CHRISTOPHER SLEBODA
& KATHLEEN SLEBODA
DR JOANNA TYBOROWSKA
PAULINE GEBAUER
& DANIEL GREMME
NICHOLAS QYLL
RAPHAËL VERONA
& SOFIA PAPAEFTHYMIOU

CARLOTTA KRÄMER

In 1953, the Swiss architect, sculptor, and graphic designer Max Bill was invited as a guest speaker at the International Design Conference in Aspen, Colorado (USA). "We came to aspen and are meeting there, all of us interested in design [...] people may never agree with our creations. Maybe people do need decoration and ugly things," he explains to his audience.

THE SIN OF DECORATION

For him, the need for decoration is incomprehensible and a concept that stands in binary opposition to modernity. Incompatible with his idea of design. At the end of his speech, Max Bill came to the following conclusion: "Typography and decoration—is nonsense." This dissociation from the decorative is more than an aesthetic program and it is no coincidence that it was formulated so dismissively at a time when the newly created profession of the designer had to establish itself with all its might as socially relevant and among the artists, the creative intellectuals. Decoration embodied in arts and crafts means unacademic—decoration embodied in femininity means worthless. This perpetuates gender constructions to this day. For me as a young female designer in 2024, it was a conscious act to overcome my inner discomfort and break through this attribution set over 100 years ago with the beginning of modernism. With the Liga Typeface, I have developed a set of ornaments that can be used to embellish—decoration for graphic compositions and typography.

In my typeface the letters have been replaced with ornaments, the true function of delivering language can no longer be fulfilled. The ornaments are distributed on the keyboard in order to use the system of digital writing. This makes it possible to integrate the practice of decorating into the handling of text and letters. There is no higher use in those ornaments than to decorate—no secret meaning, no hidden system to decipher. As for each character only stands for its characteristic play of form and inevitable presence of symbolism.

Suggested by its name, the Liga Typeface is heavily inspired by the ligature, as within type design this glyph stands for the merging of letters—the interaction of form. Forming those ligatures, by fusing two characters typed one after the other, allows the 26 "main characters" (small caps "a" to "z") to expand into 151 character variations. The characters range in abstraction as well as complexity and are grouped by certain characteristics. There are "main characters," "ligatures," and "self ligatures," describing the kind of character combination, as well as the distinction between "introverted," "extroverted," "indecisive," and "protagonists" characters—labels that provide a sense of identity for each ornament. The ligature doesn't only create interplay between the ornaments themselves but also interaction between designer and decor. Trying various combinations, typing letter after letter, watching the characters melt into ornamental arraignments, makes the Liga Typeface a playful tool for typographic decoration. Bringing together two separates that—by modernism—were made out to be contradictions.

During the Mid-20th century, when Max Bill delivered his lecture, decoration was firmly established as the antagonist of modernism. Decoration represented the superfluous, the irrelevant, and the unnecessary. It was something "extra," not inherently useful or functional. In distancing themselves from the decorative arts—seen as imbued with "feminine" connotations—designers sought to position their work as serious, utilitarian, and socially significant. To fully understand this perceived incompatibility between modernism and decoration, we must go back to the early 20th century, when Austrian architect Adolf Loos declared that ornamentation was nothing short of a crime against art and the cultural evolution.

Ornament und Verbrechen (Ornament and Crime) was first published in German in 1923, though Loos had given a lecture under the same title as early as January 1908 in Vienna. His arguments are foundational to the rejection of the decorative in modernist theory, to the extent that the modern movement can be said to have constructed itself around the rejection of ornamentation. Loos was a key figure in early modernism and his essay set the stage for the radical transformation of design that followed. In Ornament und Verbrechen he argued that the elimination of the ornament was an essential step in the "evolution of culture." He claimed to have gifted the world with an insight that would guide the modernist ethos: ornamentation was a vestige of a less advanced stage of civilization. Loos positioned himself as the harbinger of this intellectual breakthrough, though in reality, his ideas emerged from a broader conversation among architects, designers, and thinkers who were reimagining the values of progress, innovation, and experimentation concepts that have shaped the history of design to this day.

Generations of designers internalized these ideas, adopting them unquestioningly as the foundations of good design. However, underlying this seemingly neutral framework were gendered assumptions and value systems. The association of decoration with femininity, for example, played a significant role in the marginalization of women in design. As Cheryl Buckley pointed out in her 1986 essay *Made in Patriarchy: Towards a Feminist Analysis of Woman and Design*, the patriarchal context in which design evolved excluded women by designating certain types of work as inherently feminine—and therefore less valuable. Classification systems that emerged during modernism, such as "universal" or "good form," were in fact deeply exclusionary, masking their biases behind a facade of neutrality. Loos, for instance, suggested that "all modern people" would naturally understand his vision, presenting his aesthetic as a universal truth. Yet taste, as we know, is shaped by specific social conditions, and the so-called universal design was, in reality, a mechanism that allowed dominant groups—primarily Western, male elites—to maintain their cultural dominance.

"Since ornament is no longer a natural product of our culture, and therefore represents either a backwardness or a phenomenon of degeneration, the work of the ornamentalist is no longer paid for." (Loos, 1908) The work of the "ornamentalist" is completely devalued as "degenerate" and "backward" with a seemingly social argument. Allegedly concerned with the welfare of the arts and crafts, he dismantled the concept of the decorative arts with the demand to refrain from ornamentation. The "ornamentalist" can be interpreted here as the artisan whose work is now considered superfluous in the age of modernity, according to Adolf Loos.

The valuation of the decorative arts plays a major role with regard to the associated gender constructions. For within the genres of the arts, in the tense field between fine art and applied art, a hierarchy emerges that reflects current gender attributions. While architecture, which up to and including the 20th century was practiced almost exclusively by men, such as Adolf Loos, is placed alongside the fine arts in this hierarchy, textile work such as weaving or embroidery is at the lower end of this classification. This is due to the fact that the craft of embroidery was an area that was "[...] traditionally held to be female because of the iconography of the lady with her embroidery frame [...]." (Anscombe, 1984, cited by Helland 2019)

For example, there were institutions such as the Royal School of Art Needlework, founded in South Kensington in 1872, which was intended to teach "gentlewomen" the "decorative craft." Prevailing constructions of femininity were reinforced by the gendered categories of ornament, needlework, and decoration. The example of this institution demonstrates the ways in which patriarchy restricted women's ability to participate fully in all areas of design through institutional means. The resulting feminine stereotypes define practices as appropriate for women, so that certain crafts and professions are labeled as feminine.

As Griselda Pollock and Rozsika Parker argue in their 1981 book *Old [illegible] Mis[illegible]tresses: [illegible] Women, Art and Ideology*, the association between [illegible] craft and femininity can be traced back to the 18th [illegible] century. Male artists sought to distance

Liga Typeface catalog

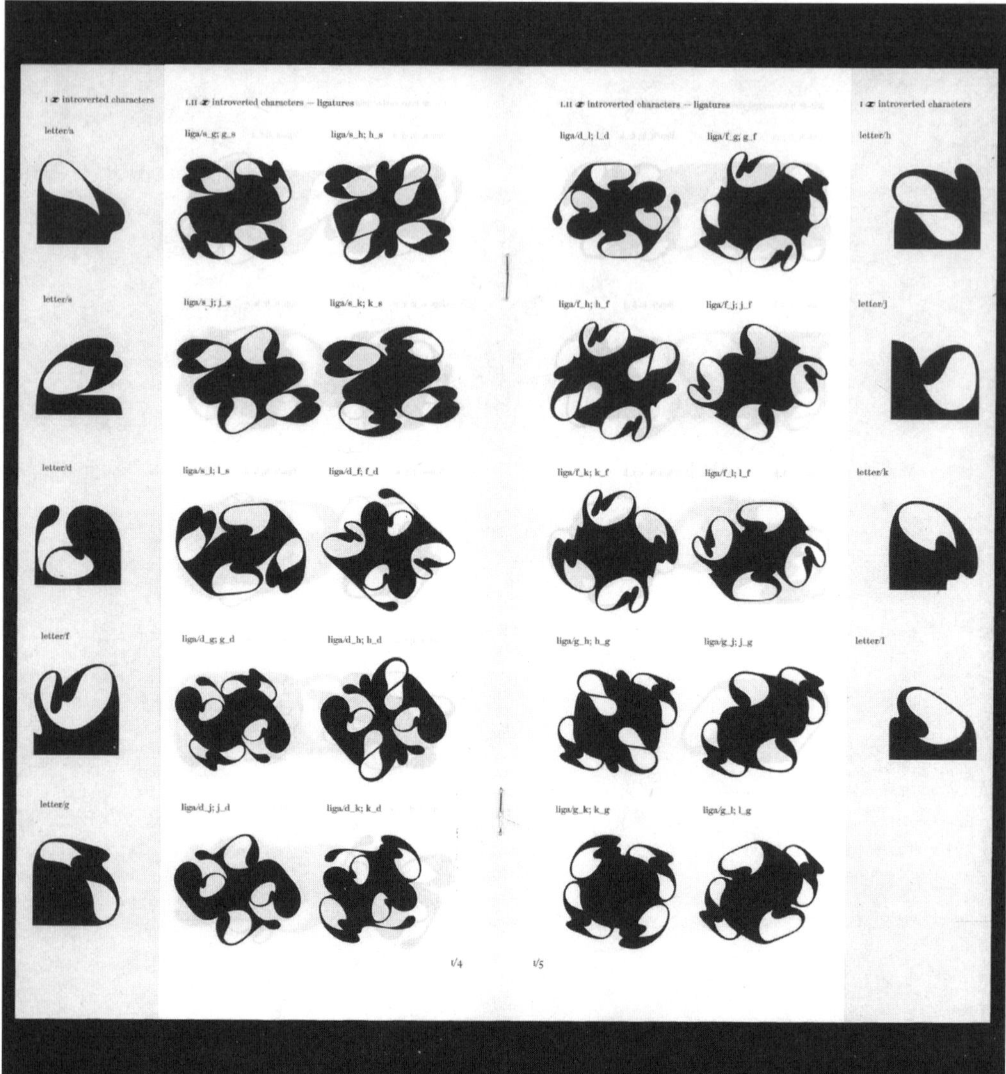

Liga Typeface catalog

themselves from the world of craftsmanship, thereby creating a new hierarchy in the arts that was, quite incidentally, based on gender differences. Loos himself reinforced this divide in his critique of ornamentation, using it to establish a clear boundary between art and craft, and by extension, between masculinity and femininity.

"Lack of ornament is a sign of intellectual strength," he declared, implying that those who embraced ornamentation lacked the mental fortitude necessary to create meaningful art. This rhetoric echoed the longstanding figure of the (male) artist and genius, which has been at the forefront of art history since the 19th century. "The central figure of art historical discourse is the artist, who is presented as an ineffable ideal which complements the bourgeois myth of a universal, classless man [...]." (Pollock, 1988) Creativity is also anchored in the figure of the genius artist as an ideological component of masculinity, while femininity, as the supposed antithesis of this genius figure, were implicitly excluded from serious artistic pursuits.

Ornaments want to attract, want to please and delight the viewer, without any sense of mission or morality: Loos condemns and rejects this purely aesthetic symbolism. In *The Trouble with Beauty* (2001), Wendy Steiner argues that the analogy between ornament and femininity is based within aesthetic history, where women themselves were seen as the ornament of their environment. "Woman [...] have been considered, for better or for worse, ornaments to society and the home. Ornaments epitomize the aesthetic; their primary function is to be beautiful in themselves and so to add beauty to the larger wholes in which they figure." (Steiner, 2001, cited by Helland, 2019) Thus, with the devaluation and exclusion of ornaments, an entire gender was implicitly excluded.

The rejection of the decorative and the associated gender constructions are embedded in the ideology of modernity. As a result, right at the beginning of the 20th century, at the dawn of modernism, women were left from the progress and discourse of modernism due to the existing connotation of ornament and the decorative. With the consequence that the decorative arts, precisely because of their devaluation, represented the only access for women to a professional occupation within the field of design. Therefore gender-specific attributions could be historically cemented. With the Bauhaus, Gropius established an institution that was intended to reflect the progressive ideas of modernism. But the clear division "[...] between the beautiful and the strong sex" and the introduction of the women's class makes the predominant hierarchy unmistakable.

At the opening of the school in 1919, Gropius welcomed the students with the following words: "No consideration for ladies, in work all craftsmen. I will fiercely combat the sole preoccupation with cute little salon pictures as a pastime." Also at the Bauhaus, gender attributions were embedded in the structure and framework of the school. A gender-specific hierarchy prevailed between the various workshops, divided into "male" and "female" crafts. The "female" crafts were generally associated with textiles and devalued as handicrafts. This can also be attributed to the fact that ornament served as a reference to foreign, non-European cultures and as it first established itself through textile art in the west, it also was linked to femininity. "Male" crafts, on the other hand, were associated with materials such as stone, metal, and wood, followed by steel and concrete, as architecture was considered one of the most "unfeminine" arts within the contemporary art discourse—based on the assumption that the so-called "weaker" sex would not be able to think spatially and was too weak to practice such pursuits. From 1920, one year after the opening, a women's class was introduced, where solely textile art was practiced. This later became the weaving workshop. Female students at the Bauhaus were forbidden access to all the other workshops, after completing the preliminary course. One reason for this gender-specific scheme was the fear of being perceived as a women's or arts and crafts school and thus not being taken seriously. To prevent this kind of publicity, even the admission of women was withheld.

The reality for women artists at this time shows that the rejection of the decorative stands for more than the rejection of an ornamental aesthetic. The connotation with female stereotypes is undeniable. Female artists and designers had to distance themselves very explicitly from this if they wanted to be taken even remotely seriously: "I don't want to even use this word because I don't want it to be used in any interview of mine, connected with my work. To me that word, or the way I use it or feel about it, is the only art sin." said the artist Eva Hesse in an interview with *Artforum* in 1970.

In 1990, when Sheila Levrant de Bretteville was appointed as the new director of the Graphic Design Department at Yale, modernist icon Paul Rand resigned in protest. He had been a member of the department since the 1950s, a period during which the Yale design program was a stronghold of modernist theory. In response to the department's change of direction and in the wake of his resignation, he publishes an article in which he is outraged by this disregard for modernism. In *Confusion and Chaos: The Seduction of Contemporary Graphic Design*, he describes in detail the decline of graphic design and design teaching and quotes the following: "[...]the academic study of the humanities in this country is in a state of crisis ... Every special interest—women's studies, black studies, gay studies, and the like—and every modish interpretive gambit—deconstructivism, post structuralism, new historicism (postmodernism), ... has found a welcome roost in the academy (and in many studios), while the traditional curriculum and modes of intellectual inquiry are excoriated as sexist, racist, or just plain reactionary." With a yearning memory of the good times—and of all those who had fallen into disdain by this new direction—he goes on to list the names of 18 men.

The process of creating the *Liga Typeface* allowed me to overcome and understand my initial inner discomfort with the practice of decorating as a graphic designer. I am aiming for the Liga to evolve into a typographic tool that by appliance is able to convey the depth and engagement inherent in the ornament. The construction of an allegedly "universal" design of modernity proves to be an extremely effective method of exercising patriarchal-colonial dominance. Ascribing decoration as a "sin" and ornamentation as a "crime" is a way of excluding non-patriarchal perspectives. This inheritance of modernity must be identified and made visible.

This is the foundation for breaking down the deep-seated gender stereotypes in design. Or, in the words of Sheila Levrant de Bretteville: "Until social and economic inequalities are changed, I am going to call good design feminist design."

ROB STOLTE

Language and letters give us the ability to express and interpret how we experience the world around us. But something is wrong. There seems to be a literal screen between us. We barely understand ourselves and each other anymore. We read and write less and less. Perhaps our alphabet is broken? It's time to look at literacy more broadly, with room for neurodiversity and synesthesia—a new literate playground where different senses work together. This is my quest for a (design) framework that revises traditional views on learning, language, and literacy, so that our way of type design can go beyond the screen and set the standard of 21st century communication.

A NEW-LITERATE PLAYGROUND

FRÖBELEN

My whole life, I have had a healthy aversion to teachers. At least, that's what I think. This likely stems from experiences in my early school years. I always struggled with reading and writing. Fine motor skills, formal rules, writing on the board—I found it dreadful. My school notebooks were filled with comments from "Mr. Daan." In red ink, he wrote: "Capital letters! This is the last time I grade such work!", "What a mess," and "Even more messy!" These are not very motivating critiques to receive at age nine.

School felt like an unsafe environment for me. Going to school was exhausting. All I wanted was to play outside. Slowly, I began to shut myself off from things. I did not want to participate or be told that "Rob is more capable than he lets on." I've often wondered how it could be that I "couldn't learn well."

For me, the transition from playing in the building corner in second grade to sitting still and learning to read, write, and do math in third grade was a difficult period. Growing up, my mother always encouraged me to "fröbel." I think the best translation is something like "to fiddle around." I thought it was just a saying and always viewed it as a pleasant but thoughtless pastime. During my research into my preschool years, I discovered that "Fröbelen" is actually a term used to describe the educational philosophy and methods of the German educator and crystallologist Friedrich Fröbel (1782–1852). Fröbel believed that education should focus on play and exploration. He invented the kindergarten and developed various "gifts," such as the block set. These materials were designed to provide children with a variety of sensory and intellectual experiences that would stimulate their

Rob Stolte's notebook, age 9

curiosity, creativity, and critical thinking. Letters were not included in the "gifts" because Fröbel believed that formal education and instruction in reading and writing should only begin when the child was at least six years old. Something must have gone wrong for me around this time. I still make spelling mistakes, do not know how certain conjugations work, and I feel dumb when I get "caught." Is my brain not working properly? Or is being literate something different from learning a language?

In the 1980s, Dutch schools developed a hyperfocus on correctly interpreting a text. There was often only one right (read: desired) answer. Just do what you're told, don't overthink. In that regard, the Dutch educate like they eat: functionally. This functional approach to literacy didn't work for me. I learned outside the classroom—skateboarding, spray painting graffiti, or playing hockey. Because I liked many different things, I often fell a bit in between and was hard for many people to categorize—though they tried: while graffitiing, I was the "posh kid," at the hockey club the "shabby creative one." While at school I drowned in formal (language) rules, outside I had the space to discover how language actually works: that it is a dynamic phenomenon. At the hockey club, I discovered that the difference between a clubhouse and a canteen lies not in functionality but in the user's culture. On the other hand, the mother of a teammate once asked me if I was sick when she overheard that I had put up some "throw-ups" on a wall over the weekend.

HOW LANGUAGE FORMS OUR REALITY

Graffiti gave me a greater spatial awareness of what is possible with letters and led me to attend art school. At the academy, I was broken down and rebuilt: forget everything you think you've learned so far. This is called Bildung and Gestalt, referring to the educational philosophy of Wolfgang Köhler (1887-1967). It's a personal process of reinterpreting the world in which you discover who you are and what you do. According to Gestalt theory of learning, there is no fixed way to teach. It is a completely situational form of education, focused on what works for each individual student. What appeals to me is that it is a holistic, building, and active way of learning. You don't learn in a linear manner (from A to B) but through a process called emergence: consequences build on consequences. This means everything is connected to everything else. This appearance can be experienced

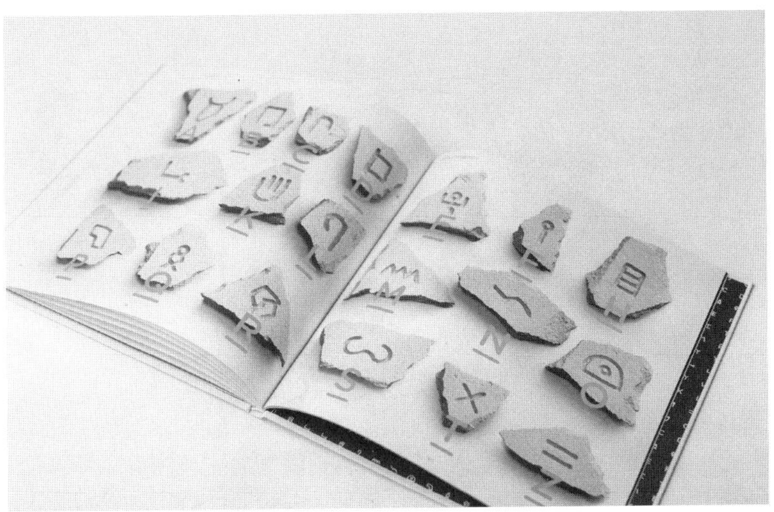

A is for Ox, published by Gottmer,
image credit: The Bookphotographer

through the Gestalt theory of perception, which states that things are first perceived as a whole before all the parts are seen. You notice patterns and relationships that exist between objects and events. The method is primarily focused on how people process knowledge and not just on transmitting content or absorbing information.

During my time at the academy, I gained insight into my struggle with letters. I started designing my own fonts, making them from physical materials, and placing them in a spatial setting. I did this, just like fröbelen, unconsciously competent. It just felt good to cut letters out of sod, create meters-high numbers from Styrofoam, and weave strings between nails to form letters. I began to enjoy it. But at the same time, I wondered how it is possible that I struggled so much with letters? Some form of dyslexia seems to be evident. In The Gift of Dyslexia, Ronald D. Davis (1942) describes dyslexia as "a different way of thinking," with strong visual and spatial abilities. He developed a method where letters are formed with clay. This process makes abstract symbols more concrete, helping dyslexics better understand and remember letters. When I read this, I realized I had always done this. In that sense, I have turned my weakness into my strength. It opened a personal exploration into what we can learn from the perceptions of dyslexics and other, atypically wired brains.

NEURODIVERGENCY: SYNTHETIC SYNAESTHESIA AS AN INCLUSIVE COMMUNICATION APPROACH

To give literacy a broader function in daily life, we must strive for what I call a holistic and inclusive understanding. It's difficult to describe your feeling or (sensory) experience to another person. In doing so, we tend to bypass words, as they can limit us. The French psychoanalyst Jacques Lacan (1901–1981) argued that from birth, we are immersed in an existing language system that influences our sensory perception of reality, our self-image, and our desires. If we aim for a more encompassing literacy, we must open up to all our senses

Untitled 002, 60 × 60 cm

Untitled 002, detail of modular element

Glyphs letter parfum

and relearn to communicate again. This requires us to create educational, communicative, and cultural environments where neurodiverse traits can flourish. A new approach to literacy might be found in synaesthesia. This is a neurological trait in the autism spectrum where senses blend. For example, people with synaesthesia might see colors when hearing sounds or taste flavors when reading words.

The word synaesthesia means together ("sun") and to experience ("aesthesis"). This shared experience not only stimulates multiple senses at once but also literally connects us. It is embedded in our language, as seen in expressions like "a warm color" or "a sharp taste." Unfortunately, we have become alienated from our senses. Before we could write, we were all synaesthetes. This can be traced back to the origins of our alphabet. The shapes of letters originated from meaningful icons with significant social implications. For instance, the letter "A" originated from the head of an ox, a very important asset those days. If we turn the "A" upside down, we still recognize the horns and head of the ox. Where the arches meet in the letter "B" is a floor plan and the entrance to a house. And the letter "C" is a throwing stick used to hunt birds. The ongoing abstraction of Western letter forms has cut us off from our sensory connection with letters. Is it possible to make the social significance of letters relevant again? One possible solution could be to utilize synthetic synaesthesia: an artificial blending of the senses aimed at developing a more meaningful expression and understanding of language. This involves approaching language through scent, taste, touch, and other sensory possibilities, which compel us to discover and appreciate new ways of communicating.

A PEDAGOGICAL APPROACH TO A NEW LITERATE PLAYGROUND

To achieve a holistic understanding, dominant cultural narratives must be questioned and, in some cases, dismantled and rebuilt. This begins with our understanding of what a letter is. To do this, we have to go back to our childhood, before the first encounter with letters. The ideas of Fröbel provide starting points for this. However, we must also articulate the understanding of the social context of letters. Where do our letters come from, and what do they mean? This allows us to enter a new relationship with abstract symbols, and even a new emergence of language is possible through other senses than just sight and sound. I propose three starting points that can be expanded:

Cultural Memory: The Voyage of the Alphabet

The alphabet is more than a series of symbols; it is a product of human history and culture. Therefore, it is important to become acquainted with the historical origins of the alphabet. This approach aligns with the idea of "cultural memory" proposed by cultural philosopher Vilém Flusser (1920–1991), who believed that understanding the origins of human communication is crucial for giving meaning to our experiences. By exploring the roots of the alphabet, delving into the evolution of writing systems and associated writing tools, we can reestablish a connection with the alphabet. This narrative approach adds deeper meaning and context to design and communication solutions, transforming the alphabet from an abstract series of shapes back into a cultural artifact with rich stories.

Perceptive Knowledge: A Multi-Sensory Approach to Letters

From our knowledge of the historical significance of letters, we can create reinterpretations. By taking full sensory perception as our starting point, we allow for a wider range of possibilities and thus more inclusive communication. The sense of smell, for example, is a highly suggestive aspect of human experience. Scents can evoke memories, emotions, and connections. By introducing the scent of an ox, a house, a throwing stick, etc., into our playground, we add a new, playful dimension to literacy. Each letter can be associated with a unique social context that is captured in a sensory state, such as taste, smell, touch. This approach bridges the gap between the abstract and the concrete, transforming the alphabet into a sensory adventure.

Modular Letter Shapes: The Cognitive Palette

By incorporating modular letter shapes into Fröbel's methodology, emergence is brought to the forefront of literacy education: when does a whole of composition, material, and experience transform into a letter and become a carrier of information? First, we see the whole before we interpret its parts. Just as art evokes a sense of wonder and expression, we can use sensory modular (letter)forms in a playful way to become literate.

If we want to introduce this playground for inclusive literacy, we must start to radically reinterpret the smallest building blocks of our language. A crucial role in this lies with type designers. Let's move beyond the screen and restore a socially and tangibly meaningful understanding of what letters are. By embracing sensory letter forms, we harness the aesthetic appeal and cognitive benefits of letter design while playfully promoting literacy. As the 21st century unfolds, it is essential to reconsider and renew our approach to learning, language, and literacy at both young and advanced ages. The artistic alchemy of sensory letter forms, synthetic synaesthesia, and a historical perspective on the alphabet opens doors to a richer, more engaging, and ultimately more inclusive path to literacy. By combining discovery through play from the pedagogy of Frederik Fröbel, perceiving the whole before seeing the parts from the Bildung and Gestalt theory of Wolfgang Köhler and developing synthetic synesthesia, we literally expand our communicative world. This creates a new literate playground for a sensory, inclusive, and deeply meaningful language journey that I would have loved to experience as a child.

ROOSJE VAN DER KAMP

I never write about subtitles. This might seem surprising given how central they are to my daily life. As a film critic, I have watched and written about hundreds of subtitled films. I'm not the only one who never writes about them: hardly any film review mentions subtitles.

LOST IN TRANSLATION

Perhaps I never mention subtitles because I hardly ever notice them. They catch my attention only when they fail: when the subtitler doesn't understand a joke, mistranslates words, or renders figures of speech too literally. At times these mistakes are so egregious that I wonder whether someone unfamiliar with the spoken language can truly grasp the film. Of course, translation always comes with loss. All translated media are forced to alter the original to make the translation understandable. What makes subtitling a strange genre of translation is that it tries to be invisible. Unlike literary translations (where the translator is akin to a literary figure who can be questioned on their choices) and unlike dubbing (which makes its artifice known by replacing the original voices), subtitles try to appear neutral.While other translations obscure the original, subtitles seem to leave the authentic experience of the original untouched. When we watch a film with subtitles, we can "think away" the text on the screen, so to speak, and imagine the original film. This "thinking away" comes so natural to the experienced moviegoer that we might forget that we are also reading when we are watching a film.

I think that subtitles are not part of film criticism, not because they are added to the film later and by someone else (this is, after all, also the case with dubbing), but because they are seen as a tool for accessibility. Subtitles are therefore not regarded as part of our experience of the film, but as a requirement to make this experience possible.

Subtitles are designed to be as unobtrusive as possible. They always appear in one simple typeface that audiences are already familiar with, such as Arial or Times New Roman. There's a limit of 42 characters and two lines. They are usually white with a black outline—in rare cases they are yellow. All of this has to do with ease of reading: subtitles should not distract from the film and thus appear on screen for a maximum of six seconds.

This means that subtitles are always compressed: in translations from English to Dutch, for example, about 30 percent of the original is left out. But, as the guidelines for Dutch subtitles dictate, anything "of essential importance must be retained." What is essential in a film? Isn't everything that is shown in the film, intentionally or unintentionally, essential? In any case, 30 percent is a lot. Imagine not understanding almost a third of what your interlocutor says, or watching a film that has been condensed by as much.

Unlike literary translations, in which the aim is to preserve as much nuance as possible, subtitles are meant to convey crucial information only. The 30 percent that is lost is essentially seen as fluff, as useless filler. Filler words (such as "uh" but also "allora" in Italian and "like" in English) are always omitted because they do not convey any information. But are they really inessential when the amount of filler words and the type of filler words can reveal details about the speaker's mental state (is the speaker nervous, for example?) and socio-economic status. A CEO is likely to speak with fewer filler words than his working class friend.

The aura of neutrality that surrounds subtitles can only exist because subtitles iron out all differences between speakers: language errors, variations in tone, and intelligibility have no place in subtitles. So while you have to perk your ears to hear what someone whispers, you never have to strain your eyes to read what is said. What is lost when we rid a film of its so-called fluff, when we boil the spoken words down to its essentials? When variations in language, tone, and accent are all transcribed into the same white, 22 Pt. Sans Serif text?

Take Gaspar Noé's Vortex. This film is about an elderly couple living together in a flat in Paris: Father, played by Italian director Dario Argento, and Mother, who suffers from Alzheimer's disease. Speech is of enormous importance in Vortex. The film is about disruptions in communication: between Mother and Father, but also between the parents and their drug-addicted son. Mother was once a prominent psychiatrist; now she doesn't make much sense. Father similarly suffers communication issues: he sometimes uses wrong words, uses strange expressions and has a thick Italian accent.

In the subtitles, Italian Father's mistake-ridden French is translated into flawless English, even though the faltering language reveals s o m e - thing about the character, who, just as h i s wife, struggles to express himself in words. That parallel between the sick Mother and the foreign

Father—a parallel that, by the way, is visually supported in the film's use of split screen—is inaccessible to someone who doesn't speak French. Now, this is not a problem for most viewers who are Western-European, like me: even if we do not speak the language, we are familiar enough with the language to detect the Italian accent.

This is not always the case. I couldn't hear any difference between the Korean of the Korean detective and the Korean of the Chinese suspect in Park Chan-wook's thriller *Decision to Leave*. And although the detective spoke several times about the suspect's strange use of words, I couldn't shake the feeling that I was missing something fundamental while watching the film. That I hadn't understood the character properly, that I hadn't really gotten to know her. I viewed *Decision to Leave* as a cold, detached film. Would I have experienced the film differently if the subtitles managed to reflect their difference in speech?

Someone who speaks Korean has a different experience of *Decision to Leave* than someone who does not. This much is obvious. And yet the idea that subtitles substantially affect the experience of a film is difficult to accept. We prefer to think of subtitles as glasses: a tool we can look through that shows us the thing as it is, without distorting it in the process. Of course, looking at a table through glasses is not exactly the same as looking at a table without them. Glasses can fog up, for instance when you drink a cup of tea, the edges of the frame can suddenly appear in your field of vision, but no one will say that someone with glasses sees a completely different world—a fundamentally different table—than someone without glasses.

I only realized that subtitles substantially change the experience of the film when I went to the short film festival in Nijmegen two years ago. I was invited to attend the festival as a jury member. In four days, I watched dozens of short films. One of the films was the short film *Exaggerations* by audiovisual artist Charles de Agustin. In this film, subtitles are not an afterthought, but the main event. In the beginning of the film, the subtitles appear to be a tool to understand the film, but gradually they take over the film completely. So much so that the only way to describe the film is by talking about the subtitles.

Exaggerations has two voice-overs and three types of subtitles. The first voice-over tells a story, a mash-up of intertextual quotes and musings on the art world. The second voice-over describes the images. Then there are the three types of subtitles: Red surtitles describe the sounds of the film and capture their sounds in images. For example, the word "eerroooo000000000000000ooooooo" describes the howling of a wolf and appears curved on screen, and the word "wo000mp" describes a hollow, electronic sound and bounces across the screen. White subtitles transcribe what the first, narrative voice-over says and yellow subtitles transcribe what the second, descriptive voice-over says. The yellow subtitles are thus an audio description of an image description. When we discussed the film with each other afterwards, a fellow judge described the film as noise music. She complained of a headache. Another jury member wondered what we just watched. Everyone called the film incomprehensible.

Exaggerations does indeed have something ridiculous about it. But it is more than an exercise in excess. By pushing the boundaries of subtitling, De Agustin points at a fundamental characteristic: its opacity. By summarizing what is on the screen, subtitling inevitably changes what is on the screen. The subtitles become part of the image and the image therefore needs a new description. In principle, this process knows no end: De Agustin could, in theory at least, continue describing.

In Exaggerations, the function of subtitling as a conduit for information is exhausted and therefore disrupted. The very attempt to relay all information on screen as completely as possible ensures that little information actually gets through. The distinction between main and secondary is lost. Descriptions become part of the story and therefore need their own description. When text appears on screen, the descriptive voice-over reads it aloud, so the text also appears in the subtitles. Often, the three types of subtitles simultaneously appear on screen.

With his film, De Agustin questions the possibility of a complete experience of a film. While watching, my eyes fly criss-cross over the screen in an attempt to take it all in. In the process, I unconsciously prioritize the subtitles. Only later, when I reflect on the movie, do I notice that I was mostly reading. When I think about the film now, I remember nothing of the story, recalling only the feeling of falling short. By trying to provide a complete experience of the film to as many people as possible, the film becomes incomprehensible to all. Afterwards, I think of the other films I watched during the festival. What else did I not see because I was too busy reading? What else did I miss?

Because subtitles should be as neutral as possible, they hardly ever use the possibilities offered by type design. Occasionally, certain words may appear in italics, in capitals or quotation marks. Cristian Mungiu's R.M.N. takes this a little further. Set in a multi-ethnic Romanian village, the film features characters speaking Hungarian, Romanian, and German, with subtitles color-coded in red, yellow, and blue—the colors of the Romanian flag.

While watching the film, I find myself continuously checking my notes, trying to remember the meaning of each color. But even then, the importance of the difference in language eludes me. The color red has no emotional effect on me. I feel exactly the same when I read a subtitle in blue as when I read it in red. By trying to make the subtitles understandable in a single glance, the film only muddled my understanding. Perhaps that is the point: Romanian might as well be red, yellow, or blue.

Filip Despotovic's speculative typeface Subtype embraces the distraction inherent to the cinematic experience. He imagines a future where tone and volume can be conveyed visually, for instance by making the experience of background music perceptible through subtitles.

His approach is far from unobtrusive. But is this lack of neutrality truly a loss? After all, even the most neutral subtitle impacts how we experience a film. Subtitles distract or conceal, just like sound can distract or conceal. Because despite what the neutrality of subtitles suggests, imperfections, distractions, and ambiguities often reflect the complexities of the original content. The loss is the point.

IAN LYNAM

As a type designer, I am supposed to love letterforms, which I do, but as far as lettering goes, there is a form of lettering that I love infinitely more than a typeface rich with connotative nuance, rigorous readability, OpenType features, multiple stylistic sets, actual small caps, and replete with formal connotation. It's a literally dirty not-so-secret that I love real graffiti. And when I invoke the term "real" graffiti, I refer to graffiti that embodies the nature of the illicit act: gestural marks that are made with an economy of form, time, and materials, applied to public or private spaces without the permission of anyone involved.

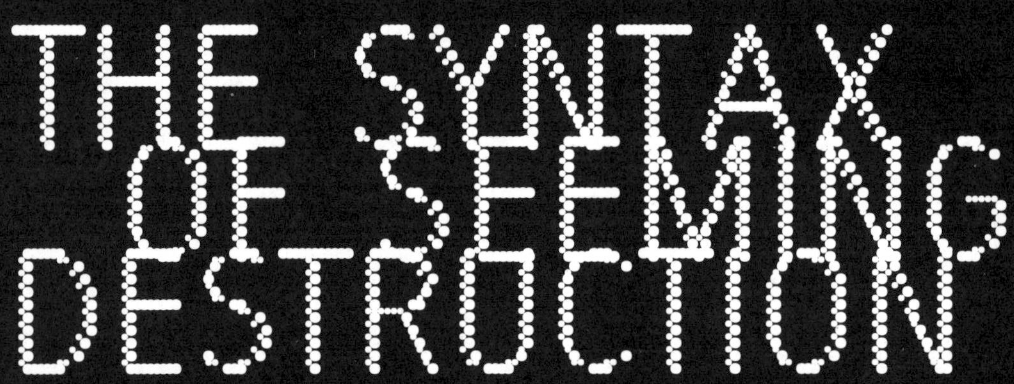

I am not writing about stencils, stickers, wheatpasting, multi-color mural-esque productions or pieces or "street art" in regards to format. Furthermore, I am not referring to sanctioned sites of activity such as walls or surfaces dedicated to the legal application of spray paint and street aesthetics. When I write about "graffiti," I am invoking sheer vandalism: the seeming destruction of public, private, and liminal spaces and properties. Some examples might be Etch Bath-mop-tagged storefront windows, spray painted throw-ups on vans, hastily marker-tagged mailboxes, profane ballpoint pen-scrawled bathroom stall writing, and Dremel tip-tagged

mirrors in rest stop bathrooms. I am referring to forms of graffiti that don't rely on permission and are evidence of the human hand behind each mark. Due to my interest in writing and letterforms, I am also specifically referring to graffiti that involves letters—be it Philly style, New York style, Berlin style, Pichaçao, placas / blocks, or the old standard, non-stylized handwriting. For simplicity's sake, what I term "real graffiti" can be most easily categorized as tagging and bombing. This is the graffiti that I subjectively enjoy looking at. I don't like pretty pictures. I like seeing the results of deliberate criminal behavior. I like seeing vandalism. Real graffiti is an expression of that which is most human—of the pack member eluding social and physical capture.

This type of graffiti tends to repeat the same message over and over, with slight variations: the adopted name of the writer, maybe the name of their graffiti crew, or in the case of bathroom graffiti, obscenity / obscenities. The former might include some additional marks for emphasis—an underline, some asterisks, or other decoration—the proverbial "icing on the cake" of unwanted mark-making. With tagging, the audience might perceive a stylistic sameness as to the tags' application—a repetition of content (name), stylistic form (particular handstyle / calligraphic approach or means of construction). This sameness helps viewers connect the dots as to the potential trail of a tagger—akin to a visual trail of bread crumbs. This content / container / site synthesis creates a discernible system within which the writer operates.

Within this system, the syntax of placement is paramount. If the audience intends to perceive graffiti as an alternate form of language, one must analyze the linguistic elements in use. Often, graffiti tends to say the same thing over and over—namely, the tagger's name. Graffiti as a system is given definition by the individual and collective sites where each tag is applied.

It is the spatial delineation of the name inscribed on a police car windshield using glass-eating acid, the linear tag that spans doorframe and door alike, the scratched name on the bus stop acrylic advertise- ment cover, the paint drip-tagged street corner, and the monumen- tal name

splashed on the side of a building using paint pumped out of an insecticide sprayer. We can put together collective meaning through where the marks are made in regards to illegal graffiti as much as through visual form.

These spatial bodies of repetition and disjunction form the lexical systems within which a writer's work exists—porous due to space and time, connected through style and content, and accretive as the writer adds to the dissemination of marks. Graffiti is a system developed much like literature, though the defining traits differ. Each mark matters, creating correlations with other marks and creating a larger framework of marks. The syntax of densely or loosely sited repetition is proof of the writer's feral determination to inject the name into the sphere of others.

The site of each mark gives further definition:

1. A public bathroom = bad
2. Someone's front door = worse
3. An ambulance = much worse
4. Trees = there is a special place in hell for people who tag trees.

Even I hate that.

What one marks gives the mark more potential power, creating a symbiotic semiotic relationship that can only be unwoven in the mind.

Viewing graffiti in regards to linguistic systems helps us understand it beyond acts of seemingly simple transgression and atavistic anti-social behavior. Writers beg for their bodies of work to be read and understood beyond mere self-expression and style. Just like literature, the best graffiti isn't "pretty"—it eludes easy classification and operates in multiple modes of meaning, provoking the viewer to potentially think about it more deeply. In opposition to a "destructive" force, it can create corpuses of reading that offer far more than we might have ever considered, should we choose to look more closely.

CHRISTOPHER SLEBODA AND KATHLEEN SLEBODA

Typography knows no bounds in our classroom. Letters are born from stainless steel chain links and bendy straws—extracted from electrical panels and brick sidewalks. We've witnessed type emerging from light flares, video glitches, and the ghostly traces of scanner errors.

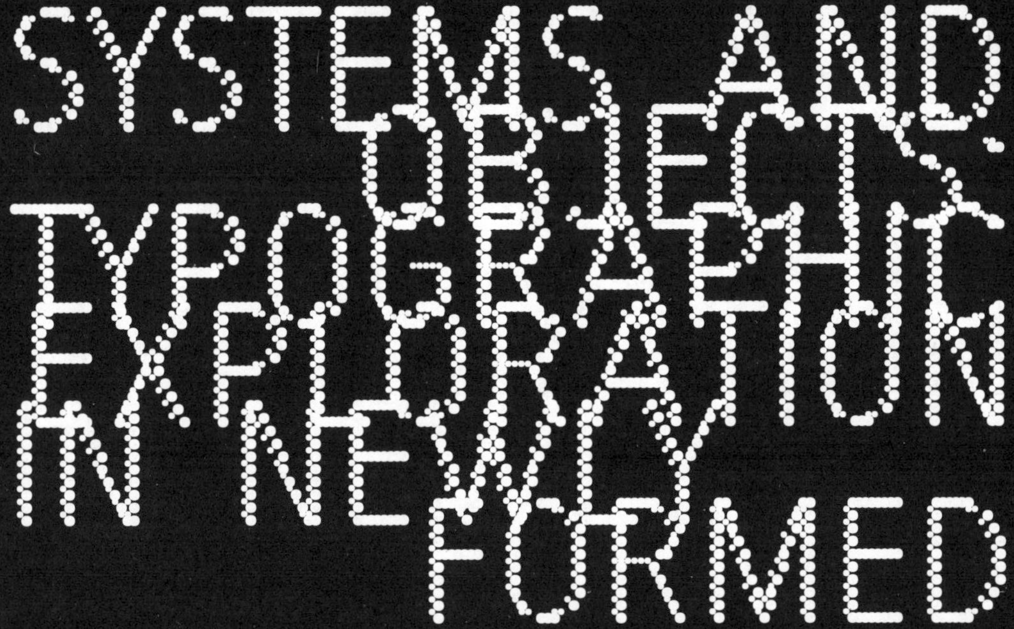

Since 2016, we've taught a course called Newly Formed at the Rhode Island School of Design (RISD). In this advanced Graphic Design studio for seniors and graduate students, we invite students to explore the boundaries of composition and typography with a focus on experimental form and image-making. We believe making and observation are both forms of research, and the course encourages generative and iterative approaches across materials, techniques, and formats. Challenging the conventional "form follows function" mindset, Newly Formed students design projects that prioritize

creativity and impact via a series of open-ended prompts. The inaugural project for the class, titled Alphabet, tasks students with creating three distinct typefaces ("A–Z" or "a–z") in just one week. Despite the challenging timeline, students consistently exceed our expectations, producing remarkable results. We've now assigned Alphabet to students in ten Newly Formed classes—it holds a singular place as the only persistent brief in the course's history.

While adaptability and evolution are central to the course's DNA—developing new briefs and reimagining the pedagogical framework have been key elements of our practice in the classroom—we've found that Alphabet's quick pace, married with the multiple lanes of exploration and execution, sets students up to work efficiently while strengthening their imagination muscles. The initial type-focused brief models the balance of creativity and rigorousness that lies at the heart of the course and is essential to prolific form-making.

Taking inspiration from works like Paul Elliman's Alphabits, Karel Martens' monoprints using found metal fasteners, and Pentagram's Mervyn Kurlansky's office letterforms, students are tasked with producing one typeface that is object-based.

Kit Son Lee selected a contour gauge as their object. Typically used to replicate or transfer the contour of an object by pressing it against a surface, this is a tool usually reserved for woodworking, tiling, or construction. Lee theorized that the customizable high-precision needles could be sculpted to produce an uppercase set of characters. Rather than maintaining a strictly horizontal orientation, Lee rotated the tool 90 degrees when necessary to create desired letterforms. Letters like "A," "H," "M," "N," "U," "V," and "W" worked best in a horizontal position to allow for the required diagonals, while others, such as "B," "D," "E," and "F," benefitted from a vertical orientation.

For another object-based alphabet, William Sumrall used LEGO® Technic pieces to create a high-contrast uppercase glyph set. The "R" features strong Slab Serifs, a LEGO®-textured thin vertical stem, a nearly solid circular bowl, and a heavy diagonal leg. The uppercase "I" flows in and out with 90-degree calligraphic serifs, while the "X" emerges from blocky vertical and horizontal pieces. For a found object font titled Cracks, Dougal Henken walked around the city of Providence, where RISD is located, photographing the abundant fractures in public sidewalks. Each letter, constructed from distressed, mostly straight lines, evokes the jagged style of death metal logos. The weight fluctuates, typically heavier at the joints where fractures meet, while curves tend to take on sharp, angular forms.

The second typeface students are asked to produce is an alphabet derived from a modular system of their choosing. This system can encompass anything from drawn forms and photographs to sculptures and found objects—the only limit is the student's imagination. We also invite students to reflect on the different elastic categories established by the brief: a modular typeface can be comprised of objects (students can approach using objects systematically), while found object alphabets may operate idiosyncratically. We show students a variety of historical examples of modular letterforms, such as Josef Albers's rigid but playful

Kit Son Lee

William Sumrall

Dougal Henken

Fabian Fohrer

NEWLY
FORMED

Gabe Melcher

NEWLY
FORMED

Rebecca Wilkinson

Schablonenschrift (Stencil typeface), created in 1931, comprised of square shapes, half circles, and triangular forms yielding predictable results, comparing this work with M/M Paris's Erosion (2004), made from similar forms but producing much more unpredictable outcomes. While Albers's system builds up the letterforms, M/M Paris excavates from solid black blocks, sculpting letterforms through removal. More recently, José Ernesto Rodriguez's Handschrift (2011) offers an organic response to Albers by utilizing forms created through the process of Xeroxing both of his hands in various configurations. The limitations of the tool—a pair of human hands—result in iconic symbols determined by the constraints of the designer's own body.

Student designers respond intuitively to modular approaches—and can often create work that is humanistic, even while working within tight parameters. Gabe Melcher, for instance, created an all-caps sans serif typeface using two rolls of masking tape—one thick, one thin. The result was raw and expressive yet refined, demonstrating knowledge of a sophisticated typographic contrast model that evoked elements of translation and expansion, though it didn't settle into either. Melcher left small gaps between each letter stroke, giving the typeface a subtle stencil-like quality. For round forms like "O," "R," and "D," he used the tape roll itself at its natural scale, rather than enlarging it to match the other letters' cap height. To complete these letters, he used repetition—six rolls for the "O," one for the "R," and five for the "D." Pieces of tape were torn rather than cut, adding texture and nuances that softened the straight lines and created visual depth. While Melcher used an object as his material of choice, it was the system of constructing shapes that drove his forms.

Lake Buckley created a lowercase condensed sans serif alphabet using thousands of Q-tips® cotton swabs. A standard cotton swab is around three inches (7.6cm) in length, and this length, in turn, determines the stroke width of each letterform. Buckley meticulously hand-placed each swab, building the letterforms line by line. The repetitive texture, formed by horizontal and vertical alignments, was further enhanced by the cotton swabs' rounded uniform ends. These rounded edges guided her approach to curves, keeping the tips tightly spaced on the inside of the curve and increasing the distance between them on the outer edge. The result is a stunning gradient of light and dark that plays with the natural properties of the material. While traditional typefaces might add weight to rounded strokes, Buckley's type became lighter and more open in these areas. The "e" consists of 74 pieces, while the "w" requires 100 swabs. Unlike Melcher's type, which avoided curves in favor of straight lines, Buckley creates graceful curves from linear elements, resulting in a typeface both intricate and evocative.

One of the most surprising systems we've encountered was created by Fabian Fohrer, who used cooked pasta—most likely spaghetti, though it may have been linguine or bucatini. Fohrer boiled the pasta al dente, then carefully crafted majuscule letterforms using cut strands. The linear nature of the pasta allowed for both straight lines and gently bent curves. However, no corner or curve could be too harsh, as the pasta would break; thus, the physical materiality of the pasta dictated Fohrer's formal decisions. Using his dinner as the blueprint for his alphabet, he redrew the forms in Illustrator, sharpening the contrast and adding openings where lines overlapped, lightening the joints and creating a sense of dimensionality.

The manipulation of physical materials for Alphabet often means that a material's properties—its elasticity, flexibility, capacity to stretch or yield, and tensile strength—establish parameters that guide form-making choices. Modular systems can also be rooted in conceptual frameworks, where grids and algorithms, rather than physical properties, shape the forms. Rebecca Wilkinson created an intricate uppercase alphabet using a system of small circles, squares, and quarter circles. Built with a modular structure 12 pieces tall, Wilkinson achieved a surprising ornate complexity, with strokes ending in serif-like forms. Letters with diagonals, like "M," "N," "R," "W," and "Y," become

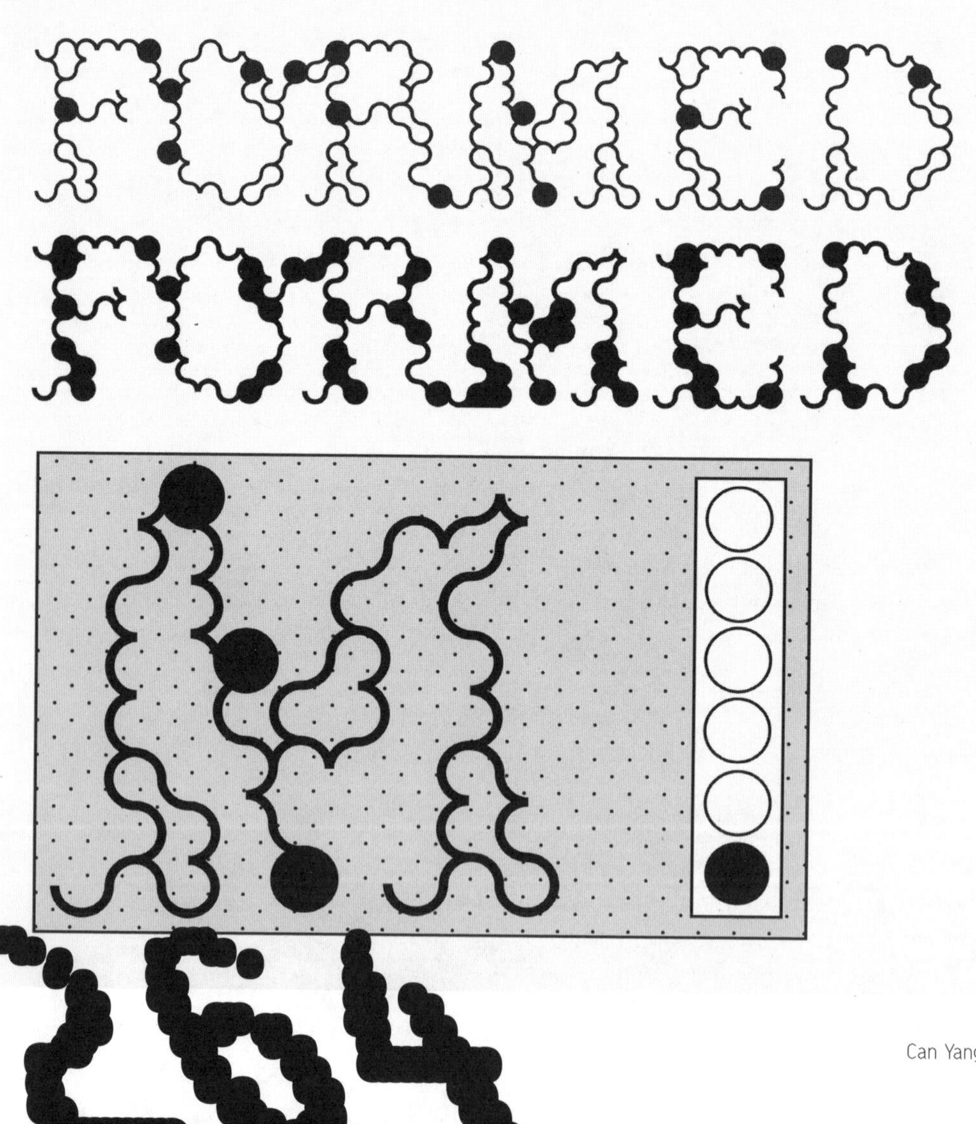

Can Yang

striking exercises in asymmetry, while "E" and "O" dazzle with symmetrical forms that border on pattern.

Halim Lee's modular alphabet system utilized an off-the-shelf Isometric Ellipse template and spray paint. Lee varied the oval widths within each letter, gradually increasing the weight either from left to right or top to bottom. The number of modular units varied, causing the cap height to fluctuate based on the ellipse sizes. The effect is an actively playful alphabet set that feels fluid and dynamic, with a sense of organic motion and balance despite its geometric structure.

One of the more intricate and complex modular systems was the brainchild of Can Yang. Yang began with a large dotted grid resembling a pegboard rotated 90 degrees. She used heavy-weight circular outlines in quarter, half, and three-quarter segments, connecting them in unexpected combinations. Occasionally, the outlines looped back,

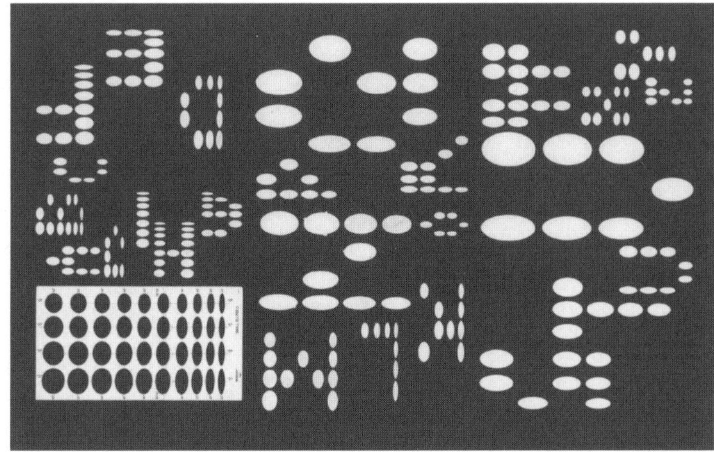

Halim Lee

Lake Buckley

Carl-Gustaf (Calle) Ewerbring

Lian Reay Fumerton-Liu

forming surprising clusters. Whenever a full circle was created, Yang would convert it into a solid black dot. A second weight was introduced to fill in any other closed counter shapes that emerged, ultimately producing both light and heavy weights. The overall effect was a blend of organic and hyper-digital aesthetics.

The third alphabet students create asks them to consider how type can be variable. This is not a functional variable typeface that designers might see available from commercial type foundries today, but what we invite students to consider as conceptually variable letterforms. One of the most inventive responses has been Carl-Gustaf (Calle) Ewerbring's. Starting with store-bought, bold-weight sans serif letter stencils typically used for DIY signage, Ewerbring poured table salt over each paper stencil, forming crisp, defined letterforms. The edges slightly rounded as the salt settled. Ewerbring then placed the black panel with the full A-Z character set onto a stereo speaker, gradually increasing the volume of sound from quiet to loud while documenting the effect of the vibrations on the salt. As the volume and deep bass intensified, the letters began to expand and blur, with some losing their counterspaces entirely. The transformations were captured on video, highlighting the dynamic shifts in the letterforms.

Another conceptually variable alphabet by Lian Reay Fumerton-Liu utilized black birdseed in a snow-filled backyard, where she painstakingly rendered an uppercase character set in a monoline script. The choice of birdseed anticipated a playful interaction between nature and design, inviting wildlife to participate in the creative process. She set up her camera to document the birds in a time-lapse, hoping to capture their feeding on the letters and the gradual transformation as the letterforms diminished in weight and eventually disappeared. However, squirrels reached the forms first, scattering the seeds in a confetti-like explosion, resulting in limited legibility of the letters.

These experiments of capturing letters in multiple states—responding to mechanical and natural forces—are meant to underline the mutability of letterforms. When, exactly, along the spectrum of transformation is legibility compromised? What forms continue to hold meaning the longest? We encourage students to create strong documentary records of their experiments and process, recognizing that the seeds of future projects and new lanes of formal exploration may be found in these inquiries. By examining the tension between abstraction and clarity, students cultivate a deeper understanding of how letterforms can evolve while still communicating effectively, ultimately expanding their design repertoire.

We estimate over 500 Newly Formed alphabets have been created over the eight years we've been teaching at RISD. With an eye towards sharing the explorations and outcomes with the broader design community, many of these type experiments have been collected and printed in broadsides which we distribute through Draw Down Books, our publishing house and book shop. This printed record has been invaluable for archiving and sharing the work beyond the institutional silo of the university where the projects occur. We've been proud to also support and carry the work of Newly Formed alumni like Sophia Brinkgerd, whose New Aesthetic series is a striking collection of contemporary typography, as well as Slanted's Experimental Type volumes which have featured a number of students we've taught.

Anchoring Newly Formed's material, formal and conceptual experiments in the rich environment of letterform creation has served as a productive starting point over the years. The alphabet is a comfortable, known set of forms (even for international students who come to Latin orthography after natively learning other scripts). The opportunity to push and pull at these known structures—understanding the forms as flexible, mutatable things—sets in place a precedent for thinking about other designed materials as inherently malleable. This approach encourages students to view graphic design not just in terms of a static outcome but as an evolving process where adaptability and innovation are key.

DR JOANNA TYBOROWSKA

Graphic design centers around the organization of information by transferring and translating the message into a comprehensible visual language. Based on a synthesized graphic structure, it vividly responds to the changing social demand as an flexible system of encrypted meanings. The issue of text legibility in the domain of graphic design is significant, considering the influence the letter has on shaping interpersonal communication and the organization of social life. Due to the functional character of the letter, the aspect of legibility is also a basic requirement for the realization of the superior function of text, which is to convey content.

THE CONTEXT OF TYPE LEGIBILITY

For centuries, the letter has been entangled in a relationship between the message it carries and its visual representation, which when read, can also satisfy the aesthetic needs of the viewer. The form of the glyph is, therefore, an embodied compromise between the established system of meanings, knowledge about perceptual processes, the current technique and technology, prevailing style or fashion, as well as the typographer's individual expression. These factors determine the form that the text adopts in public space, and determine the transmission of the encoded message. The state of the recipient's visual awareness, as well as their appropriate intellectual preparation for processing the information, is also meaningful. The alteration of the letter's structural elements, resulting in problematic character recognition, casts doubt on the legitimacy of using illegible type. A question arises regarding the relationship between the form and function of a letter, especially if distinguishing the character is genuinely difficult for the reader. Setting the limits of readability is particularly important when the text serves a specific communication purpose in a wider, social group. Currently, type characters appear in a vast range of various, interdisciplinary media, resulting in unconventional lettering forms, which open up new areas of visual experiences for the viewer. In so doing, they challenge what we perceive as legible and what we characterize as letters. The greater the flexibility in letter notation, the greater the acceptance of a new visual code over time. This process not only shapes the way one recognizes type, but also how the textual exchange of thought in its subsequent, varied scenes is comprehended.

SIGHT

The human system of visual perception evolved over time from photosensitive skin cells into a complex mechanism focused on data collection, dedicated to analyzing visual sensations. It does not actually reflect the outside world like a mirror, but rather participates in its creation during processing. When performing this activity, the human brain analyzes the physical phenomena in order to collect as much information as possible.[1] Higher-order brain areas are responsible for sensory information from down-stream sensory receptors to formulate and verify hypotheses, on an ongoing basis. The hypotheses that are put forward are not incidental, they are based on previously accumulated visual experience.

By nature, people are highly individualized in their perception of reality. Our memory functions much like a library that one constantly reaches into, in order to define a newly encountered image. The interpretation of one's surroundings is an automated human reflex, but its essence is creative participation based on acquired knowledge. What "someone sees today is derived from what he or she has seen in the past"[2] and depends on what they wish to see in the present. The phenomenon of visual awareness (defined as the ever changing and historically conditioned process of human sight development[3]) contributes to this co-creation of the our reality. This correlation determines the personal experience of every human being and their individualized image of the world. The vision formulated by the brain is only partially created by the image that actually falls on the retina of the eye.[4] The interaction that takes place is a kind of a reciprocal action between the intellect and the organ of sight, enabling the reception of the message and its processing. As Rudolf Arnheim wrote, "to some modest degree the eyesight of every human being anticipates the ability that characterizes the artist, the rightly admired ability to create patterns that, by means of an organized form, accurately interpret sensations".[5]

Humans are active observers, constantly looking for answers to questions concerning the similarity of observed elements, the logic of their arrangement, their allocation or internal consistency.[6] The image that undergoes examination by the eye is not a single, static image, but a series of fragments of a larger whole, analyzed by quick eye movements from one point to another, so as to allow other segments to be processed by the center of the retina. The six external muscles of the eyeball enable a series of fixations through jumping movements to guarantee sharpness and richness of detail. The mechanism that helps people see contours and distinguish shapes, organizes and combines the recognizable sequences and structures of its components into an intelligible whole. The perceived image is also verified through the prism of other sensations that one experiences during this interaction, such as touch or the impression of gravity. Thanks to these adaptive predispositions of the visual system, even a distorted image can be corrected so that its actual form is closer to reality.

READING

The recognition of individual words is a complicated mechanism that has been examined over many years by researchers, generating various theories. During the process of reading, the eye stops at the point of temporary fixation (lasting about 250 milliseconds) before moving to the next part of the text.[7] These jumps, called saccades, alternate with a fixation of every seven to nine letters and last from 10 to 20 milliseconds. Problems with text comprehension can arise from regressive saccades (occurring as 10–15 percent of all jumps), when the eye moves in the opposite direction to reevaluate, or additionally focuses on a given word, for longer examination to verify its accuracy. Eye-tracking technologies, analyzing processes that take place within fractions of a second, have led to the conclusion that only a fragment of the word is actually seen with maximum precision, a total of three to four letters from the focus point. Fixations usually occur in the middle of the word, with a slight inclination to the left. Information is collected from the first, main fixation point, where the word is recognized, then among the successive letters adjacent to the main fixation point. Finally, collection takes place at the point furthest from fixation, covering roughly 15 letters. At the same time, information about the length of the next words is gathered, contributing to the choice of the next place of focus.

Reading is a highly complex and automated activity that requires multidimensional engagement. Jack Post, referring to the research of the French scientist Anne-Marie Christin, describes reading as "an activity in which a person separates what is meaningful from what is meaningless."[8] It is unclear whether the key to understanding the content is the analysis of single and selective visual stimuli or a formulated and then verified hypothesis based on experience and the state of knowledge. According to researchers, reading can also be treated as an interactive process, using a number of different abilities, including both automatic recognition, synthesis, and evaluation skills. It also has access to a wide range of expertise, including formal discourse structure knowledge, vocabulary and language structural knowledge, content / world background knowledge, as well as metacognitive knowledge and skills monitoring.[9]

LANGUAGE

S i x t o seven thousand languages in the world are used for communication (of which around 2,500 are threatened with extinction). According to some linguists, this number will inevitable drop, leading to the dominance of two major world languages in the future (most likely English and Chinese). There are also some researchers who predict the emergence of an all-human language of thought, exceeding beyond speech or visual record, as pure communication between minds.[10] It is difficult however, to imagine a world in which the immateriality of thoughts deprives us of the pleasure of using the visible form of a record to show the exchange of emotions.

There are 46 different known types of alphabets that transcribe the languages of the world. Each language has a set of 16 to 60 sound units (phonemes), often greater than the number of the letters in a language, as a phoneme is also formed by combining more than one sign. A person can recognize the sound of about 100 phonemes at a speed of 16 phonemes per second, which is roughly 250 words per minute. Interestingly, studies[11] have shown that a typical reader will read a similar number of words per minute (nearly 240 words) of moderately difficult text at an average pace. In order to read at such a speed, both of these activities must be automatic.

The origins of interpersonal communication and visual art have a common source. At first, ideographic script was a pattern based on realistic and abstract signs and it functioned as a system of synthetic images representing concepts and ideas. It was only the phonographic script, ascribing syllables to signs that tied the image more closely to sound, thus subordinating it to the system of spoken language, with the appropriate division for speech. The development of phonetic script, in which the number of symbols was limited to transcribe thoughts, increased the precision of communication and slowly contributed to the emergence of the commonly used lettering code. The mechanism of assigning an image or sound to a specific idea or concept is demonstrated in the diversified visual strategy that one uses when reading. The "Phoenician strategy" assumes "correspondence between a grapheme and a phoneme" and requires the reader to "transform the substance of a word from figurative to phonic in order to reach its meaning."[12] The "Chinese strategy," on the other hand, assumes that "the reader uses the graphic image of the word as an iconic code that opens up meanings in the mental dictionary."[13]

Nowadays, social media and instant messaging users merge the achievements of phonetic script and the tradition of picture script into a modern hybrid system. It is believed that digital text, in a specially designated space, has grown closer to speech than to the written word. In the article *The Future of Text and Typography*, Jan Kubasiewicz mentions John McWhorter's definition of texting as "not script, but 'finger speech'—a loosely structured dialect that, to some extent, disregards the rules of linguistics."[14] This unique jargon, present in digital communication, is "a mixture of sound symbols, number symbols and self-referential linguistic interpretive symbols" making up a new language structure.

Early oral communication, before the development of script, was intended to consolidate the history and traditions of the com-munity, but required human presence in a given place and time. It was based essentially on memory, which is why a number of mnemonic practices were used, such as for-mal style, redundancy, rhythm, and harmony. With time, reading aloud in front of a gathered audience was replaced by quiet, solitary contact with text. The published book created a substantial distance between the author and the recipient, placing upon typography the role of carrying speech's vivid expression. The secluded reader, in order to appropriately interpret the content, was left to draw the necessary information from all the variable components in the text's formal layer. The range of these additional elements has grown over time; after the introduction of punctuation, text was accompanied by initials, illustrations, and complementary graphic elements taking into account hierarchy, composition, and color. Audiobooks however, have perversely reversed the developed scheme of silent text reading with the reincarnation of traditional oral transmission. Listening to text reduces the active reading process into a more passive broadcast, dematerializing text and all of its physical properties, in favor of the interpretation offered in the lector's voice.

At present, the process of "deep reading"—a connection with the text, in which the pace of reception allows for insightful and analytical interaction with the content—is fading away in favor of quick, superficial text scanning in search of key words. This new habit is particularly noticeable when users interact with text on multimedia devices. These multi-purpose carriers, can distract readers with a frequency of up to 27 times per hour, impairing concentration and weakening the power to remember information. For an educated adult reader with well-formed neural connections and a mature structure of analytical thinking, the new medium can be tedious. However, as Maryanne Wolf warns, the threat is especially relevant for the youngest users, who are still in the process of developing their "reading brain."[15] It is during "deep reading" in the ongoing cognitive processes that one looks for analogies, uses deduction, critical, and perspective thinking; all the accumulated knowledge about the world and about the word being read is applied. Maryanne Wolf explains this process as going beyond the wisdom of an author to reach one's own wisdom. This is where thought and enlightenment are born, and new, revealing conclusions and reflections are formulated. The development of this skill is a long-term process that accumulates all previous experiences of working with text.

People born after the year 1980 grew up alongside developing technology and in close proximity to a collective database organized in a democratic, virtual structure. The generation of "digital natives" are familiar with technology, constantly relying on the Internet and multifunctional devices with intuitive navigation. For communication purposes, they use multimedia space to participate in short, quick and extensive interactions. For "digital natives," complicated, long textual content generates problems in comprehension and remains difficult to acquire, pushing them towards short, slogan "tag lines," coexisting in a space filled with images, all of which are part of their daily lives.

At the opposite extreme of "digital natives"[16] is the patient print generation, of "digital immigrants."[17] This group, although taking advantage of the conveniences brought by the development of technology, maintains a certain reserve towards it. "Digital immigrants" are mainly familiar with a linear narrative in which the content runs in a serially systematized way within a consistently organized medium containing perceptible boundaries—that is, the traditionally printed book.

Contrary to digital text, print has material properties that satisfy one's sensual needs, through the touch of paper or the perceptible weight of the edition, making the reader aware of the volume of work. Locating the information by recalling its placement on the page by image, is another mechanism, enabled by tactual print, that helps recall and thus, allows an easier formation of mental representations related to the text structure.

Script in the context of shaping the modern man is a relatively new invention, so the reading process is also a relatively recently acquired skill. As Jan Kubasiewicz rightly points out, "on the timeline of about 200,000 years of homo sapiens' history, half of it is the development of the spoken language. People started using images for graphic communication 40,000 years ago. The invention of linear script only dates back 5,000 years. If one assumes that mankind has been around for 24 hours, script would have appeared only less than an hour ago."[18] After birth, humans are not yet fully accustomed to the reading process and our extremely flexible minds have to adapt to this activity. In response to cognitive and perceptual demands, the human brain undergoes restructuring depending on the medium or even the selected system of script with which it comes into contact. As part of the learning process, new neural connections between brain regions responsible for language, face and object recognition are formed, while existing circuits take on new roles or are pruned away.

It can, therefore, be concluded that the modern reader must be equipped with the proper tools to participate in the unique interaction with modern text. Their predisposition to do so goes far beyond linguistic proficiency. In the era of fake news and half-truths, the growing demographics of users, who superficially perceive content not only poses a threat to readability in the context of in-depth understanding of the text, but also deprives recipients of the opportunity to develop specific thought processes that advance visual intelligence.

CONCLUSION

Phonetic symbols are part of one of the oldest universally recognized social contracts. The ideogram of a letter, established over the centuries, regulates the extent to which text develops in interpersonal communication. And while each language assigns different phonemes to similar signs, extending the system to suit its needs, the fact that phonetic script has become the common denominator for culturally diverse communities in various latitudes is undoubtedly one of the most important achievements of mankind. The process of communicating at all cognitive and physical levels is a creative process that poses a unique experience for its participants. Communication is not only language, script or speech. It is the color of symbols, gestures, and calibrated behaviors, to which one relates familiar mechanisms or schemes for formulating conclusions and associations.

While the legibility of text, understood through the prism of understanding the content, assumes triggering a specific reaction to the delivered message, individual character signs have no less potential to evoke a reaction based on the presence of the letter itself, regardless of the context. The activity of reading letters and analyzing their correlation is an automatic process, that occurs despite any difficulty that the letter form may create for the viewer. The word, detached from the pure informational transmission, remains a notation with the intention of reading. Brought to life in a physical form according to a predetermined pattern—the idea of a sign—invites reading, even if its form is an integrated part of an image. In the same manner, a letter sign, although devoid of any function, will not completely lose the attributed sound.

Visual communication is subject to dynamic change and the form of the text should evolve as quickly as the visual awareness of a society expands. Text legibility can be defined as a constantly vibrating membrane, interdependent, and of flexible value, susceptible to influences. It is a complex intertwined network of connections developed over generations, on the basis of practice and natural observation. In brief, it is derived from the heritage that mankind has at its disposal, both in the natural world and in the world of art, culture and science.

1. A. Grabowska, W. Budohoska, *Procesy percepcji,* [in:] *Percepcja, myslenie, decyzje,* ed. T. Tomaszewski, Warsaw 1995, p. 29
2. R. Arnheim, *Sztuka i percepcja widzenia. Psychologia twórczego oka,* trans. J. Mach, Lodz 2004, p. 61
3. See W. Strzeminski, *Teoria widzenia,* Lodz 2016, p. 55
4. A. Grabowska, W. Budohoska, *Procesy percepcji …* , p. 12
5. R. Arnheim, *Sztuka i percepcja widzenia …* , p. 59
6. See *Psychologia. Podrecznik akademicki,* vol. 1, ed. J. Strelau, D. Dolinski, Sopot 2000, p. 357–358
7. K. Larson, *The science of word recognition,* docs.microsoft.com/en-us/typography/develop/word-recognition [access: 06.10.2018]
8. J. Post, *Rewolucja cyfrowa,* [in:] *Triumf typografii. Kultura, komunikacja, nowe media,* eds. H. Hoeks, E. Lentjes, trans. M. Komorowska, Cracow 2017, p. 152
9. E. Wolanska, A. Wolanski, *Kroje pisma ulatwiające czytanie osobom dyslektycznym,* "Logopedia" 2016, no. 45, p. 228–229
10. E. Satalecka, *The Art of Writing,* [in:] *Future Graphic Language: New Directions in Verbal Communication,* eds. E. Satalecka, J. Piechota, J. Karpoluk, Warsaw 2020, p. 95
11. See E. Wolanska, A. Wolanski, Kroje pisma ulatwiające czytanie osobom dyslektycznym..., p. 225
12. E. Wolanska, A. Wolamski, *Kroje pisma ulatwiające …* , p. 228
13. Ibidem
14. J. Kubasiewicz, *Przyszlosc tekstu i typografii,* "Powidoki" 2021, no. 5, p. 177
15. M. Wolf, The Changing Reading Brain in a Digital Culture, *youtube.com/watch?v=XmiFDLUQV8U&t=0s/* 14.07.2015, The Long Now Foundation's *Conversations at The Interval* Salon Talks, San Francisco [access: 6.10.2018]
16. M. Prensky, *Digital Natives, Digital Immigrants* Part 1, "On the Horizon" 2001, vol. 9, no. 5, p. 1–6
17. Ibidem
18. J. Kubasiewicz, *Przyszlosc tekstu i typografii,* "Powidoki" 2021, no. 5, p. 174–175.

The text is based on the thesis: Tyborowska Joanna, *Illegibility—the Dichotomy of Function and Form in Graphic Design on the Basis of Typography and Lettering Design,* 2023

PAULINE GEBAUER AND DANIEL GREMME

Architecturesque initials in ancient scripts, letterpress shadow type, and more recently, digitally extruded fonts document the desire of creatives to overcome the flat nature of letters. Now, technology is able to translate simulations of dimensionality further into interactive experiences; through perspective, spatial elements and physical properties like shadows. Why should this exclude the most used form of communication?

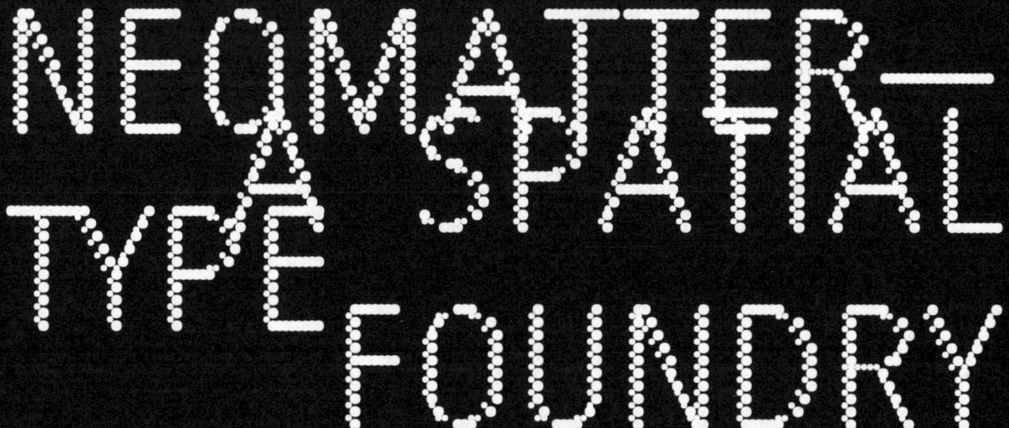

SPATIAL TYPOGRAPHY

Generally speaking, writing in all its forms necessitates the addition or removal of marks on a ground and is therefore carrying material qualities by nature, whether these are imprints of Mesopotamian sticks, ink on paper or a type shadow generating stencil. Type is material, type is a physical entity. Writing is conceptualized to lay on a surface and becomes part of the object it is attached to. In virtual spaces though, the laws of physics do not apply:

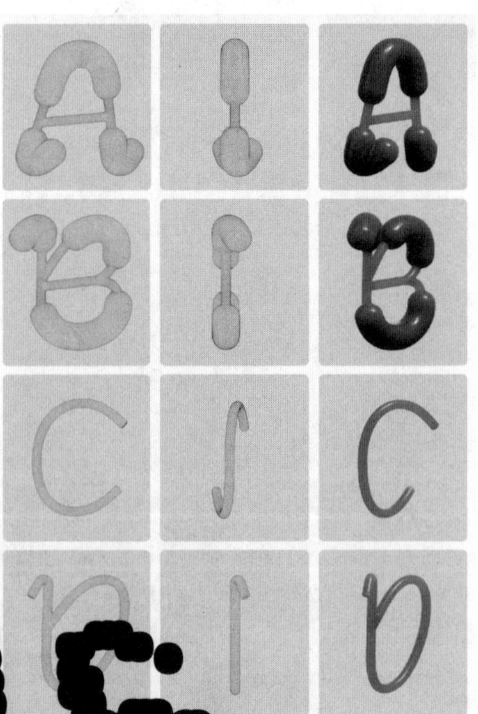

In co- op- eration with Gruppo Due

Letters can leave their ground and float around, but without depth they seem to be shadows—visible, but not tangible at all, and viewed from the side indefinitely thin. The lack of volume also causes confusion of logics between the "XYZ" environment and a shape designed just on "X" and "Y." Letters in space need to express spatial presence. The flat shape evolves into a sculpture, and it must be addressed: How does a letter look from the side, back, or bottom? How does it interact with space? Skeleton, serifs, inktraps, contrast gradients, and all other characteristics invite to be interpreted in a spatial context. Contemporary 3D and illustration software enable designers to give lettershapes volume, as often seen in Animation, Posters, and 36 Days of Type, an online challenge to design one letter a day, often in an illustrative manner. Confronted with an algorithm which prefers singular aesthetic presentations over complex design space concepts, 3D letters were rather observed as gimmickry images.

As 3D is the "natural next step" for Adobe and the creative evolution, the group rolled out features to extrude and blow up type in Illustrator, creating an illusion of depth. They serve what potential users of 3D software ask for: User-friendly tools and low-barrier entry, the two major attracting qualities. The features mentioned help bridge the gap between 2D and 3D design, strengthening client ties to the Creative Cloud ecosystem. They also serve as a soft introduction to Adobe's 3D tools, Dimension / Substance, which currently hold a relatively small market share. A move inevitably connected to the dawn of immersive experiences, such as AR, VR, and the metaverse. Apart from market dynamics controlled by monopolies, there is more to question. Although widely embraced by designers, these features bypass deeper exploration and experimentation with the spatial form of lettershapes themselves. Aren't there more refined solutions to 3D type?

Neomatter aims to provide alternatives. In collaboration with 3D Artists and type designers, we design coherently designed spatial typefaces, covering extensive glyph sets for international use, offering typefaces originally crafted as 3D objects and dimensional interpretations of conventional 2D typefaces.

ABC3D

While applying our own typefaces, we recognized the lack of a tool within existing workflows which utilizes the computer keyboard to write out 3D letters / objects on a desired path. Letters had to be placed manually, in an extremely time consuming manner (with the effort multiplying when animated). It felt like a time travel back to Gutenberg, not suited for fast paced professional contexts.

With the help of Studio Pointer*, we are developing ABC3D, a plugin to write and compose our 3D typefaces in Blender and Cinema4D. It utilizes the keyboard to write out 3D type like conventional 2D type. It brings a variety of compositional options, from placement on freeform paths, basic geometric shapes, multi-line and more.

Creative industries embrace emerging technologies like spatial computing, interactive experiences, and Web3. Blender and C4D compositions integrate into web, motion, game, VR, and graphic design, making our tool essential for staying competitive in this innovation-driven field.

NICHOLAS QYLL

This article delves into the creative-systematic process within a typographic experiment, framed by chance, variation, variables, evaluation, and selection. It explores how designers can balance structured approaches with intuitive creativity, when they need to be critical, which elements to select and further vary, and when the process reaches its optimal conclusion. The article aims to offer designers a deeper understanding of the dynamic phases that define typographic and design experiments, enhancing both their creative flow and the potential for innovative solutions.

“Imagination is the beginning of creation.”
— George Bernard Shaw

CREATIVITY WITHIN A SYSTEM

The world of typographic experiments is a dynamic playground where creative freedom and systematic exploration intersect. It is precisely in this tension that innovative design processes and outcomes emerge. Typographic experiments are not mere products of chance; they are deliberately structured inquiries centered on typography. Their aim is to generate new insights into the design of and with type, enriching design knowledge, particularly within the design community. While the process of typographic experimentation follows a methodical and structured approach, experimental typography often manifests as the creative result of these investigations. The terms overlap—though not every instance of experimental typography necessarily stems from an experiment, the two are frequently intertwined.

In an earlier contribution to Slanted magazine, "Typographic Experiments: A Method Between Research and Practice" (Qyll 2022, 2023), I explored the systematization of typographic experiments as a research method. An ideal typographic experiment follows a structured sequence, generally divided into three phases: planning, execution, and evaluation. During the planning phase, the research motivation and experimental setup are established, including tools, design operations, and components such as form, type, color, or material. However, the core of the experiment lies in the second phase, where the designer alternates between intuitive variation and targeted evaluation, adjusting design elements and reflecting on which intermediate results show the most potential to be further pursued (see also Lindauer & Müller, 2015). Even with the use of digital tools or AI, the designer remains central to the process, guiding and refining the creative experiment through iterative evaluation loops.

The process culminates in the selection of the most promising result, which is then refined and ultimately shared with the community, fostering both discovery and dissemination. But what happens between these methodical steps? What dynamics carry us from an initial spark of creativity to a completely new design solution? Would it not be beneficial to illuminate these often hidden processes to more effectively harness the creative potential of a typographic experiment?

DYNAMICS OF CREATION

The creative dynamics that unfold within a typographic or design experiment raise intriguing questions, which this text explores—based on a combination of personal experience, in-depth discussions, and various theoretical frameworks.

It all begins with a defined framework: the experimental parameters, such as tools, materials, design principles and operations, as well as type and form components, are established during the planning phase of the experiment. The designer researches relevant information, acquires the necessary knowledge, and seeks to understand the problem or creative challenge. Often, inspiration is drawn from past or researched projects or design examples, whose patterns are stored as experiential knowledge. This part can already be understood as an inspirational preparation for the upcoming creative process during the experimental execution.

But the preparation phase is not yet complete. Within the actual creative process, there is a mental attunement to the act of creation that lies immediately ahead. Cognitive processes activate relevant concepts, patterns, and examples—some consciously, others unconsciously. These inputs can draw from freshly gathered information or from specific prior knowledge, mental images, or memories of past experiments stored in long-term memory.

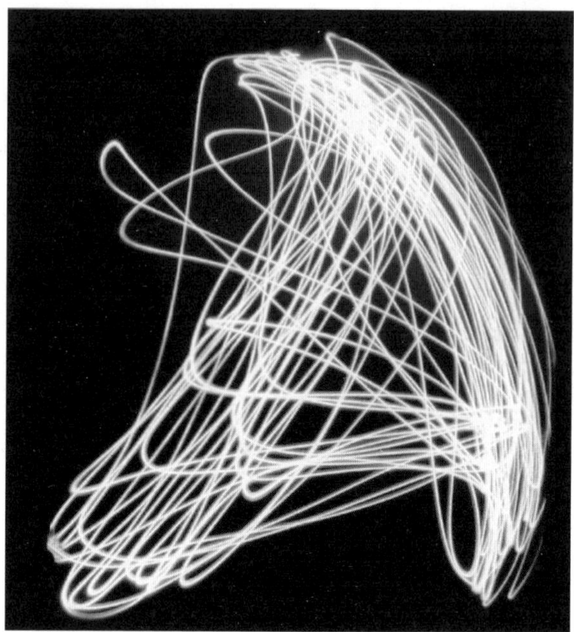

Figure 1: In my Str-alphabet project (first published in "Experimentype", 2001), the principle of conceptual blending becomes evident. Here, light movements are combined with the basic structure of letters. Through long-exposure photography in darkness, the "scriptural" movements of a light source are captured, resembling the lines of a writing instrument in their structure. The result is an experimental typography that fuses the predefined geometric forms of letters with the freedom and vibrancy of light trails.

Simultaneously, the working memory becomes active, bringing the relevant variables, goals, and operations of the design experiment into focus. At this stage, mental simulations often take place: the designer plays with vague ideas and develops early concepts that are still unrefined, yet leave room for intuitive insights and spontaneous connections. On an emotional level, the designer ideally finds themselves in a state of curiosity and anticipation—fostering openness to new and unexpected connections, both mentally and materially. This mental and emotional charge then leads the designer into the next phase of the creative process.

In the incubation phase, conscious effort recedes as the subconscious takes over. It's a phase of letting go—where the collected information and experiences are processed unconsciously. This "mind-wandering" (cf. Smallwood & Schooler, 2015) describes the mental drift that creates connections previously overlooked by the designer. Here, the "prospective mind" also comes into play—the brain anticipates possible creative solutions, setting the stage for later "Aha moments" that arise during the illumination phase. During this time, the designer steps back from active creation and allows the subconscious to generate new ideas that break away from familiar patterns. In design experiments, this often leads to conceptual combinations where elements from different domains merge, result- ing in surprising, creative outcomes (see Fig. 1). The designer allows space and time to pass with- out the pressure of immediately finding a solution. The sense that something must "mature" dominates this phase—an openness to chance discoveries or "happy accidents," which often hold the key to new forms and approaches.

The illumination phase is the moment of clarity when the unconscious mind consolidates previously processed information into a solution. This "Aha-moment" often appears unexpectedly, accompanied by a sudden intuitive impulse that is difficult to explain rationally but effectively addresses the design challenge. In typographic experiments, this frequently leads to an innovative form emerging from systematically varied parameters. Intuition plays a crucial role here—its insights are the result of unconscious processing of patterns and experiences that matured during incubation. Illumination never happens in isolation; it is a natural outcome of systematic work and unconscious connections occurring on a visual level.

During this phase, the creative flow emerges, a state of deep immersion in the design process. In the flow state, a sense of timelessness and self-forgetfulness arises as the designer is carried by an automated sequence of actions. Unconscious experiential resources are activated, allowing forms or parameters to be intuitively varied without conscious effort. The designer feels optimally challenged, with a confident sense of control even under high demands—a balance between skills and challenges that leads to a merging of self and activity. Emotions like joy, ease, and a feeling of effortless progress accompany this process as ideas seem to take shape on their own. However, when an obstacle arises, conscious thought briefly intervenes, causing the flow to dissipate before the designer returns to the intuitive creative process. This state facilitates creative breakthroughs. A deeper understanding of flow and its deliberate use can help designers develop surprising and innovative typographic solutions.

Once the first creative result emerges, the verification phase begins. The designer critically examines whether the forms meet the design requirements and the original research question. In this phase, the designer consciously assumes the role of a critic, activating analytical abilities. Both aesthetic and functional aspects are evaluated, including the readability and effectiveness of the design. Designers often face the challenge that something may be visually appealing but functionally lacking—or vice versa. This tension requires decisions that balance logical reasoning with intuitive judgment. Emotionally, this phase is often marked by frustration and relief: the designer must let go of aesthetically pleasing but ineffective solutions, in line with the principle of "killing your darlings." However, once a form meets the requirements, a sense of satisfaction arises. The verification phase is characterized by an interplay between conscious reflection and intuitive refinement. The designer relies on learned patterns and design principles while also making intuitive decisions informed by unconscious experiences. If a result proves insufficient, the creative process is reignited, and the designer enters another incubation phase.

Not every experiment leads to the expected breakthrough—and this is an essential part of the creative process. An experiment is considered unsuccessful if the chosen variations do not meet the design requirements or fail to generate new insights. This often becomes clear during the verification phase: when a creative operation does not

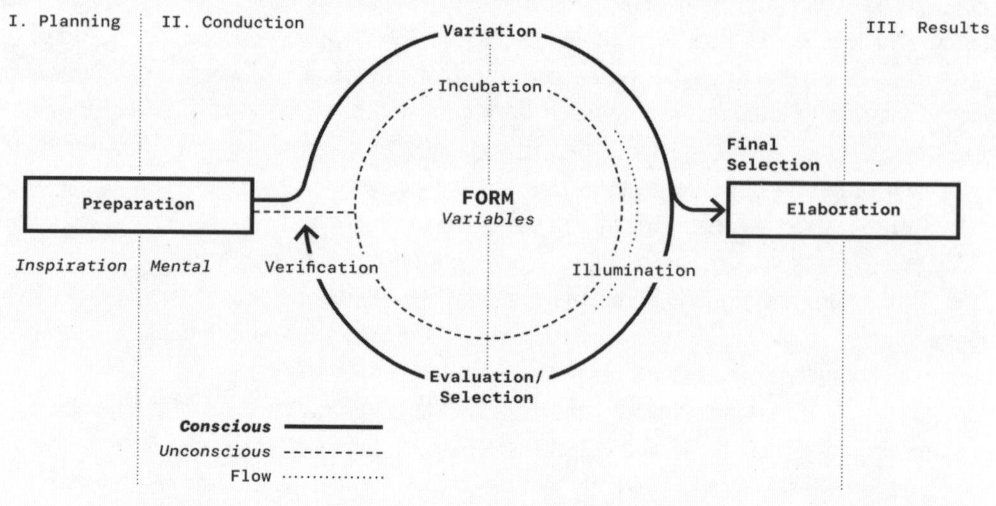

Figure 2: The graphic illustrates the creative process of a design experiment as a cyclical journey. In the planning phase, preparation serves as inspiration, while in the execution phase, it acts as a mental alignment for the creative process. The solid circle represents the conscious processes that impact the design variables—particularly the variation, evaluation, and selection of the form. While evaluation involves the ongoing reflection on the suitability of intermediate results, the verification phase ensures that the solutions align with the overarching research objectives. The dashed circle represents the unconscious phases of incubation and illumination. The flow, depicted by a dotted line, describes the (potential) intuitive experience within the creative process and facilitates creative breakthroughs. The cycle concludes with the final selection, which leads to elaboration and marks the end of the experimental process.

yield the desired outcome, it is crucial to reflect and, if necessary, start again. However, this does not mark failure but rather opens the door to reflection and reassessment. Often, it is the unexpected, seemingly failed attempts that lead to the greatest innovations. Designers should view failure as a natural part of the creative process within an experiment—one that opens new perspectives and paves the way for creative breakthroughs.

Once the outcome aligns with expectations, the final selection takes place, and the elaboration phase begins. The designer concludes the experiment by refining the final form and ensuring it meets the initial objectives. This phase transitions into the evaluation phase, where the experimental outcome is archived, prepared for final application, or published as experimental typography—whether online or in a platform such as Slanted magazine.

THE CREATIVE POTENTIAL

The creative dynamic that unfolds within a typographic experiment is fascinating and demonstrates how conscious and unconscious actions must harmoniously interact to achieve truly innovative results (see Fig. 2).

In my own creative processes, I often encounter moments when a certain openness to the unexpected leads to a breakthrough. For me, this interplay between intuition and systematics is the key to unlocking the full potential of a design experiment. Designers frequently face the challenge of balancing control and freedom. It is precisely this balance—the harmony between a structured methodology and the willingness to invite the unconscious into the creative process—that I believe is central to fostering true innovation in research-driven design. To fully harness the creative flow, it is crucial to understand and align the conscious steering of variation, evaluation, and selection with the intuitive actions in the creative phases. Only then can the space be created in which the full creative potential of a typographic experiment can flourish. To support this process, I have discovered the following guiding principles, which may also serve as valuable insights for other designers:

• Feed your mind: Inspiration doesn't only come from design. Regular exposure to visual stimuli and ideas from various fields—such as cultural knowledge, media, and everyday observations—enriches the creative process and enables unexpected connections. I encourage looking beyond your usual sources and welcoming new stimuli.

• Work within a structured framework: Set clear parameters for your experiment to establish a solid foundation. At the same time, leave room for flexibility and chance occurrences that can lead to surprising results.

• Allow time for incubation: Regularly step back from active designing to give your subconscious time to make new connections. Often, the best insights arise during these pauses or when engaging in light, unrelated activities.

• Embrace the flow state: In critical phases of experimentation, it's essential to reach a state of complete immersion. When I fully immerse myself in my work in a comfortable environment, I enter the flow state, often leading to the most unexpected and rewarding results.

Order

Visual type experiment No. 647382940473

• Be willing to fail: Failure is a natural part of the creative process and should not be feared but embraced as an opportunity. Every perceived design failure offers the chance to rethink, restart, and uncover new insights.

By understanding the creative dynamics and applying these principles, designers can fully harness the creative potential of their typographic and design experiments.

#TYPEEXPERIMENTS: CURATED SAMPLES OF EXPERIMENTAL PRACTICE (NO. 2)

Typography is far more than functional form design—it offers a fascinating playground for experiments that can continually redefine our understanding of script and communication. In the course of my design research, I regularly come across exciting projects shared under the hashtag #typeexperiments on Instagram. In this section, I present a selection of such experimental typographies—examples that impress with both their technical sophistication and their experimental approaches. This collection is not only meant to inspire but also to encourage others to explore, create, and share their own experiments with the world.

Graffiti Piece Generator

The work Order from 1996 is the result of an analog, formal-compositional typography experiment by Brad Smith (@brad.art.design). For this piece, he used found type blocks in Caslon Pro, the official typeface of the House of Commons. The experimental process, focused on formal and compositional aspects, followed these steps: The experimenter first made a copy at a reduced scale, around 25%, and then resized the copy to 150%. This proce- d u r e was repeated until all that remained were abstract word shapes. He then transferred the copies onto a c e- t a t e sheets, re-copied them, and overprinted them using a photocopier. No Photoshop or other software was used to achieve the final result. "I loved the gradual distortion, just as facts gradually fade as stories are retold," Brad says about his work. Ultimately, through this exploratory engagement with the technique, he gained experiential knowledge, which he later applied to his subsequent works.

The visual type experiment No. 647382940473 was developed by Theresa F. Hartlieb (@t.reesaa) in 2017 and explores the formal-compositional representation of the time-type relationship. A conventionally written text block, composed of repetitive "tiktoks" in the Georgia typeface, represents physical clock time and serves as the starting point of the experiment. However, "natural time doesn't 'listen' to clock time." In the next step, the experiment demonstrates how space-time distortions can affect a text object. To achieve this, the experimenter used a liquify filter in Adobe Illustrator to create more fluid and natural shapes, contrasting with the rigid, structured "tik tok" layout.

The experimental design tool Graffiti Piece Generator was developed in 2022 by Yannick Gregoire (@yannickgregoire). It automates the sketching of tags on a formal-actional level and generates randomly curved and animated graffiti pieces. Using HTML, SVG, and Javascript, the tool connects randomly plotted points through Bézier curves. It allows for adjusting parameters such as point positions, handle offsets, line thickness, and animation speed. The typeface unscii is used to reinforce the contrast between rigid programming and the creation of naturally flowing shapes.

Csikzentmihalyi, M. (2010): *Das flow-Erlebnis: Jenseits von Angst und Langeweile: im Tun aufgehen.* 11. Aufl. Klett-Cotta

Fauconnier, G. & Turner, M. (2002): *The Way We Think: Conceptual Blending and the Mind's Hidden Complexities.* New York: Basic

Georg-Simon-Ohm Fachhochschule Nürnberg (Hrsg.) (2001): *Experimentype.* Buch 1+2. Sankt Petersburg: Gradi

Koestler, A. (1964): *The Act of Creation.* London: Hutchinson

Kuhl, J. (2005): *Eine neue Persönlichkeitstheorie – Einführung in die PSI-Theorie.* In ders.: .psi-theorie.com, zul. am 08.09.2024

Lindauer, A. & Müller, B. (2015): *Experimentelle Gestaltung: Visuelle Methode und systematisches Spiel.* Salenstein: Niggli

Qyll, N. (2022): *"Typographic experiments: A method between research and practice"*, in: Slanted Magazine: Experimental Type, 40: 26–35

Qyll, N. (2023): *"Typographic experiments: A method between research and practice"*, in: Slanted Magazine: Experimental Type 2.0, 40: 258–267

Smallwood, J. & Schooler, J. (2015): *"The Science of Mind Wandering: Empirically Navigating the Stream of Consciousness,"* in: Annual Review of Psychology, 3/66: 487–518

Wallas, G. ([1926] 2015): *The Art of Thought.* Kent: Solis Press

RAPHAËL VERONA
SOFIA PAPAEFTHYMIOU

Aymara is an ancestral language spoken by approximately two million people across Bolivia, Peru, Argentina, and Chile, largely due to migrations from Bolivia. It is believed to have its origins in the Andean region around Lake Titicaca. In the La Paz department (Bolivia), the majority of the population is Aymara. As a result, the Bolivian constitution mandates the teaching of Aymara in this region—as a mother tongue for Aymara speakers and as a second language for Spanish speakers. Following these linguistic reforms, new bilingual Spanish-Aymara signs have been introduced in public spaces in the city of La Paz. With the city's 11 cable car lines aimed at easing urban traffic, it was here that I first noticed the flourishing presence of Aymara in public spaces.

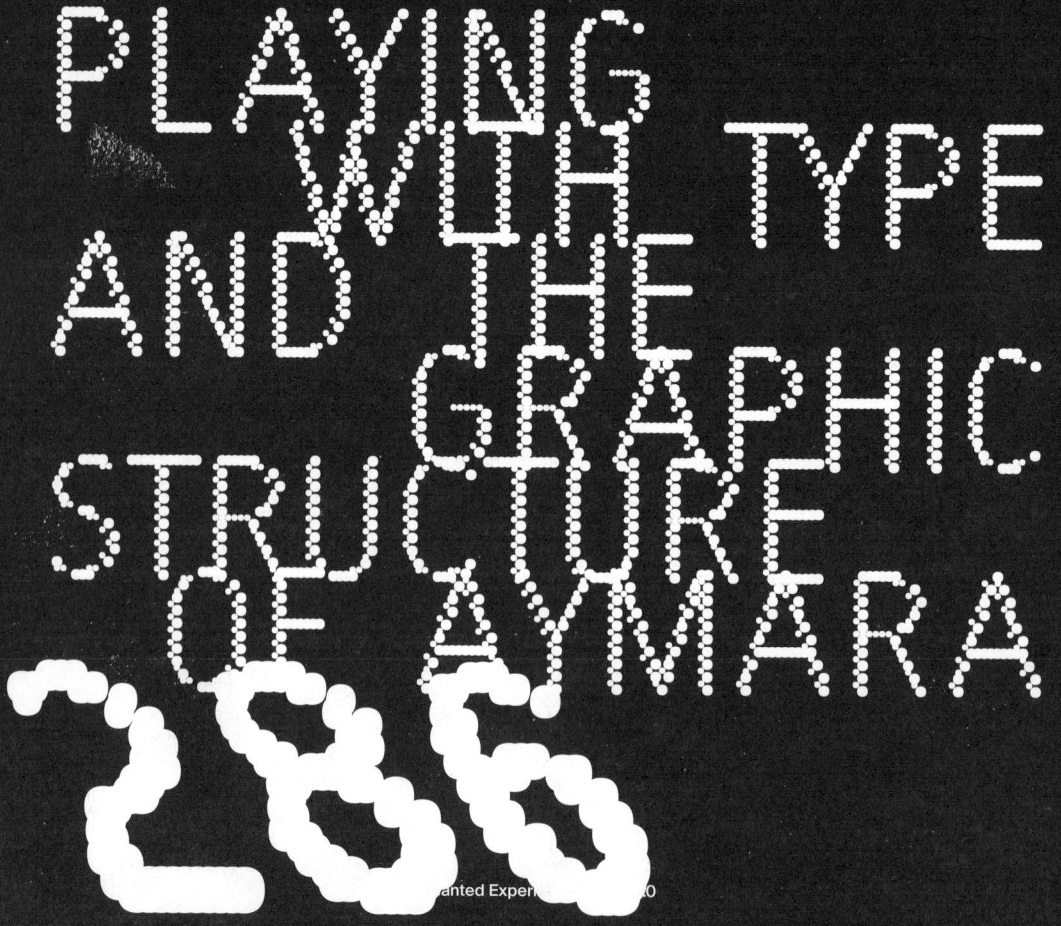

This development reflects the political and cultural shifts the country has experienced over the past two decades and serves as an important gesture acknowledging the language and culture of many of its inhabitants.

I have been fortunate enough to witness significant changes in the Bolivian society, from my first long stay in La Paz in 2003 to my most recent visit in 2023. Over these 20 years, I have made several extended stays in Bolivia, during which I worked as a graphic designer, led a typography workshop, formed lasting friendships, spent time with my in-laws between La Paz and the Yungas, and explored the fascinating city of La Paz.

Bilingual communication has also been implemented in public health infrastructures. During a visit with my daughter to the pediatric department at La Merced Hospital (Villa El Carmen, La Paz), one was struck by the sign: "Pediatria / Wawanakaru Uñjayasiña Uta." As a graphic designer / type designer, I was captivated by the imbalance in length between the two languages. It seems like a difficult typographic challenge to solve, and it's not an isolated issue in the context of this bilingual Spanish / Aymara signage. I wouldn't have wanted to tackle this using Arial or Arial Narrow, as had been done. That's when I decided to approach the problem as a type designer. From there, Sofia and I worked on designing and producing a series of typographic proposals, focusing both on composition and letter design. We were sometimes able to implement a system of ligatures and conditional alternates (calt) directly into our font files, automatically handling the composition at the level of entire paragraphs.

To better understand the stakes of our work, we explored the structure of the Aymara language in connection with cultural and spiritual aspects of Aymara culture-cosmovision, rituals, trivalent logic. We also drew from concrete examples of historical typographic proposals in other languages, such as the addition of accents and the replacement of silent letters in French, writing Arabic in Latin characters, contemporary emojis, and pre-Columbian ideograms.

The series of experiments resulting from this initial observation forms a typographic game, without any claim to hold a form of truth or orthotypographic rigor. Although I am surrounded by close family members whose mother tongue is Aymara, and who have introduced me to the logic and structure of the language, I do not speak Aymara myself, aside from a few polite phrases and counting to 20 ...

The project was initiated in 2018 and continues today. Special thanks to Vilma Mamani, Martha Quispe de Mamani and Jesús Mamani Coasaca.

1. *MORALES AYMA,* Evo (2015). Decreto Supremo N° 2477. "Capitulo III: Uso de los idiomas en la administración pública y entidades privadas de servicio público"
2. *ESTIENNE,* Robert (ca. 1530). Traité de la grammaire françoiase
3. *AL QADIRI,* Fatima; al Gharaballi, Khalid, Mahma Kan Althaman, 2010. Published in Bidoun Magazine
4. Hoedt, Arnaud; Piron Jerôme (ca. 2020). TEDxRennes: La faute de l'orthographe

Three steps to creating vertical ligatures.

Structural and letter design experiments

Structural and letter design experiments.

APPENDIX

ALPHABETICAL INDEX

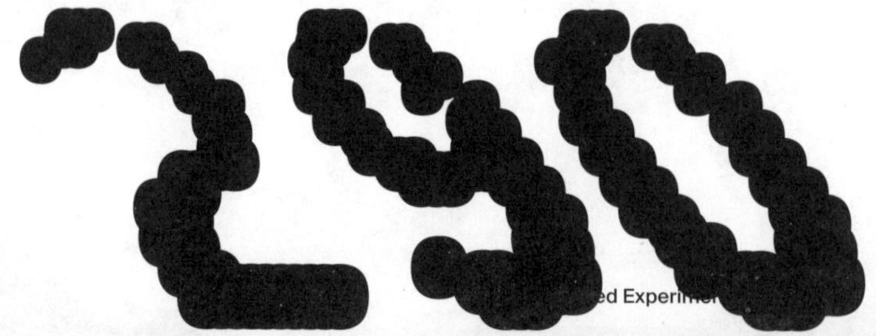

Alex Ortiga, ITA 064
alexortiga.com
@x.sy.n

Nadine Ouellet, CAN 130
nadineouellet.work

Andreas Panayi, CYP 162, 167
behance.net/andreaspanayi
@panayi_andreas

Sofia Papaefthymiou, CHE 068
@sfppfth E 286

Miyoun Park, DEU 068
mia-park.com
@mmia.park

Philipp Popek, DEU 252, 059
@philip_popek 046, 058

Youri Precht, DEU 188, 189
creal.bigcartel.com 190
@cerealk1llah

Franziska Prüsener, DEU 079
@franziska.pruesener 230

Nicholas Qyll, DEU E 278
nicholasqyll.com
@nicholasqyll

Julian Ratay, DEU 033, 216
@jutayaa

Yuliia Ratnikova, GBR 210
@centre_aligned

Maxime Rheault, CAN 130
@criterium_design

Anna Riabukha, RUS 107
unkke.space
@unkke__

Jeremy Rieger, DEU 121
jeremyrieger.com

Adson Rodrigues, BRA 040
adsonrodrigues.com

Nattapol Rojjanarattanangkool, THA 115
nattapol-rojj.info
@khaorong.khaoroi

Christine Rudi, DEU 193
@christinerudi_

Luis Rutz, DEU 088
luisrutz.de
@luis_rutz

Marie Sadlo, DEU 095, 224

Alexandra Sagalow, DEU 163
@sashdrw 249

Yavuz Sahin, DEU 233, 036
@typeshitys

Katharina Schäffer, DEU 165
katharinaschffr.format.com
@katharina_schffr

Romy Scheifel, DEU 237

Rüdiger Schlömer, CHE 158
typeknitting.net
@typeknitting

Luca Schlosser, DEU 057
@derlucamitbart

Eva Schlotzhauer, DEU 172, 243
@tzii.design

Yannik Schmitt, DEU 122
@yayaschmitt

Mona Schoch, DEU 160

Maja Schuster, DEU 198
@majaschusta

Michiel Schuurman, NLD 120
michielschuurman.com

Liad Shadmi, DEU 024
liadshadmi.com
@liadshadmi

Monica Sharoubime, DEU 021
238

Wanwai Shum, NLD 083
@shumww

Sascha Simm, DEU 152, 153
simmbild.de
@simmbild

Janell Paige Sin Fan Im, DEU 157

Jan Sindler, DEU 085
jansindler.com
@sindljan

Christopher Sleboda, USA 075
textfieldoffice.com E 259
@textfieldoffice

Kathleen Sleboda, USA 075
textfieldoffice.com E 259

@textfieldoffice

Melissa Smajic, DEU 030, 248
@melliitonin.design

Juan Solano, GRC 131
juan-solano.com
@juan_solano_rincon

Jasmin Sonderegger, CHE 047
jasminsonderegger.ch
@sandlerkoeniginjasmin

Philipp Staege, DEU 070
@bureauprogressiv

Tim Stange, DEU 222
studiomos.de
@_timstange
@studiomos_de

Alexandra Steffan, DEU 009
atelierpreto.com
@yalashhh

Sam Steiner, CHE 004
samsteiner.ch
@samsteiner.ch

Franziska Stetter, USA 017

Christian Stifani, ITA 151
behance.net/christistifani
@christian.stifani

Rob Stolte, NLD E 245
rob-stolte.52b.nl
@new_literate_playground

Moritz Stolz, DEU 170, 259
@moritzstolz

Jim Sutherland, GBR 129
studio-sutherland.co.uk
@studio_sutherland

Anna Katalin Szilágyi, HUN 135
annaszilagyi.net
@anna.jpeg2000

Cihan Tamti, DEU 093
cihan-tamti.de
@cihantamti

Lanling Tang, CHN 124
whynotedesign.cc

Julian Tillmann, DEU 027, 221

Wouter Tjeenk Willink, NLD 116
mrnelsondesign.com
@mrnelsondesign

Christian Tkaczuk, DEU 060, 217

David Torrents, ESP 076, 086
@taller_torrents

Péter Tóth, HUN 127
@peti__toth

Guillaume Tourscher, FRA 182
guillaume-tourscher.fr
@guillaumetourscher

Andreas Trenker, ITA 074
andreastrenker.com
@andreastrenker

Maria Tsilomitrou, GRC 131
studiochill.gr
@tsil_m

SLANTED EXPERIMENTAL TYPE 3.0

PUBLISHER

Slanted Publishers UG
(haftungsbeschränkt)
Nördliche Uferstraße 4–6
76189 Karlsruhe
Germany
T +49 (0) 721 85 14 82 68
magazine@slanted.de
slanted.de

ISBN: 978-3-948440-81-7
2nd edition, 2025

TEAM

Editor in Chief (V.i.S.d.P.)
Lars Harmsen, Andreas Ruhe
Co-Editing & Design
Nele Kreuger
Adelisa Ljesnjanin
Fabian Meyer
Jule Orlik
Franziska Prüsener
Tim Stange
Nihal Türkyilmaz
Managing Editor
Julia Kahl
Creative Direction
Lars Harmsen, Andreas Ruhe
Final Design
Julia Kahl, Juliane Lipp

The German National Library lists this publication in the German National Bibliography; detailed bibliographic data is available on the Internet at dnb.de

This issue features works from the course EXPERIMENTAL TYPE, a typography class held at the Dortmund University of Applied Sciences and Arts during the Summer Semester 2024, supervised by Prof. Lars Harmsen and Andreas Ruhe. The issue also includes contributions from a call for entries. Many thanks to all course participants:

Abdulhadi Aldarwich
Hannah Baumann
Jannette Bartkowiak
Anja Bolender
Lilith Alia Dolch
Beyza Duyuran
Suna Gesing
Miriam Goldschmidt
Matilda Greiner
Fabian Hoffmann
Auguste Victoria Hohage
Janett Jakubow
Özkan Kandir
Nathalie Knappik
Aysel Kopuz
Niclas Kötting
Jona Kranzusch
Nele Kreuger
Muriel Labadi
Adelisa Ljesnjanin
Fabian Meyer
Philipp Mohncke
Nassim Mokarami
Marie Nieddu
Julia Orlik
Philip Popek
Youri Precht
Prüsener, Franziska
Julian Ratay
Sonja Riedel
Marie Sadlo
Alexandra Sagalow
Yavuz Sahin
Romy Scheifel
Eva Schlotzhauer
Monica Nayrouz Aziz Sharoubime
Janell Paige Sin Fan Im
Melissa Smajic
Tim Stange
Moritz Stolz
Julian Tillmann
Christian Tkaczuk
Nihal Türkyilmaz
Tim von Bischopinck
Chanel Wloka
Pelin Yapici
Charlotte Wächter

PRODUCTION

Printing
Printmedia Solutions
Mannheim / Germany
printmedia-solutions.de

Paper
Amber Graphic, 80 g/sm
Iona®offset 350g/sm

Fonts
HARBER, 2023
Design: Benoît Bodhuin
Label: bb-bureau / bb-bureau.fr

Terminal Grotesque, 2011
Design: Raphaël Bastide, with the contribution of Jérémy Landes
Label: Velvetyne / velvetyne.fr

Suisse Int'l, 2011
Design: Swiss Typefaces Design Team
Label: Swiss Typefaces / swisstypefaces.com

ADVERTISING

We offer a wide range of advertising possibilities online and in print. For advertising inquiries please get in touch with:
Julia Kahl (advertising management / sales)
+49 (0) 721 851 482 68, julia.kahl@slanted.de
slanted.de/publisher/advertising

AWARDS (SELECTION)

ADC of Europe
ADC Germany
Annual Multimedia
Berliner Type
DDC
Designpreis der BRD
European Design Awards
Faces of Design Awards
iF communication design award
German Design Award
Laus Awards
Lead Awards (Weblog des Jahres & Visual Leader)
red dot communication design awards
Type Directors Club NY
Tokyo Type Directors Club
Werkbund Label

SUBSCRIPTIONS

Subscribe to Slanted Magazine and support what we do. Magazines via subscriptions are at a reduced rate and get shipped directly at release, for free within Germany.
slanted.de/subscription

2-Issues-Subscription
€ 40.– + shipping
4-Issues-Subscription
€ 80.– + shipping
Student Subscription
2 issues for € 37.– + shipping
Gift Subscription
2 issues wrapped as present for € 42.– + shipping
2-Issues-Subscritpion + related Special Editions
2 issues + 2 special editions for € 60.– + shipping
4-Issues-Subscritpion + related Special Editions
4 issues + 4 special editions + free issue
for € 120.– + shipping

SALES AND DISTRIBUTION

Slanted Magazine can be purchased online, in selected bookstores, concept stores, and galleries worldwide. If you own a shop and would like to stock Slanted Magazine or other publications from us, please get in touch:

Contact / Distribution DE
Julia Klose, T +49 (0) 721 85148268
julia.klose@slanted.de
Distribution UK
Public Knowledge Books /
publicknowledgebooks.com
Distribution US
Small Changes / smallchanges.com
Distribution EU & WORLD
Idea Books / ideabooks.nl
Slanted Shop
slanted.de/shop
Retail & Distribution
slanted.de/distribution

170 Moritz Stolz DEU— IT’S A MAGNIFICATION

Stolz experimented with the microscopic enlargement of printed letters on various papers and materials in order to gain a new perspective on type. This work is a hundredfold magnification of an embossing with letters on aluminum foil.